WHEN THE CHILDREN CAME HOME

Stories from Wartime Evacuees

Julie Summers

WINDSOR
PARAGON

First published 2011
by Simon & Schuster UK Ltd
This Large Print edition published 2011
by AudioGO Ltd
by arrangement with
Simon & Schuster UK Ltd

Hardcover ISBN: 978 1 445 85846 3
Softcover   ISBN: 978 1 445 85847 0

British Library Cataloguing in Publication Data available

Printed and bound in Great Britain by
MPG Books Group Limited

For Penny and Roy
Much loved and respected

CONTENTS

I look back on my period of evacuation as one of great significance to me. The experience broadened my character immensely; taught me that there was much more to my country than the suburbs of London and showed me the essential goodness of people. These things have never left me.

Robert Miller OBE

INTRODUCTION

When I am asked what it is about the Second World War that fascinates me so much I reply that it is not war but people who excite my interest: how individuals cope in a time of emergency and how such events impact upon their later lives. So when I was challenged a few years ago by a grandfather from Swindon to consider the situation that faced children returning from evacuation after the Second World War my interest was piqued. Patrick Fitzgerald, whose story features in this book, unwittingly set in train one of the most rewarding journeys I have undertaken and revealed to me a vast collection of experiences and reminiscences, both positive and negative.

It is estimated that over 3 million[1] British children were affected by evacuation at one stage or another during the Second World War. They were sent on a mixture of private and government-sponsored schemes to coastal towns, to the countryside, to Canada, the USA, South Africa, New Zealand and Australia. Some children spent six years living away from home. These children were in the minority. Most of the others spent anything from a matter of weeks or months to several years in foster homes, with extended family or living with strangers abroad. They returned, not en masse in May 1945, but randomly at stages throughout the war.

Essentially there were three waves of evacuation

in Britain and one in the Far East. The first was in September 1939 when 1.5 million women and children were moved from the major cities to the countryside in the space of three days. The second came in 1940 in response to the threat of invasion after the fall of France when over 200,000 people were moved out of danger areas, such as the coastal towns, and some 20,000 were sent to live abroad. The third wave, affecting around 1 million people came in the March of 1944 when flying bombs threatened London and south-east England. An almost forgotten evacuation took place in late 1941 and early 1942 in the Far East when the Japanese invaded Hong Kong, Malaya, Singapore and the Dutch East Indies. This book looks at the effect of evacuation on children and examines how it affected them on their return.

I was born long after the end of the war but evacuation did affect my parents' generation. Although my mother was brought up near Liverpool her mother refused, under family pressure, to have her children shipped out to America. They remained resolutely at home near Willaston and my grandmother was overheard on several occasions to say that if Hitler was going to kill her then she would prefer to die in her own bed. My father was evacuated. He was sent with his school from the Wirral to the Lake District and his experience seems to have been wholly positive. Certainly every time we return to Glenridding, at the south end of beautiful Ullswater, he takes great pride in reminding us that he and Bill Glazebrook shared a room above the post office. The rest of the boys lived in the Glenridding Hotel on the opposite side of the road. Classes were taken in the village hall and all the boys trooped off to Patterdale Church every Sunday. Evacuation features as a short, happy chapter in his war years that ended with a different but fascinating experience of national service in Vienna.

My father was lucky. He was sent away as one of a group to a structured and familiar way of life—a boys' prep school. He did not fit the bill of the typical evacuee I had built up in my mind as he faced none of the uncertainties of the 820,000 unaccompanied schoolchildren who in September 1939 were billeted with foster families in villages, often long distances away from their city homes. As I began to research the effect of wartime evacuation on a generation I became increasingly aware of the extraordinary complexity of the six years of movement of children. My father's story, contrary to my expectation, fitted in to the overall picture perfectly well. It was simply one variation on the theme. There was no 'typical' evacuee, neither was there a typical experience. I also became aware that the view of evacuation amongst the general population and, to some extent, amongst the evacuated children, has been shaped not by fact but by fiction.

Authors and novelists in the post-war era found evacuation to be a rich area for inspiration. C. S. Lewis used it in *The Lion, the Witch and the Wardrobe* as a conceit to remove the four Pevensie children from their house in London and send them to live with Professor Digory Kirke in the English countryside. Written in 1950 but set in 1940, it was based, Lewis explained, on four schoolgirls who were evacuated from London to Lewis's home outside Oxford in 1939. Four years later William Golding published *The Lord of the Flies*, which started with a planeload of evacuated children being shot down over a tropical island. Although not set in the war it again uses evacuation as a method for isolating a group of children without adults. Dramatist Jack Rosenthal also drew on his own experiences of evacuation from Manchester to Blackpool during the war when he wrote *The Evacuees*, first screened on television in 1975. It focuses on the humour as well as the sadness of the situation of two Jewish boys billeted with a foster family who have no comprehension of the cultural background of the children. Instead of producing a happy ending, he underlines the sadness and sense of loss felt by the mother as her sons return, older and changed, after fifteen months of living away from her.

In 1981 Michelle Magorian published her first novel. It was about a boy, badly abused by his mother, who was evacuated from London to the country during the war. His name was William Beech and his foster father was Tom Oakley, a curmudgeonly but caring old widower, who took the boy under his wing; both grew to love one another over the course of the novel. *Goodnight Mister Tom* is a story of trust, friendship and triumph over personal adversity. It is also one of the most enchanting children's stories and it achieved both critical acclaim and immediate and enduring popularity. In 2010 it was voted one of the most popular children's books of all time.

The upshot of this success was that the story of the wartime evacuation reached a whole new generation of children, whose parents had grown up reading *Carrie's War*, Nina Bawden's novel about a little girl and her brother evacuated to South Wales. Also fiction, though drawing on Bawden's own experiences as a wartime evacuee, *Carrie's War* centres on the children's relationships with the eccentric characters that they are billeted with. The focus of the book is not evacuation, unlike *Goodnight Mister Tom*, but the children's adventures.

In 1971 social historian Norman Longmate published *How We Lived Then*, his outstanding survey of life in Britain during the Second World War. He devoted a short section to evacuation, concentrating on the government's attempts to convince evacuees and foster families not to give up and so require the children to return to the cities that were still in danger of being bombed.

It was not, however, until almost fifty years after the end of the war that a flood of memoirs and stories of individual experiences of evacuation began to appear.

More recent books such as *I'll Take That One* by Martin Parsons, *Out of Harm's Way* by Jessica Mann and *The Absurd and the Brave* by Michael Fethney deal with bad experiences, unhappy billets, bullying and worse, as well as with what comes across as a small number of successful cases. This had the effect of making many former evacuees feel that their own, happy evacuation experiences, like that of my father, were the exception rather than the rule and had no place in the social history of the war. 'I'm afraid my story will be of no interest to you,' one interviewee explained to me as we sat down to talk about her five years living in Devon. 'You see, I had a wonderful time and loved every minute of my evacuation.' She was not the only person who prefaced her own story with that caution. Their stories are, of course, of great interest and they belong to the history every bit as much as those that have a less happy theme.

In the end I became concerned about the insistent apologies and by going back over every interview I carried out personally or read in archives I was able to establish that the majority, over 85 per cent, of the evacuees claimed to have judged the experience to have had a positive effect on their subsequent lives even if, at the time, they were homesick or lonely, or were later troubled by their return.

Michael Henderson, who was evacuated to America as a boy with his brother, Gerald, in 1940, explained recently that the first draft of his book about his and others' experiences of their American sojourn had been too positive. For him those years had been overwhelmingly happy and both he and Gerald had benefited immeasurably from their time away but then he remembered that returning to Britain had not been entirely straightforward. He wrote:

'Returning home, it was hard for us to step into the lives of parents who had survived the bombing, and more recently the V1 and V2 rockets, and would jump at any loud noise. Our parents' admonishments were met with, "We don't do that in America." Soon America became known in our family as "We-land".'[2]

For many children, even those who enjoyed their evacuation like Michael and his brother, there was not necessarily a happy ending to their story. Many found coming home as difficult, or in some cases more difficult, than they had done leaving in the first place. But this is not what their families wanted to hear and it took years for most of them to admit to others or even to themselves that this was the case. Time after time during interviews, reading memoirs and letters I came across stories of men and women who had met up with others at reunions who had been through similar experiences, and for the first time in their lives felt able to talk about how it had been for them when they came home. In general these gatherings came on the fiftieth anniversary of the evacuation. Time enough for the past to have become history and yet still recent enough to be a part of living memory. After one such reunion in 1989, Pat Crouch explained:

I'd never really thought about my evacuation in any sort of context. I mean, I'd told my own children about it and I'd looked at them when they were six and thought 'Would I have had the courage to send them away?' but that was personal. Suddenly meeting all these others who had been away, like I had, for four years, well, it released some emotions in me which must have been lying dormant. I found myself crying with one woman as we remembered how hard it was leaving our foster homes and coming back to London. As we talked we realised we had much in common. We had felt guilty about finding fault with our families, with the food that seemed so poor in comparison to what we had been used to in Cornwall but most of all we realised that it was a shared thing, not something unique and although it was painful at first to dredge up all those memories it was good to think that I was not alone. There were so many of us and we all have so much in common.

From today's perspective it is almost inconceivable to imagine a situation where upwards of a million families would agree to send their children away from home, to strangers in the countryside, or even abroad, for an unknown period. In order to understand the impact of returning home after weeks, months or years away, it is necessary to understand the reasons why the children had to go away in the first place. Children in all major British cities that were considered targets for the Luftwaffe were involved. And that was just the evacuation of September 1939. There are three other evacuations, including one overseas, to consider.

The first two chapters of this book examine the reasons behind the government's evacuation scheme and the reception that the children received when they first left the cities and arrived in the country at the outbreak of the war. The later chapters look in detail at the effect of evacuation on the children in the immediate aftermath and in their later lives. Finally the book looks at the foster families who took the children in for anything up to six years and then had to hand them back to their natural parents as the war drew to a close.

James Roffey, Founder of the Evacuees Reunion Association (ERA), which was formed in response to the fiftieth anniversary of the end of the Second World War, wrote to me in 2009:

The subject of the return home of evacuees is one that has never been given the attention it deserves. Most people believe that when they finally went home and all the feelings of homesickness were over, everything returned to normal, just as it was before the evacuation started. I know from my own experience that that was far from true. During my four years as an evacuee all I had wanted to do was to go home. I used to smuggle letters to my parents pleading to be allowed home. They had to be smuggled out because our foster parents were told to censor our letters and destroy them if we had not said that we were happy. Eventually the day came when I could go home but, to my own amazement, instead of being elated I was quite sad at leaving the village where I had lived for over four years.

The return home was a major disappointment. To be really honest I found that I no longer had any affinity with my parents. I hated London and took every opportunity to return to Sussex. As soon as possible after leaving school I got a job back in my evacuation village. I have never lived permanently in London since. However, as the years have passed I have realised just how hard it must have been for my parents, especially my mother. The little eight-year-old boy that she saw leaving in 1939 never did return home, instead she found herself trying to understand a very mature, self-reliant, twelve-year-old who made no secret of the fact that he did not like being at his real home.

The stories in this book come from a variety of sources: from first-hand interviews conducted over the space of two years; from the archives of the Museum of English Rural Life which holds an outstanding collection of interviews put together under the auspices of Dr Martin Parsons of the University of Reading to whom I am indebted; from papers, memoirs and diaries held in the Department of Documents at the Imperial War Museum; from published and unpublished books on evacuation and from the People's War section of the BBC's excellent website devoted to the Second World War. Predominantly I have focused on the human story and the individual experience of returning from evacuation.

I have made every effort to contact people and check they are happy with what is published. Some people have asked me to change their names and others have wished to remain anonymous. Views expressed by the former evacuees are their own but I take responsibility for any errors that might appear in the narrative.

Julie Summers
Oxford
October 2010

1

RUN TO THE HILLS

From the first day of September 1939 evacuation ceased to be a problem of administrative planning. It became instead a multitude of problems in human relationships.

Richard Titmuss

Of the three major evacuation movements in Britain during the war the first, codenamed Operation Pied Piper, is the most well known. It took place over four days at the beginning of September 1939 in response to the threat that the government most feared, which was the aerial bombardment of Britain's cities. From the mid-1920s attention had been focused on aerial warfare as the newest and most uncertain factor in any future war. As early as 1924 the Committee of Imperial Defence was set up to assess the potential risk to civilians and how to deal with a major attack on London. It was tasked with calculating the likely casualty figures and the probable damage to the capital's infrastructure. Richard Titmuss, in his seminal book *Problems of Social Policy: History of the Second World War*, explained how the committee worked out its figures: 'In the background was the experience gained from the eighteen German air raids on London during 1917–18, when a total of about 128 aeroplanes

1

reached the metropolitan area. During the whole war, about 300 tons of bombs were dropped by the Germans on the British Isles. These raids caused 4,820 casualties including 1,413 killed. The casualty ratio for the whole country thus worked out at sixteen per ton of bombs.'[1]

Taking into account the density of London's population at the time, the committee increased its estimate of the likely number of casualties per ton of bombs to fifty of which, they estimated, one third would be killed outright and two thirds wounded. This figure of fifty casualties per ton of bombs remained for the next sixteen years. In 1922 Lord Balfour wrote that even four years on from the First World War he expected that a continental enemy could 'drop on London a continuous torrent of high explosives at a rate of seventy-five tons a day for an indefinite period'.[2] Whilst not everyone in government agreed with Lord Balfour's warning, there was sufficient concern so that the Committee of Imperial Defence continued to calculate the capacity of the German air force to increase its tonnage of bombs year on year. Thus, a decade later, in June 1934, a new estimate was submitted by the Chief of the Air Staff and was based on an analysis of the air expansion programme in Hitler's Germany. The committee calculated that the Germans could be ready to launch a large attack by April 1939. They also considered it possible that they would start with a *Kolossal* or massive bombardment, launching 3,500 tons in the first twenty-four-hour period, which could cause up to 175,000 casualties. To put this into perspective, the estimated *death* rate would match the overall *casualty* rate of the first day of

2

the Battle of the Somme. But this time it would be civilians who would bear the brunt.

Individual politicians did not seek to delude the public. Stanley Baldwin had told the House of Commons in 1932: '. . . the bomber will always get through . . . I think it is as well also for the man in the street to realise that there is no power on earth that can protect him from being bombed.'[3]

It was not just a question of the prospective tonnage of bombs but the type of bombs that would be dropped. The Home Office was convinced that a major threat from a gas attack was to be expected and by December 1937 over 19 million containers for gas masks had been produced. The public understood the horrors of gas in the First World War trenches. Gas warfare and air raids were vividly linked in their minds and gas was the indeterminate factor in a war against civilians. However, not everyone was convinced that the most serious threat came from a gas attack. Churchill had warned, prophetically as it happened, in the House of Commons in November 1934: 'The most dangerous form of air attack is the attack by incendiary bomb.'

The great unknown for the government during the 1930s was how civilians would cope with an aerial bombardment. The horrific effects of the bombing of Spanish cities during the Civil War were well documented in the press. An eyewitness account filed by a correspondent for *The Times* the day after Guernica was all but destroyed by German Heinkel and Junkers bombers gave a graphic description:

Guernica, the most ancient town of the

3

Basques and the centre of their cultural tradition, was completely destroyed yesterday afternoon by insurgent raiders. The whole town of 7000 inhabitants, plus 3000 refugees, was slowly and systematically pounded to pieces. At 2am to-day when I visited the town the whole of it was a horrible sight flaming from end to end. The reflection of the flames could be seen in the clouds of smoke above the mountains from ten miles away . . . The town lay far behind the lines. The object of the bombardment was seemingly the demoralisation of the civil population and the destruction of the cradle of the Basque race.'[4]

Between 200 and 400 civilians were killed in this single carefully planned and executed raid and it proved, if proof were needed, that aerial warfare would be used as a weapon against non-military targets.

Evacuation of Britain's major cities became a question to be addressed at the highest level of government. In a House of Commons debate Churchill had warned:

We must expect that, under the pressure of continuous air attack upon London, at least 3,000,000 or 4,000,000 people would be driven out into the open country around the metropolis. This vast mass of human beings, numerically far larger than any armies which have been fed and moved in war, without shelter and without food, without sanitation and without special provision for the maintenance of order, would confront the

4

Government of the day with an administrative problem of the first magnitude, and would certainly absorb the energies of our small Army and our Territorial Force. Problems of this kind have never been faced before, and although there is no need to exaggerate them, neither, on the other hand, is there any need to shrink from facing the immense, unprecedented difficulties which they involve.[5]

London and its environs was thought to be the most vulnerable area with one fifth of the British population or 9 million people concentrated into 750 square miles. But other areas were also considered at risk: those lying south of a line drawn from the Humber to the Bristol Channel. The Air Raid Precautions Department, using information and advice from the Air Ministry, classified provincial cities and towns in Britain in order of vulnerability. The health departments responsible for civilian evacuation divided the country into evacuation, neutral and reception areas. But overwhelming all else was the problem of London, which was expected to be the target of the Luftwaffe in the first instance. The government's concern over how the public would react under a major air attack was based on the reaction to the German bombing of London in the First World War when over 300,000 people took shelter in the Underground stations. Titmuss wrote: 'A war of armies and navies was understood; discipline and behaviour were under control, the individual took from the group a recognised and accepted standard of conduct, and behaviour was within certain limits predictable. But how would civilians behave? They could not be put into uniform, neither given the same group loyalties nor controlled and led in the same way as was an army.'[6] By the time of the air strikes on Guernica, therefore, the question of evacuation from cities was settled in the mind of the British government.

In 1938 a committee was formed under Sir John Anderson to review the question of mass movements of people away from areas deemed to be at high risk from air raids. The Anderson Committee's report of July 1938 was presented to Parliament by the Home Secretary, who announced that the government accepted its main principles and laid particular stress on five points:

1. Evacuation should not be compulsory unless for military or other special reasons people be requested to leave a certain area.
2. Production in large industrial towns should continue for the war effort but non-essential personnel could be evacuated.
3. Accommodation should be provided in private houses 'under powers of compulsory billeting'.
4. The initial costs of evacuation would be borne by the government but those who could afford to contribute towards their maintenance should do so.
5. In order to meet the need for parents who could not afford to evacuate their children, school groups in [the] charge of their teachers would be sent to reception areas.

This last was an important point because it paved the way for hundreds of thousands of children to be evacuated from the towns and cities without their parents.

In the summer of 1939 the population of Britain was estimated to be in the region of 45 million. Of these, some 13 million were living in areas that would need to be evacuated, 14 million were living in neutral areas and 18 million were living in the districts classified by the government as reception areas. The next question that had to be settled was who should be evacuated. The Ministry of Health came up with a list of four categories: pregnant women, mothers with children under five years of age, schoolchildren between the ages of five and fourteen, and the blind and the handicapped 'whose removal was feasible'. Chillingly, those considered so severely disabled that they would not be able easily to be moved or rehoused in the country fell outside the scheme.

Although handicapped children were from the outset to be moved to camps, hostels or institutions the majority of the accommodation for the rest of the evacuees would have to be provided in private homes. To this end the Anderson Committee decided to carry out a survey of accommodation in all the reception areas. It was commissioned on 5 January 1939 and had to be completed by the end of February. The objective was not only to establish a comprehensive picture of the housing situation in reception areas but also to ascertain the number of households who would be prepared to take in children and mothers.

Choosing private accommodation for the majority of mothers and children rather than hostels was expedient for several reasons. First and foremost, the accommodation already existed and the government considered it too short notice to provide a network of hostels and camps for up to 3.5 million people throughout the country. Secondly, it was deemed more suitable for mothers and young children to go to housing judged by the committee to be 'of a standard', that is to say, adequate for family living. This was open to question, as the survey of homes carried out in January 1939 would show. And thirdly, the expense of creating accommodation for such a large number of people for what the committee believed could be a long stretch was impossible.

The government recognised that billeting was the only solution but it also acknowledged that it would be unpopular. After the Munich crisis many MPs of rural constituencies began to make their voices heard. One MP even wrote to say that 'compulsory billeting would be far worse than war'. Nevertheless, despite protests from MPs, church groups, local authorities and individuals it remained the main option with the government making the very small concession that it would construct one hundred camps, each capable of holding about 300 people. Eventually fifty camps were constructed for use as temporary housing for 'difficult' billeting cases and homeless refugees. These were built to have the future potential as peacetime holiday camps. During 1940 the camps were called into use for more permanent accommodation, particularly for disabled children who had been sent in the first instance to buildings with unsatisfactory facilities. Thus the camps were eventually requisitioned for the evacuation scheme proper.

Surplus accommodation was measured on the

basis of one person per habitable room (including kitchens and bathrooms). As housing was in such short supply in Scotland, the calculation had to be based on one person of fourteen and over per habitable room and two under-fourteens. Those conducting the survey also had to make value judgements based on such things as the age of the householders, i.e. those elderly or infirm could not be expected to receive unaccompanied children, or whether the householder would be out all day in which case that could prove difficult in terms of providing care for school-aged children.

What resulted was an unprecedented snapshot of rural Britain: 100,000 visitors investigated over 5 million homes in the course of six weeks, covering 18 million people. The figure for England and Wales, after deductions for rooms needed for other purposes such as service departments, private rental or those deemed to be too close to strategic points such as aerodromes or military establishments or, on the other hand, having problems such as inadequate water supply, was 3.7 million habitable rooms. This, fortunately, was half a million more than the government believed it would need to house the probable number of evacuees.

What the survey also threw up was the state of rural housing in 1939 which, when encountered by people coming from the towns and cities, produced howls of horror: earth closets in outside huts, poor services, often with no running water or electricity, lighting by gas or oil lamps and infrequent bus services. The survey revealed that half of all rural homes in 1939 did indeed have an outside lavatory and 10 per cent had no running water with the village standpipe being the sole water source.

One of the most far-reaching results of the Anderson Committee's report was the decision not to make evacuation compulsory. The initial impact was that no one knew until the moment came how many families would decide to send their children away. The difference between those that registered an interest and those who actually took advantage when the moment came was great. Less than half the schoolchildren eligible for evacuation in England (47 per cent), and just over a third (38 per cent) in Scotland left home in the first wave. This made it difficult for the authorities to work out how many people would require billeting in any one area but it also had an impact on the problem of providing schooling for the children left behind.

By the summer of 1939 the government had decided evacuation should be carried out quickly, efficiently and immediately before the war began. Too long beforehand and the population would not accept it. Once war had begun the bombing of Britain's cities could start within hours. With almost all schools about to start the new academic year it was decided that Operation Pied Piper should be launched on 1 September 1939. The order to commence was issued at 11.07 a.m. on Thursday 31 August with the blunt message: 'Evacuate forthwith'.

In the purely statistical sense, Operation Pied Piper was a success. The largest single movement of civilians in the history of Britain ran relatively smoothly. Hundreds of thousands of women, children and disabled were trained, bussed, paddle-steamed or driven out of Britain's major cities to the countryside. Over a period of four days 1,473,391 people left the cities for billets in rural areas of Britain under the government scheme. In addition to the unaccompanied schoolchildren on the official scheme there were a very large number of privately evacuated people, including a large proportion of children who did not form part of the official statistics but whose number was estimated over the course of the whole war to be in the region of 2 million. These children were sent away to live with relatives in the country; they were evacuated with their schools en masse or they moved with their parents away from the danger zones.

Children left for undisclosed destinations clutching gas masks, small suitcases and provisions, wearing luggage labels. Mothers pushing prams or leading small children by the hand jostled with others to find a seat on the trains and buses provided. The blind and disabled, accompanied by carers, were shepherded towards special transport that would take them into the countryside. It was a gift to the press photographers that they relished. A tearful toddler here, a stiff-upper-lipped boy there, a family group of six children waving out of a train window, a harassed mother clutching enough clutter for three hands, leaning towards a tearaway child straining at her reins.

Everyone was impressed by the sheer scale of the evacuation and the fine British spirit it showed. 'Greatest Evacuation in History Has Begun!' trumpeted one headline in the *Dorset Daily Echo*. 'Exodus of the Bible dwarfed: three million people on the move.' 'A Great National Undertaking' marvelled another journalist. 'Triumph of Planning' claimed the Civil Defence correspondent on *The Times*. The following day the *Evening Standard*'s headline read: 'Germans Invade and Bomb Poland, Britain Mobilises.' The government's planning had paid off and Whitehall was pleased with itself. In 1940 Tom Harrisson, co-founder of Mass Observation and a stern critic of the government's evacuation scheme from the start, wrote: 'Because a lot of trains took a lot of people in a little time, our leaders turned cartwheels of self-satisfaction; uncritically, un-analytically they wallowed in Maths. There was a chorus of self-congratulation, and relevant ministers ladled out congratulations to every conceivable local authority: to the teachers and mothers, to the hosts and to the children of Britain.'[7]

In the country towns and villages, mothers and toddlers, unaccompanied schoolchildren, teachers and those who had offered to accompany the school parties as assistants were squeezed into village halls, marquees, churches and schools to be selected by host families. One group going to Bedfordshire was very pleased to be sent to a smart collection area where marquees were laid out with refreshments. Tea was taken in shifts to prevent overcrowding and the whole atmosphere was that of a country fair. Then they were sent to be selected. One girl told a Mass Observation interviewer:

So far the organisation had been perfect. But the scene which ensued was more akin to a cattle- or slave-market than anything else. The prospective foster mothers, who should not have been allowed on the field at all, just

12

invaded us and walked about the field picking out what they considered to be the most presentable specimens, and then harassed the poor billeting officers for the registration slips which were essential if they were to get the necessary cash for food and lodging from the government.[8]

This situation was repeated all over the country. Children and mothers were looked over, picked, left; family members were separated, kept together, mixed and matched; strong boys went to farms, weaker ones were not chosen, well-dressed little girls were quickly selected; siblings languished at the back of the halls, clutching each other's hands and hoping not to be split up. Hard-pressed billeting officers were knocking on doors at ten or eleven o'clock at night in those first few days, desperately trying to persuade unwilling householders to take tired, grubby, tearful children, still clutching their suitcases, gas masks and wearing their now bedraggled luggage labels.

The choices that were made often had far-reaching consequences, way, way beyond what any parent, foster parent, billeting officer or tearful child could possibly have imagined. Few appeared to foresee the probable consequences.

The whole question of billeting was done on a numerical basis. Profiling such a vast number of people and trying to match background and characters was apparently not even considered by those responsible for the evacuation. As Tom Harrisson complained, the snag was the 'government's mathematical conception of the scheme. Possible solution: Another government?

Or some human mathematicians.'[9] His tongue-in-cheek remark was not entirely unfounded. Paper, paper, paper—reports, timetables, maps, surveys, numbers—but nothing about the human beings that made up the statistics. Little thought had been given to the impact on the human side of the scheme. Harrisson wrote:

It was when they arrived at these new homes that the troubles began—troubles which the authorities had left to look after themselves, apparently assuming that in such emergency human nature would rise to the occasion and a miracle of adaptation be performed. In this assumption they were naturally enough not correct, and in spite of the whole-time efforts of teachers and those in charge of local billeting arrangements, the chaos of the first days was such as to send many of the evacuees straight home in disgust.[10]

In the same paragraph he sounded the word of warning that would echo across the country over the next three months. It was not enough simply to send people away from the cities and into the countryside without thinking through the consequences: 'Under any circumstance such a vast scheme needed not only competent *technical* planning, but also competent psychological and social planning. And once begun, it needed constant supervision, objective criticism and analysis, constructive leadership, using all the channels of opinion forming and habit stabilising.'[11]

When town met country and country met town

the shock was intense on both sides. For the ensuing weeks and months both sides waged a propaganda war about each other. From the country came the cry of horror that the mothers and children from the cities were verminous, lousy, badly dressed for the country and ill-mannered. From the town-dwellers came the squeal of disgust at cottages with outside earthen lavatories, oil lamps and cold-water taps in sculleries. There were tales of children who demanded chips and beer for tea, who ate soup with a knife, who slept standing up, or believed that beds with sheets were laid out just for dead people, children who had never used a chamber pot before. From the other side came stories of girls being used as unpaid maids, boys being kept back from school to work on farms, mothers told to take themselves and their children out of billets for the whole day and roam the lanes, of children forced to use an outside privy in the middle of the night and eat unaccustomed food, often killed and plucked in front of them, of boys in despair at the lack of things to do. R. C. K. Ensor wrote in the *Spectator* on 8 September 1939 that many of the mothers who had arrived in the Home Counties: 'were the lowest grade of slum women—slatternly malodorous tatterdemalions trailing children to match.'[12]

An observer, speaking to villagers in Cheshire in 1939, concluded that 'the village women were very indignant that their beautiful black-and-white village was spoiled by these women in shawls. They were Catholics, on top of it.'[13] At other times the class system, so stratified in pre-war Britain, came in for a side-swipe: 'He will lose family life in the midst of all them servants,' one mother moaned to

15

another observer from Mass Observation. 'And so on. Thousands of cases in our files, atrocity stories about our own people which exceed anything yet about our enemies. Is that a measure of the national unity so constantly trumpeted by King, Halifax, Chatfield, Stanhope and other lords?'[14]

Amidst all the upheaval and drama of the first wave of evacuation, of the disrupted school days and unsatisfactory billets, individuals on both sides struggled to bring some order, comfort and goodwill to the situation. 'It must not be forgotten,' wrote Harrisson, after listing a catalogue of disasters, 'that in *a very large proportion* of cases foster-parents did make their adopted families *happy*. The vast majority of children enjoyed being evacuated.'[15]

One of those was Dorothy Carlile, a seven-year-old from East Manchester who was evacuated at the beginning of September by train with some hundred children from her school. Her father was a bricklayer and her mother a shoe-fitter. They had discussed evacuation before the war, Dorothy recalled, but when the day came she was simply sent to school and the next thing she was taking a train out of the city. 'It was really all a big adventure,' she explained. 'In the end we only went about seven or eight miles. Some of us went to Hollingworth, others to Tintwistle and Broadbottom. But it was evacuation nevertheless and we were away from home.'

Dorothy was dropped off by the billeting officer, with two other little girls, to live with Mrs Parr and her stepdaughter, Maud, who they knew only as 'Miss Parr'. Mrs Parr was out when they arrived, so that the girls were left to play in the field in front

16

of the house until she came home. The house was a converted stable and Mrs Parr, who was in her seventies, was a well-travelled ladies' maid who turned out to be a kind and generous foster mother. The house was sparse but more comfortable than Dorothy's own home in Manchester and she was struck, even as a very little girl, by the beauty of their surroundings.

The cottage was basic with no electricity and cold water that came from a spring up the garden. The three girls slept in one bedroom at the top of the house until it was winter and too cold, when they were moved downstairs to sleep in the warmth.

The only horrid thing I remember was the privy in the garden which was emptied once a week. Otherwise it was a basic but lovely cottage. My own home was a terraced house in Manchester that overlooked the tripe works of United Cattle Products. It was on a very busy road and the smell from the works could be horrible. Eventually my parents moved to Ashton so that my mother could catch a bus to visit me at the Parrs' every weekend. I was very happy there but I still wanted to go home to live with my parents.

Eventually her mother agreed and Dorothy left Mrs Parr and went back to Manchester. She moved to her parents' new house at Ashton. Her own school, Wheeler Street School, had not reopened, so she had to go to St Clement's, a school in a deprived area of the city. Her mother was so anxious about her daughter's education that she

17

persuaded the school to let her take the exam to Manchester High School. Dorothy passed the exam and joined the scholarship class where she was teased by some of the girls about her background. 'My father says you live in a slum,' one girl taunted. Dorothy replied: 'You should have seen where we used to live!' She survived Manchester High School and went on to read medicine at Sheffield University.

The impact of evacuation on Dorothy was profound and positive. She acquired a great love of the countryside and a respect for other ways of life. She felt she benefited from Mrs Parr's lifetime of experiences of travel and knowledge of the world beyond Manchester. She realised she was fortunate that she was not moved far from her home so that her mother could visit her regularly and that kept the vital link of family life going strong for the two years she was away. The biggest disruption in coming back from Mrs Parr's was not adjusting to her home again but finding her feet at a new school.

Eddie Harrison was evacuated from Manchester to Market Drayton where he had the advantage of a far superior education to the one he had received prior to the war. During the autumn of 1939 most of the evacuees returned so that only five children from Mansfield School remained in Market Drayton and he was soon absorbed into the Senior School where he was no longer considered to be an evacuee but just another pupil. He was immensely fortunate in his billet as well as in his education:

Mrs Hughes was a natural foster mother. She treated us as one of her own: she got cross if

18

we stepped out of line and we were well disciplined, but fairly. She was a fantastic woman and my brother and I were very devoted to her. Evacuation was a wholly positive experience for us and we benefited not only from a change in lifestyle but also the excellent education. My sister-in-law is as clear about this as we are. She feels we did well in life as a result of our wartime experiences.

On his return to Manchester Eddie won a place at Manchester Commercial School and studied there until he was fifteen when he had to leave school to support the family as his father was unable to work. Although his formal schooling was curtailed he had received sufficient and good quality education so that he could reap the benefits in his later years.

Not all evacuee children were as fortunate as Eddie Harrison. Disruption to education was a major issue for many and it was something that took months to resolve. One of the problems that faced the local authorities was that evacuation had not been compulsory, so that when whole schools were evacuated from urban areas to the country it was not necessarily the case that all the children would follow. This left the problem of what to do with the children who had remained behind and indeed, very soon after it became clear that there would be no major air attacks, what to do with those children who had returned to the cities. Official figures show that by January 1940 over one third of mothers and children had returned home leaving only about 570,000 evacuees in the reception areas.[16]

For the children whose schools succeeded in evacuating the majority of their children as a group, the experience was often successful and the ties to the temporary home have lasted in some cases a lifetime. Doris Cox lived in Bow in east London before the war and was evacuated with her classmates from Coburn School to Taunton. The school set up in Taunton and established such a name for itself locally that the 268 students had a real sense of identity and pride in their own school. Some went back to London during the course of the autumn of 1939 but enough stayed for the school to continue to function and when the bombing started in London children from Bow who would have qualified to join the Coburn School in normal times were accepted into the school in its new location. The school eventually took over the Bishop Fox School in Taunton and continued to thrive. Doris felt strongly that the education of the girls did not suffer and they had a strong sense of identity, both of which helped to make the evacuation to Taunton less unsettling.

'What I miss most about my past life,' explained Doris, 'is the loss of my cockney accent. I so love to hear it when I come up to London or if I come across someone who speaks with a cockney accent down here in the West Country. That was the major victim of my time as an evacuee. For the rest I believe I had a much easier time than others.' Born in December 1927, she was already nearly twelve at the outbreak of the war. She had won a scholarship to Coburn School and spent just a week there before the war broke out and she and the school were moved to Taunton. This, she is certain, meant that her attitude to evacuation was one of welcoming an opportunity. 'I don't think I gave much thought to my mother, I'm not sure any of us did. It was all just such an adventure for us.'

Doris and her mother were living with her grandmother in the late 1930s as her parents had split up when she was five. Doris's mother was the youngest of eleven children and Doris herself one of twenty-five grandchildren, so although she was the only child of a single mother, she had been used to an enormous extended family. She has scant recollection of her father and knows little about him other than that his name was Ritterbund and that her paternal grandfather was a German Jew and her grandmother a Russian Jew. He was a waistcoat-hand or tailor and worked as a journeyman so that he contributed only irregularly to her mother's allowance. Doris saw him just once before the war that she can recall and never again thereafter. 'We never did know what happened to him. He must have been killed in a bombing raid but no one ever found out how he died. Years later I went to St Catherine's House and discovered that he had been a twin. I didn't know that at the time.'

Like many children she was moved several times as people got used to the fact that some evacuee children were to stay for the duration. Her first billet was very happy but that lasted for only six weeks. The next two billets in Taunton were unsatisfactory. 'We were moved to a very poor family who were quite snobby. They would say to us: "When you are talking to people do you mind not saying you come from the East End? Could you say you come from North London?"'

21

Eventually she was sent to a hostel where she felt completely at home. Matron was an excellent cook and the other children seemed to be contented there too. That lasted until another billet was found with a Mr and Mrs Hann. There she and her friend, Dorothy Mackay, thrived for nearly three years.

In 1944 Doris left school and returned to London to work in a post in the Civil Establishment Branch of the Admiralty. Her mother, Lily, meantime, had remarried and had had a baby daughter with her new husband. They were living in Hackney, so close to the Liverpool Street to Cambridge train line that the house shook all night as the trains rattled along the tracks. After three days in London their home was hit by a bomb and Doris found herself tucked under the stairs in her mother's house holding her baby half-sister. 'It was then that I learned most definitely that it is people that matter, not material things. I think I became hardened as a result of being bombed. Not tough, just philosophical about life. After the bombing I left London and went back to Taunton where I worked for the Admiralty in their Hydrographic Department doing most interesting work. Not long after the war I met my husband, a policeman, and I have stayed in the area ever since.'

It was only when her mother was dying that Doris really considered what it must have been like for her to have been alone in London without her daughter during the air raids. 'Looking back now I think that Mum was glad that I didn't have to go through the Blitz and that I was safe in the South West. I was luckily spared most of it though I was

22

in Liverpool Street Station in the buffet during a rocket raid, which was a hairy experience. The war did not affect my relationship with my mother; in fact it made us closer.'

Thinking about the overall effect of evacuation, Doris is sure that she benefited more than she suffered from living in Taunton. She is certain that the fact the school was kept together and so many of the girls remained there for long periods increased the sense of being part of a group.

What I learned during the war was that children are very tribal. It was good to be in a group of girls from the same school all belonging together. We formed a bond that has lasted in some cases up to the present day. We were sometimes resented, even years later, by the girls from Bishop Fox's School for taking away the boys, but that's natural. What I do know is that during the war things came into very sharp focus for me. I find that even today I know more about girls I was evacuated with than I do about people who I met after the war. It stripped life back to the bare essentials and in a way that was one of the most interesting aspects of it.

For a large number of children, keeping their school together was not straightforward and evacuated city schools struggled to rub alongside the village schools, which very often had to share premises and work on a morning shift one week, afternoon shift the next week rota, so that the classrooms and facilities could be shared. As a result these children's education was disrupted and they frequently found they were unpopular with the village children and their parents who resented the incomers.

Had the German Luftwaffe pilots emptied their bomb bays onto London as predicted, the reception of the town children and mothers in the country might have been different. As it was, the resentment grew very quickly as parents asked themselves why they had been forced to evacuate their children and host families wondered out loud what all the fuss had been about and why they were being put upon. The reception areas wanted the children out; the authorities in Whitehall wanted them to remain; the children had no say. It was a profoundly unsatisfactory situation.

Despite some searing criticism of the mothers who took their children to the countryside in 1939, not all of them were 'slatternly malodorous tatterdemalions' and many who made themselves a life in a rural community for the duration of the war were very happy. Valerie Clayton was just four and a half when she left the city with her mother and little brother: 'I fell in love with everything we saw in the woods and fields in our adopted home. The smell of wood burning and primroses, violets and cowslips always make me think of those blissful days. Now I have to make a special trip just to see a few cowslips. I am going back this year to recapture old memories.'[17]

As already seen, official evacuation was aimed at predominantly working-class families living in the densely populated inner city areas of the major industrial towns and cities. Although statistically it is true that more rural working-class families made their homes available to incoming evacuees, some host families in the countryside, small towns and villages were middle class. The result was that some of the city children, especially those who spent years with their hosts, became accustomed to a new, different and more prosperous lifestyle. Going home was a test and it did not always work out satisfactorily. Barbara Lamb's foster family had a car. At the end of the war they drove her back to London but she would not let them drive her up her street, not because she was ashamed of her home, she explained, but because she knew it would make her parents feel uncomfortable:

> I really came down to earth when I got home. I'd seen the other side and now I was back on the working-class side. It must have been terrible for Mum seeing me being fussy. You see, I'd been used to a big plateful of everything. My hosts had been very wealthy landowners and I had had everything I wanted. That was the first problem. The second was that when I went home I spoke like someone who came from a cultured corner of England, much to my family's disgust. And to my mum's horror I kept comparing the two lifestyles. That was really sad for her but I didn't realise how hurtful it was when I said at mealtimes 'Is that all there is?' and things like that.

Barbara found living in London miserable. At school she was teased for her 'posh' accent. She felt that she had no friends any more and she found home life tiresome. Eventually she emigrated to Australia, where she found the relaxed attitude towards class much more to her liking.

Barbara's experience was by no means unique. One of the selling points of evacuation had been that it would be a great leveller: all classes mixed together and learning about each other's customs. The reality was often far less comfortable than the government had imagined, and it caused friction not only between children and parents but between siblings who had had different experiences. Baroness Shirley Williams, herself evacuated to America for part of the war, wrote in 2009: 'Comfortable middle-class England was unaware of these differences, and that was why having evacuee children from the big cities bivouacked upon them in the first two years of the war came as such a great shock. I suspect evacuation had a lot to do with the radical change in public attitudes between pre- and post-war society.'[18]

Elizabeth Green was billeted with a wealthy family in a large, clean house that was a glaring contrast to home. When her mother came to visit she found herself embarrassed by her mother's manners but almost more annoyed by the foster family's smirks at her mother's manners. Worse still was going home to the flea- and mouse-ridden hovel above the shop that was her real home. She summed up her discomfort by writing: 'I really loved my mum and dad and little brother but I know which type of home I preferred and that was an awful twist.'

Beryl Carter was evacuated from Stretford Road School in Manchester to the home of Lady Worthington in Mobberley in Cheshire, a distance of a mere dozen miles or so but to an entirely unfamiliar world:

> We four older children were evacuated together without our mum, who was evacuated with our baby sister to a different house in the same area. We came from a small terraced house with no bath and no garden to this magnificent place with a croquet lawn at the front, an apple orchard and extensive gardens. Lady Worthington was in her nineties I believe, so we were looked after by the butler and a maid called Lilian. It was lovely and even today when I smell mown grass it reminds me of our stay in Mobberley.

Beryl remained there for a matter of weeks before she was moved. The children left the Worthington household and were split up and went to live with different families, which did not please their father, so he brought them all back to Manchester before the end of 1939. She went on: 'I loved being in Mobberley and I would have thoroughly enjoyed my evacuation if I had been with my mother. My brother and I used to talk a lot about our memories of that time and we agreed that it was a good experience but for the fact we were split up from Mum. I don't think it changed me but it gave me a different view of life.'

Beryl and her siblings were among 350,000 children who returned to the cities during the autumn of 1939. The lack of air raids, parents' loneliness without their children and the government's insistence that families contribute to their children's upkeep in their foster families all helped to fuel resentment of the evacuation

27

scheme and a determination to bring children home. The press was full of opinions on the failure of the evacuation scheme with a special correspondent writing in *The Times* in January 1940: 'Evacuation was originally planned as a temporary, quasi-military operation to save children and mothers from a few weeks of intensive bombing. Whitehall did not foresee a complete and prolonged dislocation of normal education.'[19]

At the beginning of the war the major problem for the government was persuading parents to keep their children in the countryside, despite the lack of air raids. It was decided that from the end of October 1939 parents should contribute to help support their evacuated children. The amounts involved were less than the official weekly billeting allowance of ten shillings and sixpence per child but the scheme proved to be more trouble than it was worth and tipped the scale for many parents towards demanding their children's return.

The ties to home were too strong for many families, although this did not always meet with sympathy from the host villages. The Reverend Oldham from his vicarage in Brockham Green in Surrey deplored, in a letter to *The Times*,

the selfish attitude of parents who insist on coming to the countryside on a Sunday by Sunday basis to see their children, in fact they even come during the week and have the temerity to complain that they are missing their little ones. Frequent cases are brought to my notice of children being taken home with the selfish excuse that, as one mother wrote, 'We cannot stick the loneliness.'! While one appreciates the feelings of parents, surely something can be done to prevent this senseless withdrawal of children into danger zones.

The government ran advertising campaigns in 1940 warning mothers of the danger of bringing their children back to the cities but with limited success. By May 1940 only one householder in five registered an interest in sending their children away from the cities if heavy raids began. The campaign was stepped up when the German invasion seemed imminent but local authorities found it difficult in some areas to persuade people to accept evacuee children, especially if they had had a bad experience in September 1939. One historian cited the case of Hungerford where of thirty-one wealthy homeowners asked to receive their share of new evacuees in the summer of 1940 only one agreed. Things got so bad in Windsor, where homeowners objected vociferously to taking evacuees, that the local newspaper recommended the council consider setting up concentration camps to segregate the evacuees from the town's residents. Some householders were taken to court for refusing to house evacuees. A woman in Leicestershire had her case heard in the High Court. She argued that she had taken two children in September 1939 and had paid for clothes, food and even a holiday for them but without warning the parents had arrived to take the children home and she was bitter over the lack of gratitude. The case resulted in her being required to take evacuees in the future. She said: 'I told the billeting officer that there appears to be one law for the parents and one for the householder.'[20] Even if householders relented they could still make evacuees feel unwelcome by forcing them to use outside lavatories, or forbidding the children from making any noise or using any room in the house other than their bedrooms and the kitchen.

John Hart explained:

I can remember my mother telling me after the war how she had trawled round the Hampshire village she was evacuated to day after day with my older brother in the pram and my sister on foot. The couple she lived with did not want her in the house with the children during the day as they made too much noise. She was not allowed to use the kitchen and the only tap she could use was across the yard where there was no light at night. My mother was not a strong person and she did not have the courage to stand up to Mrs S. and tell her that her attitude was deeply unchristian. In all fairness Mrs S. had had the experience a year earlier of a woman [an evacuee mother] who turned out to be a thief, but that was no reason to tar my poor mother with the same brush. Eventually another woman in the village took pity on Mum and let her rent a little cottage on the edge of the village. That worked out really well and my mother started doing hair again—she had been a hairdresser, you see. And the irony was that she was so good at perms that Mrs S. used to have her round to do her hair. She stayed in the village until

1945 and I was born there about a year after my dad was invalided out of the Army and came to live with her. We still go back there but I never did meet Mrs S. who made Mum's life so difficult.

On 10 May 1940 two things happened that changed the course of the war and began a new era in Britain. Hitler's army and the Luftwaffe launched the Blitzkrieg and Winston Churchill became Prime Minister. The most immediate effect of the offensive in Holland and Belgium was that the British Expeditionary Force was woken from its post-1918 slumber and brought sharply to its feet. It found itself woefully ill-equipped and trained to cope with the German onslaught. Just twenty days after the attacks commenced, Britain was involved in another immense evacuation. This time it was the evacuation of troops from Dunkirk, over 330,000 in total. Heralded as a great triumph and a victory by the government, the troops knew only too well they had been beaten into retreat and felt little of the glory that was being celebrated in their rescue. Of their original number, 30,000 had been killed or wounded and almost the same number were missing or had been taken prisoner, and most of their equipment remained in continental Europe.

The swiftness of Hitler's domination of the Low Countries and France had shaken the British government and the military. It also had a significant impact on the general population and, despite everything the government did to dampen anxiety about an invasion, there was a very real and keenly felt fear that Britain would be next. In a way that the threat of air raids at the outset of the war had never done, the urgent threat of the invasion concentrated people's minds. Historian Michael Fethney wrote: 'With the occupation of Denmark, Norway, Belgium and Holland, and the collapse of France imminent, the so-called Phoney War was decidedly over. To add to the mounting apprehension in Britain, newspapers described through April and May how Nazi bombers were attacking civilian refugees as they sought to leave the war zones.'[21]

The Joint Chiefs of Staff warned the Cabinet two days after the capitulation of France: 'We must regard the threat of invasion as imminent.' It was not surprising that people felt anxious about the prospect of Britain's future. The overwhelming reaction of parents to the perceived threat of Nazification of Britain was to put their children beyond the reach of the Germans by sending them as far away as possible. Middle-class families and those with independent means flocked to take up the generous offers from America and Canada to offer safe-housing for their children, either on a one-to-one basis, or as part of a school evacuation scheme, or as part of a group scheme, often set up privately by bodies such as the Quakers; or Anglo-American companies, such as Kodak and Ford; or through academic exchanges: over a hundred children from the homes of Oxford academics were invited to live with families in New Haven in the summer of 1940, as part of an exchange with Yale University.

The government had to be seen to act on behalf of children and families who did not have the means to place their children beyond the new danger. Their first concern was that many of the evacuation areas considered 'safe' reception areas in 1939 were now deemed to be at risk of attack or invasion. These were towns along the south coast such as Hastings, Dover, Folkestone and Portsmouth as well as towns up the east coast as far as Harwich. Tens of thousands of schoolchildren and mothers with toddlers had been evacuated to these areas, as had hospitals and homes for the blind and disabled. As many as possible now had to be evacuated again to new safe areas, along with the children of those coastal towns and villages.

The evacuation of 1940 was significant in number, although not as large as the 1939 exodus from the big cities. Almost 213,000 children were on the move. They travelled by train and bus in all directions, criss-crossing the country as they made their way to their new homes.

But it was the evacuation abroad that really caught the public's imagination. Offers of safety and care from the Dominions had trickled in from the late 1930s onwards. Canada and Southern Rhodesia had been particularly keen to encourage Britons to send their children there but these kind offers had by and large been ignored by the government, not least because of the problem of getting the children across the seas. The other reason was that the government had not wanted to separate parents and children by such insurmountable distances. In the early summer of 1940 this changed.

The man put in charge of official overseas evacuation was Geoffrey Shakespeare. Initially unsure, he eventually became convinced that it was a sensible policy. His views chimed with those of the general populace, the public responding wholeheartedly to the idea. Churchill strongly opposed it because it smacked of giving up and took valuable resources and attention away from the war effort on the home front. He made no secret of his irritation with the scheme, as this comment in the War Cabinet minutes from 1 July 1940 shows: 'A large movement of this kind encourages a defeatist spirit . . . entirely contrary to the true facts of the position, and it should be sternly discouraged.'

The Children's Overseas Reception Board scheme, which became known by its sobriquet CORB, was launched in June 1940, just a month after the Blitzkrieg brought the Phoney War to an end. Three days earlier Circular 1515 had been sent to all education authorities and independent schools giving guidelines for the possibility of an evacuation scheme abroad. Even then it was not clear that the War Cabinet would give permission for its go-ahead.

In a matter of just two weeks CORB had received applications on behalf of almost half of the children eligible for the scheme, 211,448 in total. Michael Fethney, himself a CORB evacuee sent with his brother John to Australia, suggested that it was possible that, had the scheme remained open (the lists were closed on 1 July 1940, just ten days after the launch), an even larger percentage of eligible children would have been signed up for evacuation overseas. (The story of the 'seavacs' and their experiences, though small in number in comparison with the domestic evacuees, is an important part of the evacuation picture and will be told in detail later in this book.)

Meanwhile, as children were being sent abroad and moved to other parts of the country, the Battle of Britain commenced and the bombing, so desperately feared in 1939, began in earnest in August 1940. Children who had returned to the cities were sent back to safety and by the time the Blitz intensified in September 1941 the official figures for evacuees away from home totalled 1.3 million.

Later that year an evacuation took place that barely registers on the radar of wartime experiences but it had a very profound effect on those caught up in it. This was the evacuation of women and children from the Far East, principally from Hong Kong, Malaya and Singapore, although a significant number of families were also evacuated from Manchuria. Initially this far corner of the British Empire was distanced from the war. Some men had returned to Britain and joined up but many remained in their posts, notably those working for the Colonial Office, which included a cross-section of professionals such as doctors, nurses and engineers as well as plantation owners, lawyers and bankers. Malaya contributed large amounts of rubber towards the war effort until 1942. Their families, many of whom knew no other life, remained with them. As the war progressed and spread across the Middle East and beyond, the American Ambassador in China ordered all women, children and non-essential staff to be evacuated. Hong Kong, highly vulnerable on the coast of China, was aware of the danger to its colonial families and they too were evacuated in July 1940. The order to leave Malaya and

Singapore came much later, in fact after the invasion of those countries by the Japanese, so that their flight was hasty and latterly, in Singapore, conducted under attack.

Most families from the Far East were sent to Australia or India. Some went to South Africa and a number returned to Britain. They wanted to be among family once their own livelihoods in the Far East had been lost. In all nearly 12,000 mothers and children were evacuated from British overseas postings in the autumn of 1941 and the early spring of 1942. For them evacuation brought a complete change of life and for many it meant that that change was for ever. They had no home to come back to in the post-war era and for nearly a third of the children there was no father to return to. The death rate in the Japanese prison camps, both military and civilian, was shockingly high. Of those imprisoned in Thailand and Burma alone, 27 per cent perished of disease, brutality and neglect.

A fourth evacuation in Britain came in 1944 and this was in some ways the most real in the sense of being an emergency evacuation because people were fleeing from a new and deadly enemy—the V1 bombs, the Vergeltungswaffen, the vengeance weapons. These Buzz Bombs or Doodlebugs were unmanned cruise missiles that flew day and night, raining terror onto the South East. The true fear came not from their droning noise but from the silence that came as the engine cut out and the bomb tipped and fell. All accounts in diaries, letters and fiction speak of that ghastly moment when the buzzing stopped and the bomb plunged towards the ground. Brenda Bancroft had come back to London to live with her grandmother, having been evacuated to Oxfordshire earlier in the war. She recalled the bombs clearly: 'They made this awful click-click sound in the skies as they went over. It was the silence when they cut out I remember most vividly. I truly learned the significance of the term "pregnant silence". Can you believe me when I talk about the sound of silence? But that is what it was.'

The damage they caused to London's housing was almost parallel to that of the Blitz three years earlier: 1,127,000 to 1,150,000 houses damaged or destroyed. The casualty figures for civilians were lower than in 1941: 23,892 as opposed to 92,566 killed or injured in the Blitz. But the effect to morale was terrible. Author Ruth Inglis described the V1s as 'the last sting in the tail of a dying aggressor, but they successfully injected the slow poison of despair into the exhausted population of Great Britain'.[22]

Between July and September 1944 over 500,000 mothers and children or expectant mothers left the Metropolitan area on the government's assisted private evacuation scheme. This time there was no organisation of billets in rural areas; the government merely helped to finance travel out of the capital. In addition, 100,000 unaccompanied children were sent from the Metropolitan area to the country in the last government-backed evacuation scheme of the war, so that the total number of official evacuees accommodated in rural Britain in September 1944 was only 200,000 fewer than during the Blitz in 1940–41.

Some evacuees moved to the countryside and then back to the city, only to be moved out to the country when the threat of bombing became more serious. It could prove to be disruptive not only to their education but also to their sense of stability.

Wally Boater from south-east London was born in 1934 and grew up in Poplar with his parents, his two younger sisters, grandparents and extended family all living in a row of small terraced houses in Follet Street. In September 1939 he was evacuated with his mother and two sisters to Wantage in Oxfordshire. They were lodged in one room of the local vicarage and, from what Wally can remember, it was not a particularly happy experience for his mother who, at twenty-five, missed her husband, her family and above all her way of life in London. They remained there for four months until his father visited them and brought them back to London. Wally's grandfather was sufficiently concerned for their safety, despite the lack of aerial attacks at that stage, that he found them lodgings in Canning Town where Wally was sent to school, the second in four months.

As the threat of invasion became a pressing concern in the spring of 1940 Wally and his mother and sisters were evacuated once again, by coach, to Oxford. 'We had been sitting in a shelter for the whole night before we were evacuated. The bombing was terrible and all the doors and windows in the house were blown out so it was clear it was not safe to stay any longer. I remember getting on the coach—it was a green and white one. I don't think we had any idea where we were going. Well certainly we children didn't and for us it was all a great adventure.' This time his father came with them to see that they were safely settled in a nice home before he went back to London to work. Wally remembers arriving in Oxford on the

Marston Road. They were all exhausted after their sleepless night and were sitting on a wall like sparrows waiting to see if anyone would offer them lodgings when a lady called Mrs Lewis came up to them and said, 'You'd better come in for a cup of tea.' Wally explained:

She was a dear lady and she obviously took pity on us all sitting there looking bedraggled and tired. My clearest memory is of being shown into her son's room at the back and playing with a little train set. We lived in Mrs Lewis's front room for several weeks and tried to settle down a bit. Dad went back to London but his factory had been bombed so he came back to Marston and eventually found work at a foundry in Cowley. The house next door to Mrs Lewis's, 447 Marston Road, became vacant and we were allowed to move in. After that, well, the whole family turned up: my aunties Nell, Peggy and Betty, Aunt Maisy, her boy Alan, my granddad and his wife plus Aunt Wyn, Johnny and Joyce. Then there were my parents, me and my sisters. It was a bit of a squash in a very compact three-bedroom house.

The biggest upheaval for Wally was in his schooling. For the third time in a year he was sent to a new school and he found it difficult to settle at first. There were a lot of evacuees at Star Lane School in Marston and a further influx of London schoolchildren in the autumn of 1940 meant that the class sizes were seldom less than forty and there was continual fluctuation within the school, which was housed in the Congregational Church, until the end of the war.

Our family was poor but we were not down-and-outs. We survived on our rations plus fruit that we could pick locally and soon we began to keep chickens so that we had eggs as well. As a little child I had no knowledge of the country. I'd never seen a cow and as far as I can remember there were no trees on our street in Poplar, so life in Marston was completely different. On balance our life as evacuees soon settled down into a routine but it never felt completely secure. Mum always used to talk about how we would 'go back home' but we never did. At one stage all our aunts and cousins left and then the house felt big and lonely. The result was that I have never really been able to relax. I was always concerned that I would not have enough money and I found it very difficult to settle and work for someone. My first job was doing newspaper rounds at the age of eleven and thereafter I knew I would have to take responsibility for making my own living. I left school at fifteen and got an apprenticeship with a coach works in Oxford but I only lasted six months there. After another unsuccessful job I decided I would work as a freelance gardener and I have done that ever since, with a short break for National Service in 1952. I bought a Morris van and some scales and sold vegetables in the village. Eventually I had a market stall and then I bought a field to expand my little business. It was not that evacuation was an unhappy experience for me, it was just disruptive and left me with this feeling that I will never be able to stop working.

2

RELATIVE STRANGERS

Will they rest,
Will they be contented, these
Fledglings of a cuckoo's egg reared in a
    stranger's nest?
Born of one people, with another bred,
Will they return to their parents again, or
    choose
The foster-home, or seek the unrented
    road?

From 'The Evacuees' by Norman
Nicholson

Of the estimated 3.5 million mothers, children and disabled people who were evacuated over the course of the Second World War only a handful, less than 2 per cent, were repatriated officially. The returns were piecemeal rather than an orderly surge as had been the case with the major evacuations in 1939, 1940 and 1944. The lengths of time children were away varied. Some were away for only a matter of days. One boy came home the day after he was evacuated from Bootle to Blackpool. His only memory of evacuation was the indignation he felt that the family he was billeted with helped themselves to his emergency provisions, including a precious tin of corned beef. Another woman refused to get off the bus in the Dorset village she was evacuated to and returned

42

to Southampton despite the protests of the driver.

Most, however, spent longer in the countryside although many were back home by Christmas 1939 and of those a sizeable number never left home again. A structured homecoming was rare and often children found themselves being taken away from foster families with little notice or explanation, which could be deeply distressing for both the evacuees and the hosts. Some came home unexpectedly but the majority found their way back at times that suited them or their families. The exception to this was the children sent abroad on the government scheme in 1940 and who were repatriated by ship in 1945 and 1946.

Plans for returning evacuees to London officially were considered as early as August 1943 and detailed planning began in the spring of 1944 but was disrupted by the arrival of the V1 rockets. The official evacuation scheme was closed on 7 September 1944, the day before the first V2 bomb fell on the capital. Families were already beginning to drift back to London and the press was full of anxious reports about the inherent dangers of unofficial returns. Six days later the government repeated its warning that the danger from rocket attacks was not over and Herbert Morrison spoke of the trials still in store for Britain 'before the allied armies have rooted out the last of the vipers' nests.'

The even greater long-term issue facing the government was the serious lack of suitable housing in the major cities. In London alone over 850,000 houses in a parlous state awaited urgent 'first aid' repairs while the number of schools able to accommodate returning children safely was inadequate. Many had been damaged by bombs but a number had been requisitioned. The Leas School on the Wirral, for example, had been used as a rehabilitation centre for the Royal Air Force from 1939 and the buildings were not handed back to the school until well after the war.

Despite warnings from government ministers and pleas in the press, evacuees continued to pour back into the cities. As late as April 1945 the government said: 'Make no move until the official word to return is given you.'[1] The telegram to set in train the official return was sent out to local authorities on Wednesday 2 May 1945. It was believed that up to 500,000 mothers and children would take advantage of the return scheme on special trains to reception areas in the Metropolitan area. In the event just one tenth of that number came back that way.

Little advice was offered to parents on how to deal with their returning children. The scheme suffered from the same problems as its predecessors in that it was designed to deal with transportation, to minimise disruption in the city reception areas and to reduce the risk of families gathering where there was no housing for them. What the scheme failed to address was the psychological impact of how evacuation had affected children and would go on to affect families for weeks, months, years and, for a few, a lifetime. Although some help and follow-up advice had been provided by local authorities on the advice of the Ministry of Health, it was not universal nor could it address all the problems faced by individuals.

The return home was at times more traumatic

than the departure had been. Settling down after months or years away took time, with adjustments needed on both sides. For some this came quickly and children were scooped up into the familiar world of home and family life. But for others it could take much longer and there were children who found it hard to live with relative strangers. One little boy, Robert, who aged three had been placed with three elderly spinsters in Devon, came to love his foster family so much that he shocked his mother when she eventually visited him. At bedtime he knelt down by his bed and prayed: 'O God, don't let this woman take me away; she says she's my mother, but I want to stay here with my aunties.'[2]

Rita Jennings was older than Robert but she too found it very hard to readjust after five years away:

I did not want to return. I cried most of the way back and when I first saw them I hardly recognised my parents. They felt like strangers to me. They spoke strangely, dressed differently and wanted affection from me, which I could not give. Evacuation from eleven to sixteen ruined my family life for good—even now when my mother is ninety the gap is still there on my part.[3]

The respected British psychiatrist John Bowlby, who developed one of the century's most influential theories of personality development and social relationships—attachment theory—was asked by one former evacuee why some children had developed depression in later life. It had to do, he explained in a letter to her in the late 1980s, with the reception children received from their parents on their return from evacuation. What mattered most was how the parents reacted to their children's homecoming, how they coped with the changes, newly adopted attitudes and recent experiences. This could go on to have a major impact on how well or not the children coped as adults and those who had a very difficult homecoming would, he suggested, be more vulnerable to depression than those who had not.

For a very few children (official figures gave 29 children out of 9,000 who still remained in the countryside in 1945) there was no return because they had been abandoned by their parents. Others returned to discover a new baby or, more unexpected still, a different father. Some children had no home to come back to as it had been bombed and destroyed; others had lost siblings during the war and their families were grieving. For others still there was no ceremony or welcome. They would arrive at home one evening and be back in school the following day, and told to 'get on with it'. The fact that this was expected of them not only by their families but also by society at large is summed up in a single action by the BBC, explained Dr Martin Parsons: 'When war was declared in 1939 the Mickey Mouse cartoon that was running on television was stopped in mid-flow. When the BBC ran the cartoon again in 1945 it was re-started at exactly the same point it had been stopped at six years earlier.' Life, implied the BBC, was to proceed as normal.

But what was normal? Felicity Hugh-Jones was evacuated with her three siblings for four years. The two younger boys went to one couple and

Felicity and her sister were split up and sent to different homes so that she saw her brothers and sister infrequently. The effect of all this had been to make her internalise her own feelings. She wrote: 'I don't think we talked much between ourselves about our experiences. Children tend to keep miseries to themselves. After the war the four of us were separated by schools and college. I don't remember talking to the parents much about it either; perhaps it was reluctance on both sides. With relatives or new friends, guilt at my comfy war kept me quiet, and how did one describe it all anyway?'[4]

Fear at leaving a much-loved foster family was a common theme. One girl who spent five years in Cape Town spoke to former overseas evacuee and author, Jessica Mann, and said: 'I was terrified of leaving people who had become my family, I was really quite unwilling to go, but I was also terribly ashamed of my reluctance.'[5] This feeling of split loyalty and guilt is a common theme for children who were evacuated abroad and realised that they would be regarded by their peers as having abandoned the country in its darkest hour. It was not something they could discuss with their parents, many said later. It would have sounded so disloyal to say they had not wanted to come home and yet that is how many felt, having been well cared for abroad.

Similarly Jean Huckstepp, who was evacuated to Wales at the very young age of three and a half, remembered feeling happy with her foster parents from the outset: 'Being so young I have no recollection of anything before living in Hirwenydd in the village of Beulah. Mammie and Jack were a

47

wonderful couple, already in their sixties and had brought up twelve children of their own, so they had plenty of experience and they treated me exactly like one of their own family.' She had an idyllic childhood, being treated like a treasured grandchild and although she received regular parcels and letters from her parents in London she felt at home with her Welsh family.

I count myself very, very lucky to have been brought up by such a loving, caring couple. I lived with them for five years and it broke my heart to leave them and the friends that I had made. It was the only life that I knew. I could speak and understand Welsh, I felt Welsh and to me it felt as though I were leaving home. Although I was going back to England to live with Mum and Dad and my sister and brother, I'm sure that the situation didn't really make me as happy as it should have done. I was going to live in a completely different world and I didn't know what to expect.[6]

Jean's sister had also spent the wartime years in Wales, although with a different family. She had similar problems coming to terms with home life in London after the war. Jean was fortunate that her parents were understanding and made it possible for the girls to visit Wales:

It took my sister and me a long, long time to settle down with Mum and Dad. My brother had already returned home quite a while before us so he was fine. All we wanted to do

48

was to go back to be with our Welsh families so Mum and Dad arranged for us to spend our long school summer holidays with them each year. My sister and I used to speak Welsh to each other at home sometimes, which used to annoy Mum and Dad. I have kept in touch with my Welsh family and have been going back 'home' for over fifty years.[7]

Lack of communication could lead to misunderstandings that might take years to resolve. Iris Charos had been living very happily with a family in Devon when her mother arrived, without warning, in 1942 and took her and her sister and brother back to London:

I can remember leaving the farm and not wanting to speak to my mother. I was twelve by then. She seemed so remote, she seemed detached. She didn't even seem happy about taking us home. I really didn't want to go. I can feel, now, that overwhelming sense of loss as we got further and further away from the farm, getting on the train coming home. I can still feel it. I could almost weep for what I lost and Mum never understood. It was like a bad dream and was even worse when we arrived in London to find there were still occasional air raids. There was also the fact that we came back to a different house. But when the Doodlebugs started my resentment at being brought home to the smells of cordite and ruined buildings and a very, very restricted diet on strict rations really came to the fore and I asked my mother why she had brought

49

us home. She told me 'That is past. We don't need to talk about it now.' It soured my relationship with her until she was an old lady when I relented and cared for her but I never broached the subject again.[8]

It was not until two decades after she had been removed from the farm in Devon that Iris learned that the reason her mother came to collect her was because a letter had been written saying she was homesick and wanted to come home. By then her foster mother was dead and she could not ask her who had written the letter but she wondered whether it was from the son who had been less happy to have the evacuee children living with them than his parents. She also realised that it was only her and not her two siblings who had been so unhappy to be back in London. She concluded: 'Mum never seemed to understand and I am sure that was the reason there was never any warmth until much later in life when she needed looking after.'

For other families there was a sense that even if children could talk to their parents they would not necessarily be understood. Anthony Thwaite told author Jessica Mann: 'It created an unspoken rift with my father and mother; I think I felt I didn't need either of them. My mother, in particular, was aware of this, though we hardly ever spoke of it. My mother lived on well into her nineties, and was perhaps increasingly aware how, emotionally, she had "lost" me. I was a devoted and dutiful son, but—after those four years—I didn't really need her.'[9]

Other children did not recognise until much

later the impact of their own evacuation on their parents. Jill Murch wrote in 2000:

I only realise now, as I've grown older, how anguished my dear parents must have been— worried about the welfare of my sister and myself and distraught at the loss of their home together—although at the time we were not alone—a huge number of families had similar, often worse, sadness. Accepting the love and care which we did not question, my sister (I believe) and I (for sure) recall the war years and especially our evacuation as a huge adventure and it jolted my innate curiosity and fascination with other peoples and ways of life, which has never left me.[10]

Jim Bartley came back to London after being evacuated with his school class and found that his parents had moved house. Their old place, he was told, no longer existed. So he settled down to life in an unfamiliar house but with familiar people. At first it did not seem so strange. Until he thought about it:

I certainly do not have any bad memories of that time but it has left me with one curious feeling: all the time I was evacuated I used to tell myself that one day the war would be over and I could go back home. After the war we were living in another part of London and then I made my way to where I used to live. The whole area had been completely obliterated in the first few days of the Blitz. I was quite unable to find the spot where my

51

house once stood. This happened more than fifty years ago. I have lived in many other places. I now have a grown-up family of my own, I am a grandfather. I have a lovely house but somehow I am still waiting to go home.[11]

Home in an emotional sense had disappeared for many children. Tom Welsh came back to a broken home. His father had been captured by the Germans at Dunkirk and had spent the war in prison camps in Poland and Germany. His mother had remained in Manchester with his baby sister and had fallen in love with another man. When Tom was sent home as one of the few thousand who were returned by train, he was met by his father at the station and taken to the house where he had lived with his parents before the war. The house was still there but everything else had changed. Tom's father dropped him at home, explained that he was going out and said, 'Oh, your mother doesn't live here any more. She's got another man.'

Home life for many families had been severely shaken up and it took time for people to re-establish relationships, even hierarchies within the home. For many mothers this was particularly difficult. For six and a half years they had had to hold their world together, to cope with rationing, bombing, separation, anxiety, loss and often very little in the way of relaxation. Yet everyone expected them to go on coping, to reunite the family and to deal with whatever came home. Pam Hobbs had high expectations when she returned from the East Midlands. 'When I dreamed of reuniting with my family, I used to think everything would be the same. Now I discovered it had all changed. Faithful to the end, Mum had written me with weekly updates, but it took my homecoming for the reality to sink in.'[12] What she had not expected, she wrote later, was to feel so lonely. 'For months I had literally dreamed of being home, back with my family in a noisy kitchen and a cosy front room. Now nothing was the same. Not the house, not my family, not the daily routine—and definitely not me. I felt disassociated from my family—like a person on the outside looking in. A stranger.'[13]

Pam Hobbs soon settled down and became her mother's closest ally and best friend. She was proud of how her mother had coped during the war, showing such resilience during the bombing and keeping the household going under extremely difficult physical and financial circumstances. After the war Pam's parents stayed in Kent and lived quietly. Pam moved to Canada in 1950 and took up a career as a travel writer. The experience of evacuation and the opportunities offered to her by her education increased her horizons and helped her to move away from the life she might have lived had it not been for the war.

When John Carter left Walthamstow in 1939 he had no idea what was happening to him. He thought evacuation was going to be an exciting adventure and he was not disappointed when he arrived in Langham in Rutland. He and his friend Terry lived in comparative luxury on a farm owned by a lovely, welcoming woman called Mrs Smith. The cold douche of the evacuation experience for John was not the going away but the coming home. He found himself comparing his parents to the

Smiths at every turn. His father drank beer and swore; Mr Smith did not. His mother was illiterate and worked in a shirt factory. Mrs Smith was educated and cultured. She cared about their clothing, food and schooling. His mother, he wrote, 'was a typical cockney Mum: a kiss one moment and a smack the next'.[14] His father was a staunch communist sympathiser; the Smiths were patriots and read the *Daily Mail*. It left John with an uneasy sense of not quite being able to accept his own home after the war:

Reviewing those years with hindsight, it is obvious that like anybody's childhood experiences, they profoundly affected me on a lifelong basis. Due to Hitler, I was unwittingly given the opportunity to break out of the feckless, somewhat haphazard, cockney way of life which, but for the war, would probably have left me with a limited education and much more limited horizons and aspirations. Whether I would have been happier is of course quite another matter. Certainly nearly three years with the Smiths unsettled me for life back in Pembroke Road and left me with a permanent feeling of shame for my parents and their home; and perhaps a sense of guilt for such shame. Physically, mentally and socially, evacuation was all gain for me, but psychologically I'm sure it left scars.[15]

Amelia Brown spent three years living happily in the Rhondda Valley with a kind family who treated her well but never tried to take on the role of her natural family. She described herself as a very secure child from a loving home with two older brothers and a baby sister. Although she knew she would miss Wales, she could not wait to get home and see her family again. Amelia's mother was overjoyed to see her daughter, now ten years old, and little Carol was thrilled to have her big sister at home. Unfortunately the homecoming was not a success. Although the house was intact and her brothers and sister safe, Amelia felt miserable. She was consumed by jealousy and resented her four-year-old sister deeply. 'Carol had taken that part of my mother's affection that I used to occupy before I went away and I hated her for it. I hated my mother for betraying me. I did not like being at home one bit and I made my mother suffer. Now, when I think about it, I feel ashamed. So many stories of this time tell of parents rejecting their children but I rejected my mother and my sister.' Amelia was sent away to boarding school and there she met other girls who had suffered far more than she had as a result of the war and this put things into perspective for her. Her relations with her mother eventually improved, but she found it a disconcerting experience. Only when Amelia became a mother herself did she gain any inkling of how hard it must have been for her own mother when she rejected her in 1944.

What is striking about the stories told by evacuees is that in the immediate post-war era this topic was barely, if ever, discussed. It was simply taken for granted that children would adjust to life. Reunions, often not held until half a century later, seemed to act as a release valve for many evacuees who said that they had never talked before about the problems of coming home. 'When people ask me about evacuation', said Joan Crystal, 'they only seem to want to know what it was like when we went away, not when we came home. Yet for me coming home was much, much more difficult than going in the first place. Leaving was an adventure, coming back was a wrench but I could never have talked about that with my parents.' Many write that they only really started understanding what they had been through when their grandchildren asked them what had happened to them during the war.

Not all children within families reacted to evacuation in the same way. Nigel Bromage and his twin brother, Michael, spent two years during the war on a farm in South Wales. They shared a room, they went to the same school, they experienced the same foster family and saw the same sights in the countryside. They were seven years old when they arrived and nine when they left. Yet they had two completely different and opposing responses to their evacuation. It was a subject that was never discussed between them and Nigel only learned of how homesick Michael had been from his sister after Michael's early death at the age of fifty-two in 1984. Why did one brother feel that he had had a bad time while the other, Nigel, loved every minute?

The boys were born in December 1932, the joint third of four children. Their older brother, Ronald, joined the navy at the beginning of the war and their parents decided that evacuation was the sensible course of action for the younger three. Nigel and Michael were sent first briefly to Eastbourne, then to Windsor, where they spent a short time in the same billet as their fourteen-year-old sister, Margaret, and finally they were moved to Carmarthenshire where they were billeted on a farm at Golden Grove near Llandeilo. In all there were twelve London evacuees from the same London school in the local area and they were taught together in a separate class at the local primary school by their teacher from London. It gave them a sense of belonging, Nigel explained:

Miss Warren was wonderful with us. She was very good at keeping us informed about what was going on and why it was important for us to remain in Wales rather than go back to London, where the Blitz was crashing all around. We, in a funny way, understood the situation and at no time do I remember either Michael or me feeling that we were abandoned by our parents. We used to get regular post with comics from them and although my mother only visited us twice it was enough to reassure us.

Mr and Mrs Williams, Nigel and Michael's hosts, were farmers on a small scale. They had twenty cows, all of whom had to be milked by hand, and the sole aid was a horse who towed the main farm machinery. 'The only horses I had ever seen up until we arrived in Wales were the coalman's horse and the rag and bone man's horse. Now here were proper working animals on a farm and I got to know them and enjoy them.' It was hard work at times. The Williamses had one son who helped on the farm and a niece who worked with them as a maid. The Bromage boys were not expected to undertake heavy work—their job was to collect the eggs and help out with feeding the cows and sheep. Nigel also remembered having to 'stone' a couple of large fields, which involved collecting stones after the horse had ploughed. In the summer they got to help with the harvest, loading hay onto the carts.

Later on, Nigel was proud to be trusted with taking the empty milk churns, by cart, to the collecting point on the road on the high ground above the farm. But his greatest sense of achievement was when he was allowed to ride Lil, the farm mare, on his own, to the local smithy about three miles away to have her re-shod. For Nigel there was really no downside. 'I mean, occasionally Mr Williams could be a bit harsh but no more so than he was with his own son. If he and Mrs Williams did not want us to understand something they spoke in Welsh. By and large I was immensely happy there. The way of life suited me and I learned a lot from watching the seasons change.' A high point for him was the birth of a colt to the working mare. He saw the foal minutes after it was born and he still remembers it as one of the most exciting events of his life. 'My mother was staying at the time and I knew Lil was going to foal and sure enough, early one morning, I realised it was all about to happen. I rushed upstairs at about six thirty in the morning to wake my mother. I wanted her to come and see this amazing birth. It was so thrilling.'

In 1941 the Williamses sold their farm and moved to Fenny Stratford. At the same time, Nigel's father, who worked at the Woolwich Arsenal, was due to be relocated to the new

Ordnance Depot at Donnington in Shropshire and so the family was reunited. They remained living near Telford for the rest of the war and the boys both went to Adams' Grammar School in Newport, one of the leading grammar schools in Shropshire. Nigel said:

As I enjoyed my experience on the Williamses' farm so my brother did not. I do not think I was particularly aware of it at the time because I was so enjoying myself. Thinking back now I'm slightly ashamed to say that I was never homesick. I loved every minute of it. It was only later that Margaret, my sister, told me how homesick and unhappy Michael had been. It is not perhaps surprising. We were very different personalities—he an introvert, I an extrovert. He tended to opt out of activities around the farm, I volunteered for everything. Yet at school we were close. We stood back to back and no one bothered us. I think initially we had a bit of a reputation though it was not that we were rough, it was simply that London children were viewed differently to begin with.

During their time away evacuee children often developed a love of living in the countryside. For many it enriched their lives; for some it changed them for ever. 'Wessex saddlebacks and large whites are two of my favourite breeds of pig,' said John Brasier, former Principal of Merrist Wood College of Agriculture and Horticulture in Surrey. 'After three years as an evacuee in Hertfordshire I was happiest when I was in close proximity to farms and, especially, cattle, sheep and pigs. Later, much later, when I had by then returned to Hastings to continue my secondary education, I hankered for a career in agriculture much to the dismay of my parents and my headmaster.'

At the outbreak of war John was eight and his younger brother, Michael, was four. Their lives in Hastings were not affected by the war until 21 July 1940 when they and hundreds of other children, locals and evacuees from London, were sent away from the coastal town by train and bus to Hertfordshire. Before they were evacuated the Hastings schoolchildren were told that they were going on a tremendously exciting adventure. 'We would live in the countryside with cows and grass and sheep grazing in the fields, fruit orchards, corn crops, potatoes and so on and we would be living off the cream of the land.' Being the son of a plumber, John's experience of the countryside to that point was very limited but it was with a sense of optimism mixed with a little apprehension at the responsibility of having to look after his younger brother that he set off.

In 1942 the children were split up. John won a scholarship to Hastings Grammar School, which had been evacuated to St Albans, and Michael returned to Hastings to live at home. Eventually, in the summer of 1943, John returned to Hastings for the summer holidays. 'I had begged my mother to let me leave Hastings Grammar School and go to an ordinary secondary school in Hastings. She and Dad were very proud of the fact that I had won a place at the grammar school and she was reluctant to let me give it up.' In the end she agreed and he was sent to the Hastings Emergency Boys School that later became Hastings Secondary Modern. For him it was as if he had gone from one extreme to the other. From being bitterly unhappy and lonely he was cheerful and happy living at home once again. His schoolwork improved and he went from being at the bottom of the class in every subject to being the top in all subjects except music and art. 'My mother was wonderful although I think she wondered for some time whether she had done the right thing by allowing me to return home and leave the grammar school. I think she was worried about what my father might think. In the end I never did know what he thought as he never voiced his opinion one way or the other. Sadly we did not have a very happy father–son relationship.'

John summed up his experience of evacuation during the war:

> It must have formed the foundation of my philosophy of trying to understand and consider other people's points of view. It did have a profound effect in that respect. I always listen to what other people say, not necessarily agreeing with them but hearing them out. As a college principal of course that is a pretty important part of managing a large and complex college and making the right decisions. The other thing is that I like to give people what was not offered to me—a chance to express their views and have them heard in a fair and impartial manner.

What made a good or bad evacuation experience was highly subjective, as was an easy or difficult adjustment to home life. However, there is no doubt that for those children who were unable to see their parents during their time away, the postal system was relied upon as their foremost means of telling their parents about their new lives.

The value of correspondence and communication during the war is often underestimated and certainly it was the case that letters back and forth between family and evacuees were of great importance. For the children they were frequently the only form of contact with their mothers and fathers and at the beginning, at least, they mattered enormously as they provided a link to a familiar world. For the parents, letters were of equal importance and their appearance or non-appearance was often dependent on how much store the host family set by them. Some foster parents read every letter that a child wrote home and sometimes even censored them, others were less anxious about how they were portrayed to the natural parents and encouraged the children to write while others still left it to the children themselves to decide how often to communicate. And then there was the decision taken by the individual parent or child as to what to put in a letter and what to leave out. It is clear that some editing went on and this had an impact on how well things went on the eventual return.

Ten-year-old Rose Clarke explained to an interviewer that she and her seven-year-old brother, Alf, had been separated in the village in Wales where they had been billeted. Alf had been sent to live with a mining family who went down the pits whereas she was with a family whose father worked above ground, 'a nice family' as she described them, who had two little girls of her own age. Her two major concerns during the months she spent in Wales were whether she would get behind with her schoolwork and how she could explain to her mother what Alf had been up to. She used to meet him regularly in the street on her way back from school as he was coming back from the mine:

Apart from the layer of grime, his hair permanently looked as if it needed to be cut. As they gave him half a crown [for going down the mine] he was very wealthy, or he would have been if he had not smoked. If we met in the street one of us would say, 'I've had a letter from my mother.' It was difficult to believe we had the same mother. My brother was very bad about writing home and my mother used to ask me if he was all right. I felt very old and responsible about the issue as I knew she would be very worried and upset if she knew how dirty and unkempt he was. So I told her only the things I thought she would want to know. I felt quite guilty about this but I felt it to be better than the truth.[16]

When the two children eventually returned home to London the clash of cultures surprised them all. Their mother was astonished by their thick accents and Alf, who had spent almost four years speaking nothing but Welsh, found it difficult to switch back to English so that Rose spent several weeks interpreting. The other surprise was that there was a new baby to get used to. Rose had been told by her mother in a letter that there was to be another family member but Rose was far from excited when she found out. It just seemed like something else for her to have to worry about; first Alf and now this new baby. What would happen, she kept asking herself, if her mother died and she had to be responsible for the new baby, Alf and the ration books? She felt like a premature adult even though she knew that she was very immature in herself and desperately lacking in confidence. All these worries spun around in her head and the result was that she began to behave like a little girl: 'It took a long time to adjust to home life again, because I had held myself tightly in rein whilst away. I seemed to regress, dissolving into tears if only looked at, a development which infuriated my mother. She said if, as I said, I had not cried whilst away, why did I have to do it now? Once bottled up again I did not cry for many, many years.'[17]

Joan Clarkson found that she was equally restrained when she returned from her evacuation experience in Northamptonshire: 'Apart from when I went home I think I lived in that period totally without affection. It made a bit of a mark on me. There was no one I could actually talk to, no one I could confide in . . . I just bottled it up inside, and although no one had ill-treated me physically, I was not loved. As I've got older I think I understand it more, but as a child I was withdrawn. It was a very hostile place to be.'[18] Like many others with similar experiences she found readjusting to emotional life at home very difficult. The separation had affected her relationship with her parents beyond repair:

When I came home eventually, although I had enjoyed the last year, I did not trust anybody for a long time. I never confided in my parents again. It was something, a barrier that was there. I think it was because I kept asking to come home and they would not let me. I was unhappy, and although they explained it to me in their letters and when I came home on holidays, it was something that I, as a child, could not understand. I think I lost my confidence in them. I learned to trust again with my husband and I gave lots of affection to him, as I do to my children and my grandchildren.[19]

By the time Bill Rolstone got back to London in 1944 he had been through five schools and several billets in Somerset. He admitted he ran amok. 'When I returned London was still being bombed with Doodlebugs. My mother was out at work all day and my father was away in the war. I just ran wild on the streets and became something of an urchin. With my Somerset accent I got bullied quite a bit and was always in scraps. That was until my Dad came home.' Bill's father had been in the Army since the outbreak of the war. On his return he found one rebellious, hard to handle twelve-year-old son and a second, extremely sickly ten-year-old boy who had suffered severely from rheumatic fever. It cannot have been a very easy homecoming for him but he seemed to take the attitude that now he was home order would be restored.

My dad disciplined me from the moment he arrived home from the Army. From then onwards I had to be home on time, I had to be polite, I had to do what I was told. The effect was astonishing, even to me. Although I was a bit rebellious at first I responded really well and got on famously with my dad. I really needed that strong hand to keep me under control. He understood me and I respected him. I'm just sorry that I couldn't bring myself to stay with my foster father until the end of the war. He did so much for me but in the end he was not my dad.

For those who returned in 1945 their homecoming often coincided with the reappearance of fathers, older brothers and sisters who had been in the forces. This provided its own excitement and tensions as family members jostled for position and attempted to make sure their story was heard first and loudest. Juliet Sanger's return from America in the middle of the war dovetailed with her brothers' leave from the forces. David had been home for a week and her brother Richard for just twenty-four hours so that her parents had gone from having no children to all three within the space of just a few days. Juliet's mother was so overwhelmed that she collapsed on hearing that all her children would be at home but soon recovered and was delighted by her beautiful daughter whom she had not seen since 1940. 'I was no longer the shy eleven-year-old tomboy they had said goodbye to, but a sophisticated young lady with shoulder-length hair falling over one eye. It was wonderful for me that David was there, as he acted as a buffer between me and my parents and all the mixed emotions we felt. None of us was quite sure how to behave . . .' She was not unhappy to be home, merely unsettled by the experience of living once again with her boisterous and energetic family that she had missed so terribly when she was abroad. She settled quickly into school and unlike many others, was not troubled by the curriculum or school rules, though she was a little put-out that other girls were aloof and perhaps even a little jealous of her adventures in America.

It took her, she wrote, a long time to feel completely at ease with her parents for they seemed a lot older to her than they had before she left and she had become introverted and unwilling to show her feelings. However, as other girls returned from abroad during the course of the next two years she was able to help them to share the difficulties of coming home and getting used to life in Britain. They had something in common, which she did not with her family, and this gave her comfort.

Having a common experience helped children to form close bonds. Equally, having differing experiences could mean the opposite. Joan Risley (née Yates) summed up her post-war life in an interview in 2010: 'I am different from my family. I was not brought up with them.' Life has been very kind to her, she maintains and she feels she is one of the lucky ones.

The first evacuation in 1939 was not a success. She had been billeted, with her sister, Ivy, in Beccles in Suffolk. The journey itself had been exciting enough—they had been taken by boat from Dagenham docks to Lowestoft on a paddle steamer called the *Daffodil*—but life with Mrs Pipe, a deeply religious lady who would let them sing only if they sang hymns and who made them attend church and Sunday school three times on a Sunday, was miserable. By the beginning of 1940 Joan and three of her eight siblings were back home with their mother in Dagenham. As the threat of the German invasion became ever more serious the question of whether or not to evacuate the children came up again. In the end Joan was determined to go but this time she was the only one to leave home. Her mother could not make her change her mind and by September 1940 she was on her way to Northampton by train, this time without her sister Ivy or brothers for company.

Although only nine years old, Joan was an assured, pretty little girl with red hair and an outgoing personality. When she arrived at Duston, 5 miles outside Northampton, she was selected at the local Women's Institute building by Mrs William Watts, who had no children of her own. Auntie Hilda, as Joan was asked to call her, took her by the hand from the hall where the children had been waiting to be selected and said: 'Don't worry, I've got a little playmate for you.' Joan had hoped to stay with two other girls that had been on the train with her, but Auntie Hilda assured her kindly that she would soon see them again but that for now she was taking her on her own.

'I arrived at six o'clock on 22 September 1940 and my first sight of Uncle Will was him sitting at the table at home eating bread and butter. On the table were tinned pears. I was astonished. Where I came from these were an untold luxury.' After tea Joan was introduced to the little girl who lived next door, Sheila, who turned out to be Auntie Hilda's niece. Sheila was eighteen months younger than Joan and they soon became great friends. Because Hilda and Auntie Nora, Sheila's mother, were twin sisters, there was two-way traffic between the two houses for the whole time that Joan lived in Duston. She became the child that Uncle Will and Auntie Hilda never had and she was brought up as one of the family.

Imagine what it was like for me, coming from a family of eight, where we had very little, to live in a beautifully clean cottage with my own bedroom and a playmate who shared everything with me so generously. I could not have been luckier. Auntie Hilda treated me like a daughter. She was strict with me and I couldn't get away with anything, but she was incredibly kind and fair. Before I went to school I had to wash up the breakfast dishes. It was a really good grounding and I knew where I stood. On Saturdays, after I'd finished my jobs, which were things like shelling peas or peeling potatoes or going shopping in the village, my time was my own to spend with Sheila. Sometimes she used to help me with my jobs to make it quicker. I had my toys and my books in the shed, that is where they were kept, but occasionally I smuggled a book and torch upstairs to my bedroom to read. I had a beautiful high feather bed in the front room. On summer evenings I would watch the sun setting on the bedroom wall until it disappeared. Auntie Hilda used to bring me a china jug of water to

69

wash in every morning. I was a guest, you see, a very welcome guest, but nevertheless they never tried to take the place of my own parents, which I really respected them for.

For five years, from the age of nine to fourteen, Joan lived with Auntie Hilda and Uncle Will. She learned everything, she said, that she needed for life. Her education was not just academic but social and practical as well. She received only one visit from her mother in all the time she was away. By this time her father was ill and had not been able to work so she knew that it had cost her mother a great deal of effort and hard-earned savings to make the trip. But she also knew that her mother was relieved that her daughter was safe and happy in Duston although she has no idea what her mother and Auntie Hilda made of one another. They were together for only a few hours but it must have been strange for Joan's mother to see her daughter in different surroundings. She recalls a little sadness when Auntie Hilda advised her not to go back to London to be a bridesmaid for one of her sisters since it was at the height of the bombing and Hilda was afraid she would be killed.

For Joan the five years she spent in Duston were some of the very happiest of her life. Whilst she was not spoilt, she wanted for nothing:

Auntie Hilda was a wonderful tailoress and dressmaker, so I soon became the best-dressed evacuee in Duston. And she never once asked my mother for a penny towards any of the clothes she made for me. If I

70

needed new shoes I was taken to Northampton to have them fitted. In addition I was lucky enough to be taken on trips around the local countryside, most often on foot or sometimes on the bus as the family had no cars. We went to rabbit and bird shows in neighbouring villages, we went walking along the river and sometimes we went further afield on bank holidays, to places like Bedford.

At fourteen Joan left Duston in order to find work. She knew by then that Auntie Hilda very much wanted to adopt her so that she and Uncle Will could send her to college. They were prepared to pay for further education and were against her leaving school and going back to London to work but they did not interfere with her wishes, so Joan got a job working in the office at the Co-op in Stratford East. She remembers the very tearful parting in Duston when she left Auntie Hilda and Uncle Will to make her way back home. 'Auntie and Uncle reassured me there would always be a home for me here if I ever needed one.'

Joan returned to live with her parents. That was not easy:

I found it all so different when I got home. I remember sitting on a sofa with a feeling of not belonging. By that time we were really poor. Dad was still ill and unable to work. He spent his days sitting in a chair at home doing nothing. He was not a good husband to my Mum, but he did love us kids. Another problem was that the house was not as nicely

71

kept as Auntie Hilda's and that troubled me, though I didn't say anything about it. Mum did not have time to do much housework as it took her all her time to do the shopping and cooking for the family. My family all commented on how I talked different so I had that strange feeling of not quite belonging yet wanting to be there because they were my family.

Gradually Joan began to readjust to London again and she realised that she had to come to terms with the fact that she had had two lives in the time her siblings had had only one. 'I soon got used to being with Mum and she got used to me. But with my siblings it was more difficult. They are my family and I am very fond of them but they never went away like I did so they don't understand that I have had these two lives.'

Uncle Will and Auntie Hilda continued to play an important role in Joan's life, as did Sheila. Every year Joan would spend her one week's holiday in Duston and every year Uncle Will would say to her on her arrival: 'Come on in, Joan, your room is always here waiting for you.' And it was. The house was as clean and comfortable as ever and the affection and kindness they had showed Joan during the war never faded. It was wonderfully reassuring for her. But she was proud too and she wanted to show them that she was capable of looking after herself so she saved what little money she had left over from her wages after she had given her mother the lion's share and bought good quality shoes. It mattered to her that Auntie Hilda and Uncle Will did not think that all the kindness and education they had offered had gone to waste nor that she expected them still to be responsible for her.

In 1954 Joan took her fiancé, Edward, to meet the Wattses and was delighted that they approved of him. When they were married in 1956 Auntie Hilda and Uncle Will, Sheila and her parents came to the wedding. The friendship with Sheila endured and has now lasted seventy years. They grew up together, they married within two years of one another and they have holidayed together. Their children know one another and the bond of affection goes far deeper than just friendship.

Auntie Hilda died in 1980 and Uncle Will in 1984. This made Joan feel terribly sad and her only consolation was that they had lived long enough to see her two daughters. Not long after Uncle Will died Joan received a letter from a solicitor telling her that he had left her a sum of money in his will. 'All I can say is that the love and kindness they gave me was worth more than any money I could possibly have had. They showed me love and they gave me an education for life. I can honestly say that evacuation changed my life from what it might have been had I remained in London.'

Sheila Shear also had life-changing experience as a result of evacuation. As past-president of the League of Jewish Women and an energetic organiser at the Nightingale Home, a care home for Jews, Sheila leads a busy life. She is on first-name terms with most of the prominent members of the Jewish community in London and holds strong opinions. How incongruous, therefore, that she, her sister Myrtle and her parents spent the war years living with a Christian bachelor in

Chesham.

At the outbreak of the war, Sheila, Myrtle and their mother were evacuated to Hunstanton, which was not a success. As was so often the case, the families who took mothers with children found it more difficult to cope with the incoming guests than those who took unaccompanied children. Sheila remembers her mother having to walk around Hunstanton all day because she was not allowed to remain in the billet during working hours. After three weeks she had had enough and she took the children back to London where her husband had remained, running his business selling chemist sundries in Brixton. Sheila recalls:

My father had muscular dystrophy which meant that he was slightly handicapped and certainly unfit for war service. So he continued to work in his business throughout the war, going regularly to the East End to do his buying. We lived in a Jewish quarter with a very strong sense of community. I remember that when food got a bit scarce he used to barter mascara or leg make-up as booty for extra food. Come to think of it, that's very enterprising. I never remember going hungry in the war years but we were not wealthy and my parents had to struggle to make ends meet.

The children remained in London during the Phoney War but as the Battle of Britain began in the summer of 1940 their father once again decided they should move out of London. They took a train to Chesham and the four of them traipsed around the town with a little overnight bag and their silver Sabbath candlesticks, which were precious to her mother. They knocked on several doors and as it got dark a woman took pity on them and let them stay the night. For the next few weeks the four of them lived in a tiny room with no windows, their father travelling up and down to London on the early train. If he were ever late on the train they would all worry that something had happened to him in London. It was no way to conduct family life, even during a war. So they moved back to London for the second time.

There was a communal shelter close by their block of flats and Sheila remembers spending nights in the shelter on bunks or camp beds. 'It was quite an eye-opener down there, I seem to remember. There were buckets for use as toilets and on more than one occasion there were people fornicating. Life certainly went on around us in that shelter.' As the bombing got worse so her parents began to wonder whether it was safe to keep the children in London. Then, on the night of 29 December 1940 London received the most serious raid yet:

We had decided to sleep in the flat that night and we heard the air-raid wardens shouting at us to come down. My father carried Myrtle downstairs to a brick shelter built in the grounds of the flats. There were bombs falling all around us, incendiaries and other devices. It was so loud and frightening. That made up my parents' mind and the following day we decided to evacuate. So, it seems, did the rest of London. We took a train to Reading but there was no room for us there so we spent the night in the Town Hall and then came home the next day. Father had had enough. He sent us to Chesham, where we had spent some time that autumn. 'Hello Mrs Ripps,' said the billeting officer, when we turned up in January, 'I knew we'd see you again. We've got the perfect place for you. 26 Blucher Street. Go and knock on the door.'

Sheila, Myrtle and her mother went to knock on the door and there began a chapter that became one of the happiest of their lives. It did not look auspicious from the start, however. Number 26 Blucher Street was a small terraced house with a parlour, a kitchen and a scullery on the ground floor and two bedrooms upstairs and a tiny attic bedroom, which Sheila had to herself. There was no hot water, no electricity, and the loo was outside in the garden. Cooking was done in the scullery on a gas cooker and there was a butler's sink that had cold water. The house was owned by a bachelor called Harry Mayo who was an upholsterer by profession and worked for a company called Brandon's in the same street.

He had never encountered a Jewish family at close quarters and they had never been guests of a non-Jewish household for such a long period of time. Sheila explained:

There were some very funny moments, I have to say. He had never come across our customs or traditions before and it took time to get used to them. But Uncle Harry was the kindest person you could ever imagine. He took us into his house and without a moment's hesitation shared everything with us. He had the kitchen, we had the parlour. He had one bedroom upstairs and my mother, Myrtle and my father had the other. I had my lovely little attic room with a view over the garden. In the spring of that first year my mother explained to Uncle Harry that we were coming up to Passover and that there were certain customs that we had to observe. Uncle Harry was fantastic. He didn't flinch. He merely said to my mother: 'Well, well, well I never. Who'd have thought it? I always thought Jewish people must be good but now I know for sure.' And with that my mother could relax and share all the Jewish festivals. She always invited Uncle Harry to join us and he always took part. It worked the other way around too. We were invited to his sister, Nell's, on Christmas evening and we used to go along for supper and to sing and play games. There we ate plum pudding for the first time, we pulled Christmas crackers and saw the lovely decorated Christmas tree. It was all great fun and seemed such a long way from the constant air raids, bombings and shelter life we had left behind less than a year earlier.

Harry got to know more about their Jewish customs:

Over the years which followed we became his

family, he became our beloved uncle, and we were proud of the way a single gentile man and a traditional Jewish East End family learned to live together in such difficult and trying circumstances. At Passover Uncle Harry ate matzos, the unleavened bread which Jewish people eat for this week-long festival, on Sabbath he enjoyed 'kneidlach' a delicious matzo meal dumpling in chicken soup, which he insisted on eating with a knife and fork and not with a spoon as we had always done. He even fasted with us for twenty-five hours on Yom Kippur because he thought it would be unfair for him to eat when we were not permitted. The fast is difficult enough, but alas on one occasion he began his with bacon and so suffered an unbearable thirst all day, but stubbornly refused to give in and waited to break his fast with us on some more conventional Jewish cooking.

Slowly but surely Uncle Harry became a more and more significant figure in Sheila and Myrtle's life. He understood the value of education and even though he did not have children of his own he took great trouble to help them with their broader academic education. He would buy books for them, or let them read his own books. He spent hours reading to the children and used to enjoy helping them with their schoolwork. On special days he would even let them read from his encyclopaedias. The children knew always to ask and he never refused, but they were constantly aware that they were there as his guests and could take nothing for granted. Sheila learned to play the piano and that was something Uncle Harry encouraged. He would sit with her when she was practising and encouraged her with patience and tact. He was also an enthusiastic artist and the girls learned the delights and mysteries of mixing oil paints and of washing watercolour onto paper, as well as the care needed in creating pictures. 'He introduced me to the joy of looking at paintings and my family has several of his pictures which we treasure.'

Although they became as close to him as family in many ways, they respected his privacy. They knew, for example, he liked to take a nap after lunch but they also knew that he did not mind them watching him working on his paintings. They also used to watch him shaving:

His shaving routine, which took place in his downstairs room, was a daily ritual. He used an open 'cut-throat' razor and sharpened it on a leather strop, lathered his face and then carefully scraped off his beard. Myrtle and I watched with awe, afraid to speak or move in case we distracted or jogged him and were very relieved when the razor was washed and placed in its little plush velvet box until the next day. In fact, Myrtle, who was four and a half years younger than I was, saw more of Uncle Harry than she did of our own father because Dad only ever used to have Sundays off as a full day in Chesham whereas Uncle Harry was with us the whole time. Mother used sometimes to leave us with him if she had to go back into London or go out somewhere and she knew that we were completely safe in his company.

When Sheila's grandparents came to stay Uncle Harry moved out of his bedroom and insisted on sleeping on the floor downstairs. Sheila remembered wonderful exchanges:

Neither grandparent spoke English and Uncle Harry of course had no Yiddish but he showed no surprise when Grandmother would bring her pots, pans, plates and cutlery and take over a corner of his kitchen to do her kosher cooking. Although Grandmother didn't speak any English she was a great communicator and she managed to convey her delight with Uncle Harry by stroking him and saying: 'Ah, Mr Mayo, Mr Mayo!' He didn't seem to mind at all and would join in on evening meals whenever he was invited.

On 8 May 1945 there was an enormous celebration and street party in the Broadway in Chesham to celebrate VE Day. There was singing and cheering, people danced around the war memorial and talked excitedly about the future. The bells rang out from the church for the first time in six years. Uncle Harry was nowhere to be seen. Eventually Sheila's mother found him in the garden. He was standing with his back to the house and he refused to come inside and join the celebrations: 'Everyone in the world is happy today,' he said. 'Everyone is happy except for me, because you are leaving.' Sheila remembers her mother's immediate reaction: 'We'll stay until the new school year begins.' She told him on the spot. That way he would have three months at least to get used to the idea of their returning to London.

When the time came for them finally to leave Chesham and move back to London in September 1945 they insisted that he should remain closely involved with the family 'which you will always be a part of', they told him. Thus began a new era in their relationship. Sheila explained:

Uncle Harry took up coming to see us once a week on Thursdays and in 1946 he even came on holiday with us when we went to Bournemouth. My mother used to make a parcel up of all the food that Uncle Harry liked and he would receive that each week. At Christmas there was a bumper hamper of all his favourite food plus ties, socks and other goodies. And each year he would come on a special mission to buy a new hat from Dunnes. We would all traipse along to the shop and watch as he chose the same hat each year. I remember, he would try several on but he would always come back to the style he liked and felt at home with.

For Sheila and Myrtle going back to live in London was 'a real culture shock. Like coming out of one world and moving into another.' The family was now living in the Spitalfields area, which had been severely bombed. As they saw the devastation for the first time since 1941 they realised how very lucky the family had been not to lose anyone in the raids. By now Sheila had been to several schools both in London and Chesham. The family moved

81

to south London in February 1947 and Sheila had to commute to her school in the East End. During the severe winter of 1947 school was interrupted and Sheila began to lose interest in formal education. So she left school and went into her father's business.

Uncle Harry Mayo continued his weekly visits until he was well into his seventies. Eventually the visits became fortnightly and then monthly but he continued to make the trip to London until he was too frail to travel. He also continued to give the girls sixpence pocket money a week until they were each twenty years old, by which time it had increased to two shillings and sixpence, and when Sheila married he gave her £20.00 (the equivalent of about £420 today). In January 1976 Uncle Harry's nephew phoned to say that just before Christmas he had been run over by a car on his way to visit his niece in hospital. The injuries had been fairly minor but after two weeks, sadly, he had died. He was ninety-four years old. Sheila said: 'Uncle Harry had always said that he did not believe in the Church. He was not even sure that he believed in God but he was without doubt the truest Christian I have ever met.'

Neither Sheila nor her mother had been back to Chesham since 1946 as Uncle Harry had been such a regular visitor to their flat in London but they felt that they had to go to his funeral.

My mother and I travelled by train to Chesham. The town seemed smaller, the hills not as steep as when I was a child, and memories came flooding back. When we got to Chesham we were treated like the closest

82

members of his family. In fact, in the church—and this was the first Christian funeral my mother and I had ever been to—we were put to sit in the front row, in front of Uncle Harry's nieces and nephews. It was only then, I think, that I really appreciated how much our little family had meant to him and had gone on meaning to him all his life. The vicar's moving eulogy reminded us that Uncle Harry's life had had great quality. And then it was all over, no more talking, no more flowers, no more Uncle Harry. We returned to London in the knowledge that we would never go back to Chesham again. We had no reason to. The following day we each received a letter from his solicitor containing a cheque. In the envelope was a note that read: 'A very small token of my very great affection.'

Sheila's life was immensely enriched by her evacuation to Chesham and the four years with Uncle Harry Mayo. It was not just the fact that she and her family were made to feel so welcome in the home of a person whose religion, culture, traditions and ways they had no experience of, but that he welcomed them so openly and broadened the children's horizons in such a variety of ways. That he also became an adopted member of her family was not unusual in the post-war era and it is a sign of the strong relationships that could build up as a result of the dislocation of evacuation.

The belief that evacuation added to their life's experience is something expressed by a large number of evacuee children who feel that their side of the story, the good side, is not trumpeted loudly enough when the subject crops up in the media or in literature. 'There were many successes,' Norman Longmate wrote, 'but understandably it was the failures that made the headlines.'

So many children felt privileged to have been exposed to experiences they would never have had if not for the war: Welsh male voice choirs, classical music, theatre, church, new foods, spring flowers, farmyard animals and country traditions. And for those who went abroad: cultural differences ranging from comparatively classless societies to a different education system, as well as things such as dancing, skiing, ice skating on frozen lakes to back-country hiking and vast, unpopulated landscapes so very unlike the cities they had left. Tony Moore returned to England from America at the age of fifteen and in 1998 he wrote: 'In some ways the experience of the evacuation did not end with our return to this country. I came back influenced by the kindness and richness of the experience and I have remained conscious of it through the years.'[20]

3

THE ANGUISH OF ELDERS

Sending you away has been, in some ways, a tragedy. I still think it was the right thing to do, even though events proved different from our fears. But it has been heartbreaking to miss these years of your lives. We shall meet again as almost strangers.

Ted Matthews to his daughter Judy, 1944

Understandably, evacuation stories focus on the children who were sent away from home. But what of the mothers? What of the parents and grandparents who were separated from their children and did not know for how long? The agony of letting go a beloved child is something that most parents would find difficult to imagine. For many whose children were sent away on the government scheme in 1939 it was the first time they had ever been separated from their children and the impact on those parents left behind is seldom considered. In fact, parents are often condemned for taking the decision to send the children to live with unknown people in an unnamed part of the country for an unspecified length of time.

When planning for the evacuation from the cities the government concentrated its propaganda on the mother's conscience. In 'Paying the Piper', Margaret Simmons, daughter of a former evacuee and researcher in war studies, asked the provocative question: 'Why did none of the mothers ask why the evacuation scheme was called Operation Pied Piper?' The sinister connotations of the traditional story of the Pied Piper of Hamelin, who takes the children away for ever after the Mayor and the elders renege on paying their debt to him for ridding the city of Hamelin of rats, seems not to have rung any alarm bells. Yet, as Simmons argues, 'Like the City of Hamelin, the wartime "Pied Piper" scheme overlooked mothers' voices in how the scheme was organised, despite them being heavily involved in its orchestration. The cost of paying the piper was a high one both in Hamelin and in Britain in the Second World War.'[1]

What is often forgotten is that the men and women who were parents in the 1930s had lived through the First World War and many of the fathers who had fought in the trenches knew all about the horrors of warfare and would have done anything to spare their own children from those atrocities. Time and again one reads of a father saying: 'I didn't fight for four years so that my children could go through another war.' Though few of the women, other than those who had served as nurses, would have witnessed the war first-hand, they knew about the appalling losses, they knew about the injuries and horrors of the trenches and they knew, above all, that the threat in this war was aerial attack that would not discriminate between civilians and military targets.

The role of women in the Second World War is well documented in terms of their work in all manner of war-related industries; however, it is often overlooked that some of these women were

86

first and foremost mothers, whose traditional role was that of wife and homemaker, with few rights and usually little say beyond the running of the house. It is remarkable that many accounts from evacuee children explain that it was their father alone who took the decision to send them away. The pressure on women to combine their caring, home-based role with their new responsibilities towards war work as well as to cope with the fact that their children were torn away from them was great and it is hardly surprising that some of them found it hard to bear. 'I felt a cold hand on my heart as she clambered onto that bus in Church Street,' one mother said of her daughter's parting, 'never have I felt so torn. It was for her safety but the pain was all mine in those first few moments and I felt guilty for days at having let her go. I was unable to concentrate on anything. I was all anxiety until I heard she was safe in Hertfordshire. It was only then that the tears came. She had gone and it felt like for ever.'

Another woman remembered her aunt telling her years later what happened on the fateful day when she and her four siblings left home:

Your mother ran all the way back from the school with the tears coursing down her cheeks. She didn't seem to mind who saw her in that state. Once or twice she pulled up her pinny and wiped her eyes but that just made her face look worse. She pushed open the front door and ran into the kitchen. I ran across the road and went in through the open front door. There she was, sitting at her place at the kitchen table, with all your five place settings laid up for breakfast. Her eyes were glazed over and she was sobbing 'They've taken my babies.' It was the saddest thing I had ever seen and the worst of it was that I knew your father, my brother, had talked her in to letting you go. For at least a week she would lay the table for all of you, just in case you came home. And by the by, as you didn't, she began to get used to it and threw herself into all different kinds of voluntary work but she never lost that haunted look in her eyes. Never, not till Freddie came home. I don't think she ever forgave my brother for letting you all get taken away.

Some historians of the evacuation have suggested that there were mothers who were pleased to be rid of their children so that they could enjoy the freedom of a working life and indeed begrudged them coming home after the war. The accounts of mothers' anguish are far more frequent and documented, whereas the tales of those mothers who were glad to be relieved of the children come mainly from hearsay. One child described, seventy years on, the scene when the bus left taking her and her sister away from their school. The mothers had not been told when the children were leaving but it had been made clear to them all that it would be too distressing for the children if they were there at the moment of departure. However, word had got around in this street that the bus was about to leave and suddenly a group of women, including her mother, were seen running full-tilt down the street behind the bus. Her mother tried to catch up with the bus but she could not. At that moment when she realised that she had lost the race she held her apron to her face and just stood there, frozen to the spot. It was a terrible sight for the child looking out of the back of the bus, and into adulthood she could remember the intense distress conveyed in that single gesture.

Another girl, Jean Barnes, explained that she understood, with hindsight, that her mother knew instinctively that the separation would cause an irreparable rift between them, which turned out to be the case.

In the end I was away for two years. The irony was that it was not so very far from Newcastle but once I had left mother had no excuse not to work and this meant that I could not come home to see her nor did she have more than very infrequent opportunities to come and see me. When I returned I was thirteen and I had developed in every way imaginable. There was but a shadow of the little girl I had been when I left. Although we lived together until I left home to go and live in the nurses' hostel we had little in common. She used to look at me in a sad way and now I think it was because she was trying to find something she had lost. When Mike and I had children, however, she was in her element and was a fabulous grandma. She poured all the love she had held back from me onto our kids. She knew that I knew this and we both loved it, so it was a happy ending and I'm glad she lived into her eighties and could see her grandkids grow up.

The evacuation scheme was voluntary but enormous pressure was put on families to do the right thing by their children and allow them to go to the safety of the country. Although it was often the grandparents and fathers who held sway in the decision-making, the government, with all its propaganda, urged mothers not to hold their children back in the cities. Government ministers made radio appeals imploring parents to get the children away from danger; every home received a leaflet in 1939 claiming that 'the main way to avert the enemy's intention of creating panic and social dislocation is by removing children from endangered areas.'

Whilst accounts tend to focus on the prospect of children not knowing where they were going, nor for how long, nor when they would ever see their parents again, it is sometimes overlooked that for many children the initial evacuation was seen as an exciting adventure, albeit one that was not always so thrilling when they arrived at their destinations. John Carter was delighted at his first taste of evacuation:

I stared down puzzled at the line of weeping Mums and others. I wondered why they were all crying: surely, we were just going away for a sort of holiday. Now of course, I can appreciate the heartache and emotional misery such partings must have caused for adults, with the very real fear that we might not see each other again given that all the experts (e.g. the air marshals, politicians and senior civil servants, and pundits like H. G. Wells or pacifists such as Bertrand Russell) had forecast an aerial terror which could destroy London in a week. But to seven-year-olds like me and my fellows, evacuation was an exciting expedition.[2]

For the mothers, however, there was nothing positive about saying goodbye to one, two, three, four or more of their children and not knowing where they were going, nor to whom they would be sent, nor when they would see their little ones again.

The women's magazines were no more supportive of the wavering mother than the politicians. They too chided women that they should cooperate with the government: 'Don't fight the recent evacuation plans. They are wholly for the benefit of your children,' admonished the editor of *Woman's Own* in 1941.

If your children have an opportunity of going off to the country, don't grudge it to them because you will be lonely. Apart from their health—and none of you can deny that space and fresh air and country food are best for growing boys and girls—they will benefit enormously from new experiences and new friendships. They will have a better chance in the future with every single new thing they learn . . . you will give to them a better chance than you had yourself. It is you women who will have to build up the future. You can lay the first bricks with the health and education of your children. Use the best bricks you can. Stand up [to] Hitler's Blitzkrieg yourselves.[3]

The emphasis on the mother's responsibility to fulfil her patriotic duty was underlined by the government poster campaign in 1940 after the gradual return of children to the cities during the Phoney War. The Ministry of Health wanted mothers to regard caring for evacuees as 'a national service' and ran a series of advertisements showing women being praised for taking on the responsibility 'She's in the Ranks too!' trumpeted one poster. Another was more sinister and direct. Also issued by the Ministry of Health, it featured a mother sitting beside a tree in the countryside with a town in the distant background. Frolicking before her are two little boys and behind her, in ghostly outline, is Hitler in uniform whispering into her ear 'Take them back! Take them back!' The mother looks anxious and confused. The caption along the bottom reads in red: 'Don't do it, Mother. LEAVE THE CHILDREN WHERE THEY ARE.' The implication was that mothers would be regarded as traitors if they ignored official advice and brought their children home. In September 1940 an editorial in *Woman's Magazine* suggested that if French women had had more children, and in particular sons, to defend its shores then maybe it would not have had to surrender. The pressure on women to comply, cope, work and organise was immense and the admonishments meted out to them for unpatriotic behaviour and weakness were delivered without a trace of irony. Women were encouraged to be attractive and cheerful, as well as being brave, competent, thrifty, patriotic and motherly. They were responsible for keeping the home together, for working for the war effort, for looking after children, for sending their children away, for taking other people's children in—or all of the above. They were expected to go on country walks and read books, enjoy flowers and music. They were encouraged to be letter writers to keep up the spirits of the troops, they were to knit to clothe the forces, they were to bake for Britain and pickle for the future. It was bewildering.

One of the difficulties for mothers was that when the children left their family home they also left their control and although some foster parents were immensely thoughtful and wrote to the child's parents to inform them of developments or ask permission for this or that, many foster parents treated the children as they would their own. This led to serious tensions. Even those with the best intentions inevitably made some decisions that would not have been made at home. Thus foster mothers were on the receiving end of criticism and the children had to listen to often unguarded comments about their parents. Jessica Mann remembered her mother telling her that she looked simply awful when she came home from America: 'with long matted ringlets, lots of fake jewellery, a sickly pink, frilly dress. The very first thing I did was to take you to the hairdresser.'[4] Jessica's hair was cut to within half an inch above her ears and her mother dressed her in grey flannel divided skirts. Hardly surprising that when she reached what she described as the age of rebellion she swished around in long skirts and stiletto heels.

Some children found the atmosphere they encountered in their foster homes unsettling if they had different standards from what they had been used to at home. They had to adjust in one direction and then, at the end of evacuation, in another. Margaret Hanson spent seven years in Canada from the age of eight. 'Intellectually I knew my parents cared for me, but emotionally I felt they'd abandoned me,' she told Ruth Inglis in the late 1980s. The family Margaret was billeted to had completely different standards from her own: 'I found it distressing that my foster mother would do something that my mother wouldn't have done. She had her hair permed and she wore lipstick . . . My foster mother wanted me to be "pretty pretty", but my mother had not approved of my being vain. In the end, she gave up on trying to prettify me and let me be an intellectual.'[5] Concessions had been made on both sides. In 1946 Margaret's mother arrived in Canada to bring her home: 'By that time, my accent was so Canadian that I couldn't convince people I'd originally come from England. She was insensitive to North American manners and she wasn't dressed like other people . . . Here she was in a conventional, middle-class, professional Canadian home with a daughter who had turned into a little conformist.' On her return to Britain Margaret Hanson found the schooling to her liking and she soon settled but, she wrote: 'You couldn't say I was a happy teenager. Happiness didn't come until my maturity. In a way, I had to grow up when I was eight.'[6]

A challenge for mothers was what to do with their lives now that their children had left. It was not the same situation as when children left home in the normal way. Everything had been cut short and become disjointed by the war, so that mothers had to invent a new life for themselves. They were encouraged into war work and for some this was liberating and rewarding. However, for many the desire to visit their children was intense and this was often made more difficult by limited free time as well as the distances involved and the problems of getting around Britain on public transport. For many it was not an option for them to become weekend parents, though those who succeeded in doing so found it rewarding, reassuring and ultimately easier when the children came home.

What must it have been like to have to decide it was in your child's best interest to be separated from you? And how difficult would it have been when the children wrote, as they so often did, to say they were miserable and lonely? Doing what was sensible or 'right' was not necessarily happy for either mother or child. A letter from a foster mother in Canada to a mother in Liverpool in 1944 summed up their plight. She wrote: 'You must be torn between anxiety to see these lovely children of yours and the fear lest they encounter danger. It is difficult to use one's head when one's heart is pulling in another direction.'

In 1940 Phil and Patricia Mare sent their two younger children to live with Phil's brother, Dennis, and his family in Vancouver. Seven-year-old John settled down to enjoy a blissful and carefree childhood in the countryside around Vancouver. Patricia, known always as Suzie, was far less happy and she wrote long letters to her mother begging her to let her return to Britain. Phil Mare was a captain in the Royal Navy and Suzie's older brother, Charles, had joined up aged seventeen as an able seaman. Her main concern was to get home so that she could join the services and do 'her bit' as the rest of her family was doing.

Eventually her parents decided it would be better to let her come home than force her to remain in Vancouver and they arranged passage for her aboard a Swedish cargo vessel, the SS *Vaalaren* that left New York as part of a convoy sailing to Swansea. There were just eight passengers aboard ship, including Suzie. As the convoy passed just south of Greenland enemy submarines were spotted and the skipper of the SS *Vaalaren* decided to leave and make a run for England. It turned out to be a fatal mistake. The ship was torpedoed and sunk the next day, on 5 April 1943. There were no survivors. When John returned to Britain at the end of the war aged twelve he was shocked to see his mother had grey hair. He was later told his mother's hair had turned grey overnight when she had learned that her daughter had been lost at sea.

In many accounts written in the recent past, children, now parents and often grandparents themselves, have reflected on how hard it must have been for the mothers to cope with their returning children. Wartime mothers are often blamed in recent analyses for being unable to understand what a child had experienced or how much their little son or daughter had grown up and changed during the months and years he or she was away. Few parents recorded their feelings in letters or memoirs but several children spoke later about how difficult it had been for their mothers to adjust to the jump from a little, dependent child to an apparently confident person three or four years older:

My parents felt it was important not to let me come back to London until the bombing was over so that in the end I was away for four and a half years. I had been loved and well cared for by my foster parents and I found it very difficult to start over again with my own parents who seemed older, a little formal and somewhat in awe of the twelve-year-old girl in their house. Years later my mother told me how she had wanted to hug me and kiss me as she had done when I was seven but she had not dared. Now I think how bitter that must have been for her, to lose the closeness to her only child, but at the time I didn't want her to come too close.

Some children, now adults, are still critical of their parents' decision, incredulous that they could have chosen to 'abandon' them to strangers. Pola Howard had a bad experience as an evacuee and felt wronged for many years after the war:

My brother and I felt very resentful towards our parents and blamed them for sending us away. We felt we had been abandoned, even more so toward the end of 1939 when the great drift homeward began for a considerable number of evacuees, perhaps because families wanted to spend Christmas together. We felt more desolate than ever at that time, we thought we had been rejected and forgotten.

My brother and I would say how we would have preferred to have taken our chance in London, rather than to be sent to live with people who had no love for us, little sympathy, and in some cases were totally lacking in understanding and tolerance. It was many years before we realised just how very deeply our parents cared for us, and many more years before we contemplated whether, given their situation, we might not have done the same thing.[7]

Deirdre Hart, who was evacuated as a five-year-old, confessed to her older sister that everything she had told her parents when she got home about her foster parents being cruel and not feeding her properly was made up to make them feel guilty for sending her away. In fact she had been well looked after and her foster parents had been kind and loving. By the time she told her sister the truth her parents were dead and she regretted deeply not having been honest with her mother, in particular, after the war. Others admitted to making their parents suffer: 'I made it as hard on my mother as an eight-year-old can when I returned five years later. I kept complaining "I want to go back to Aunt Madeleine." I suppose it was only natural but it must have been very hard on my mother.'[8]

Milly Squib tried to keep her children with her. She was just twenty-four years old in 1939 and had four children. She was expecting her fifth by the following summer. The family lived in Bermondsey and by 1940 they had been bombed several times. When the firebombing began towards the end of the year she decided she would have to send the three oldest children away. By then they were nine, seven and five. They went to Newhaven.

I wanted them all to stay together. The woman they were staying with took a dislike to my little boy and she made his life hell. My eldest girl phoned home one night and she said, 'Mum, Georgie's run away.' Of course I left the toddler with my mum and we went down to look for him. We found him with a woman just up the road. She knew what was going on and she took him in. He was friends with another little evacuee boy that was staying with her and he told her that the other lady was cruel to Georgie. She used to make him go without his food, and she'd sent him up to bed with no dinner. It was bad enough to have a war on and the children having to go away from home without people picking on them.[9]

Milly took the children back to London but her husband was not happy with them all back in Bermondsey with the bombs dropping around them so as soon as the new baby was born and was old enough to travel they were evacuated again. This time Milly went with them. She was not going to risk having the children being picked on by other families. The result was that although not all her billets were good and she often had to work very hard for the householders she lived with, she was able to protect the children and give them as normal a childhood as the war would permit.

Rose Brittain sent her three children to the country in September 1939 and remembered the terrible pain and sadness she felt as she saw them leave their home: 'I had three children who were evacuated with the school. I did not see them off because I was too upset. For the first two days after they went I could not eat I was so upset about them going. My eldest boy, James, was nearly thirteen, and the others were ten and seven. He would not be parted from the other two and so they were left until last to be chosen.'[10] Fortunately the children were very happy in Cambridgeshire. They lived in a manor house with Mrs Rowe, a member of the Women's Voluntary Service, and her husband who was a farmer. The Rowes had had six children of their own so were well used to a houseful. When Rose went to collect her youngest son, who had contracted bronchitis, James decided he wanted to stay with the Rowe family and he remained with them until he was fifteen and old enough to leave school and go to work. 'We still keep in touch with the family. There could not have been a better family and I do not regret having to let the children go on evacuation.'[11]

In 1940 a survey was conducted of the parents of 275 children still in the country.[12] Ninety-four per cent of the mothers said they believed their children to be happy. When asked where their information came from the mothers cited visits to see their children, letters from their children or letters from the foster parents which they believed to be true. However, when asked how they felt about their children being away nearly 50 per cent of the mothers said they were terribly unhappy because they missed their children so badly but it was often not possible for them to get their children back home. The main reasons given were that the cities were still too dangerous, travel was difficult, the fares were expensive and there were no schools for the children to go to if they did come home. This last is doubtless true. School medical services, school meals and milk schemes had been suspended in the most vulnerable areas as the authorities anticipated the evacuation of all schoolchildren. In London and Liverpool these were completely withdrawn providing an immediate problem about what to do with the quarter of children who had not been evacuated. In London in 1939 there were just 12,000 school places for a pre-war population of more than 190,000 school-aged children and many of the buildings had been taken over by government or military departments so that even if the schools did wish to reopen, it was made more difficult through lack of premises.

As the war progressed the whole question of schools in the major cities became more vexed. Damaged by bombing, they often became structurally unsound, so that according to official figures on school attendance, it was not until the summer of 1941 that the percentage of children attending school in London reached anything like the pre-war levels of 87 per cent. In November 1939 there were just 70,000 children in London of school age but that figure rose to 192,000 at the end of the year and by May 1940 to 242,000. Without the provision of adequate schools tens of thousands of children suffered from a year or more of disrupted education. This was another reason why the government was so keen to keep children who had been evacuated with their schools in the reception areas.

Once children did come home the cracks in some cases began to show. And it was often the parents who had to bear the brunt of a child's difficulty in adapting to home life. Diana Deane-Jones, who went to America in 1940, reflected on how difficult it must have been for her mother when she returned. She had left as a nine-year-old and returned at fourteen:

I was in a daze, very tired, even before the journey. It was about midnight, pitch black outside. Somebody had a flashlight. I saw Daddy and recognised him at once. We all stumbled out of the carriage and I hugged and kissed him. I was a great shock to them— so tall. Then I saw Mummy, but I did not recognise her at first. She had white hair and looked very tired. I think she was shocked by how much I had changed. She kept looking at me out of the corner of her eye when she thought I was looking at something else. I tried to be grown up and not show any emotion. Now I think how much that must have hurt her. I recall her turning away from me in the taxi with tears in her eyes. It was not the happy homecoming she had expected. She had waved goodbye to a child and I had returned almost a young woman.[13]

For Diana's family there was the added sadness that her older brother, Ralph, had been killed in 1942 flying over Africa.

My mother, I think now, felt that she had lost both her children, one to death and the other to a different life. But the story is not such an unhappy one. My father realised after a few days what was going on and he took me aside and explained what a dreadful time my mother had had. Gradually I began to let her back into my affections and once she was 'in', so to speak, I never let her go again. She remained my best friend until the day she died in 2002 at the age of ninety.

Most people talk about their experiences of evacuation either from their own personal perspective or from that of their mothers. This is not surprising. However, it would be wrong to conclude that evacuation had little impact on the lives of fathers. Letters and diaries written during the war show clearly that the safety of wives and children was in the forefront of most fathers' minds, especially those with families in the big cities. For men who stayed at home, evacuation was often as difficult for them as for the mothers. Ted Matthews, a father of four girls who sailed for America in August 1940, wrote in his diary on 10 August, during an air raid:

I feel as if I had committed some horrible crime. There are mines strewn across the oceans, submarines lying in wait to torpedo them, aircraft searching to blow them to pieces. Yet I cannot but believe that the crime of exposing them to these dangers is less than the crime of keeping them at home to be the possible victims of an invading army. Every minute that passes takes their ship further and further away from that danger. If ever my children read this, I beg them to forgive me for doing this thing. They have no conception of what it has cost to make this decision. They will never know the agony which I suffer at the thought of them tonight.[14]

Another father, Neville Hughes, was unable to go to see his four-year-old son, Martin, off to Canada. Only women were allowed to accompany the children in this particular group to Liverpool. He wrote a letter that gave voice to his feelings: 'Darling Boy, this is a little note to bring you your Daddy's love on your big adventure. Just say to yourself "Daddy loves me very much" and be sure that it won't be very long before there is another big ship for all of us. Always your loving Daddy.' Martin was nearly nine when he next saw his father and he didn't recognise him, but walked straight past him on Euston Station in August 1945. 'Three weeks later I was posted off to prep school and then on to boarding school. I never really got to know my father but I know that he felt those years of my childhood, when I might normally have been at home, were stolen from him, and he mourned that.'

Stolen years are a recurring theme in the evacuation story. Many parents spoke of the sadness they felt on missing out on cherished years of childhood, times that could never be recaptured. Four or five years out of a child's life represented a large slice, sometimes more than half of their life to date. One girl reflected that the five years she spent in America from the age of nine to fourteen accounted for more than a third of her life.

The other thing I sometimes hark back to is the waste of time I spent worrying and trying to adjust. For the first two years I was in the US I was in a state of perpetual mild-homesickness, sometimes more acute than others but always there. Then I settled happily for three years and was fine. And then the cycle started all over again. I was back in England and desperately homesick for my American family. That also lasted for about two years. So for one quarter of my childhood to the age of 16 I was in a state of flux. Five years out of my parents' lives was a much shorter spell by comparison but I know that they regret the loss of those five years more than any others.

Heather Hodge looked at the lost time for her parents:

My mother and father were most upset because my sister had grown into a young woman and I was quite big and very self-assured for my age. I did not want a fuss made and yet in a way I did. I felt I was too old for anybody to cuddle me and make a fuss of me but I needed something. My mother said, many years later, that if such a situation had ever occurred again she would not have let us go away. Five years out of your children's lives was too much and at one point she began to think that she would never see us again.[15]

Joan Herring saw things slightly differently: 'Apart from being such important years to a youngster, anyway, it seems, looking back, like another world, a dream period that I remember so much of. I can't remember the following five years so clearly. Evacuation gave intensity to life because we were surviving an unnatural time in our lives through a war, the outcome of which never seemed as sure as the politicians declaimed.'[16] That her parents had missed out on this intensity was a double blow for them she felt.

Many families had two or even three members coming back who had had wholly differing experiences and, despite the odd bump along the way, they found that life resumed if not as before then at least with a semblance of familiarity. However, there were problems of adjustment when children had changed so much there was no longer sufficient common ground for the relationship to start again. This inevitably took longer to rebuild and in some cases it was never fully righted. It was not always so serious however. The way in which the children viewed their parents anew could be comical. John Mare, whose sister Suzie had been torpedoed in 1943, returned to Britain from Canada at the end of the war to meet again his grey-haired mother and his father, who had been invalided out of the Navy. He told his friend Penny, who later became his wife: 'My mother wears lipstick and powder. They drink and smoke and even the dog is called Whisky!'

Research has shown that the length of stay away made less difference to the effect on the child coming home than might be expected. This may seem surprising but as historian Martin Parsons explained:

The children left the platform at Waterloo or Liverpool Street or Birmingham or Liverpool Lime Street and they had no idea at all, if or when they would ever see their parents again. The effect of this uncertainty cannot be over-emphasised. Little boys and girls as young as five, some even younger, clutching their suitcases, were torn away from their parents for who knew how long. That is the real shock of the separation of evacuees from their parents: not the fact that they were leaving but the fact that they had not a clue when they might meet again.

Children, Parsons pointed out, need something familiar to cling onto, whether something physical like a favourite teddy bear or blanket, or something less obvious like a familiar smell or favourite corner. What few parents and psychologists understood in the immediate aftermath of the war is that on arrival at their new homes children often quickly formed new attachments.

Jimmy Vickers was eight when he arrived in a village near Corwen to live with a childless farmer and his wife. He had grown up in Norris Hill and when Liverpool was evacuated he was sent with his class to North Wales. Mr and Mrs Jones were not unkind to him but they had no comprehension of what a child from the city was used to. He found the countryside dark and frighteningly quiet. In the evenings he was sent outside when the Joneses wanted peace after supper. It was a terrifying time for him and he dreaded being told to leave the kitchen for his walk. As the spring came he noticed the nights were getting lighter and one evening he spotted a carpet of snowdrops under a tree beyond the farm wall. He had no idea what the flowers were called but the tree became his own private oasis, and he visited it every evening. As spring

107

warmed the ground, the snowdrops were joined by crocuses and eventually, by late March, daffodils. But it was always the little white harbingers of new life that made him feel happy inside.

When Jimmy returned to his family home, a terraced house with screaming babies and shouting adults, he was at once relieved to be home but in desperate need of the peace he had learned to enjoy in the countryside near Corwen. Liverpool had been badly damaged during the Blitz and the area around Norris Hill was dilapidated and bedraggled. One day, on his way home from school, the spring after he had come back from Wales, he was walking through the park when he saw snowdrops. A tiny clump in comparison to the great drifts he had seen the year before, but there they were. He picked a small handful and took them home.

I remember so clearly walking into the house with my little handful of snowdrops. It was as if I had a bunch of happiness in my hands. I gave them to my mum who, distracted by the squawking baby, said 'What do you want with them there snowdrops? They'll only die if we put them in a vase. You should never have picked them. Here, give them to me.' And with that she plonked them into the bin. I cannot tell you how devastated I felt by this. It still takes my breath away and brings tears to my eyes when I think about it now, all those years later. It was not that my mum was unkind. I think she loved us all in her own way, but she just didn't get me. After that I never picked another flower again.

Although Jimmy settled down to life in Liverpool after his return from North Wales and got on quite well with the rest of his family, he knew he was different from them. Mr and Mrs Jones had not been rich farmers, so it was not that his head had been turned by a wealthier lifestyle. It was something more intangible, he explained. It was an appreciation of silence, of solitude and of peace, which was lacking in his Norris Hill home and would always be lacking, for none of the others had ever experienced it.

Mum was a good woman in her own way. I know she missed me when I was away, though she never wrote to me. She couldn't write, in fact. My aunt Gwen wrote for her. But Mum just didn't understand why I was different after the war. It used to make her cross. She didn't like me going off for walks on my own or trying to get the other kids to be quiet. But I got on. You know, you do as a child. You just accept you're a bit different and get on with life. But when I eventually did have my own place outside Chester, I planted snowdrops everywhere. Not crocuses or daffodils, just snowdrops.

Snowdrops for Jimmy had become a symbol of something that made him feel happy and secure. Audrey Watts found comfort and reassurance in something even less tangible but equally important to her. In September 1939 she was billeted with a friendly Catholic widow, Mrs Ellis, and her sister, Miss Cousins. Every Sunday they took her to mass.

Audrey explained:

I had absolutely no idea what any of the service meant because it was all in Latin. There was a lot of chanting and bells, there was incense and murmuring but it was all rather beautiful and lovely. Well, when I got home I was so pleased to see my mum and it was just so exciting to be back in London. Only after a few days did she get down to asking me in detail about my time with Mrs Ellis. I told her about going to mass and she hit the roof. Mum had been brought up a strict Methodist and she was horrified that I had been 'Romanised', as she put it. I can recall sitting there thinking to myself, 'I don't know why Mum is so upset, it's not like I joined in or anything.' But it became a taboo in our house and I was duly frog-marched off to Chapel every Sunday morning. As soon as I left home I converted to Catholicism. Mum's aversion to it had pushed me towards finding out more about this lovely, rich, musical, friendly religion. But I don't think at the time it was the religion that I liked as much as the fact that mass was beautiful and everyone in the church seemed to be happy. Mum never did come to my daughter's christening. It remained something that separated us. The war did that. It separated people for the strangest of reasons.

Some mothers found the change in their children bewildering and failed to come to terms with the child that returned after evacuation. The

110

relationship between the mother and child could be changed for ever, with the child finding a closer relationship with the foster mother. Such was the case with Donald Bayley. As neither of his 'mothers' ever spoke of how they felt about this, the story has to be told through the child's experience. Don was born in West Bromwich in 1933. He was the second son and third child, with a young brother, Philip, who was almost five at the outbreak of the war. Two more children were born during the war so that by the time Don returned to live at home they were a family of six children. Don's father was a railwayman.

He worked all his life for the railways and he was really proud of the fact he worked for the Great Western Railway, GWR. It was known in those days as 'God's Wonderful Railway' and he used to joke with us that LMS stood for 'ell of a mess'. Eventually Dad became foreman of one of the big yards but he had no education. He had started working on the railways at the age of ten so that was all he knew. There was no expectation that we children would do anything other than leave school as soon as we could.

Don admits that he was a handful as a child and he did not always behave for his mother, so that he spent quite some time in the late 1930s living with his grandmother in order to give his mother a break, or at least that is how he read it at the time.

When war was announced on 3 September 1939 it came as a complete surprise to Don. He knew that his mother had organised gas masks for them all but he was sure that no explanation was given as to what they were for: 'We were taught how to put them over our faces. It was horrible and it seemed hard to breathe. The rubber around my cheeks always vibrated when I breathed out. It didn't dawn on me that it was the same for everyone. The gas mask was in a neat little box with a string attached which went over my head and I was told I must carry it wherever I went. No one ever told me why.'[17]

An inquisitive child, Don did not often find answers to his questions so he learned to listen and not to ask why. Thus when his parents told him that he and his older brother and sister, Geoff and Pat, would be leaving West Bromwich to live somewhere safer for a while he did not question it but rather looked forward to an adventure. Phil, at that stage not at school and thus deemed too young to be evacuated, was to stay behind but he cried incessantly and begged to be allowed to go with the older three, so in the end Don's parents agreed to let him be evacuated as well, on the condition that he live in the same home as Pat.

All four children were evacuated to Lichfield, about 20 miles north-east of West Bromwich but a world away from anything familiar to them. The first shock of evacuation was that they were split up three ways with Don and youngest brother, Philip, being scooped up together by a couple called the Morleys. This rather threw Don as he had expected to go with Geoff and for Pat to be responsible for their little brother, who spent much of the first day crying so a great fuss was made of him, which did not please Don: 'I was so lonely. Everyone made a fuss of Phil. It didn't seem any

112

better for me here than at home.' However, things looked up when Don realised that the Morleys were living just down the lane from the family that had taken Geoff. As Don went down to the garden gate on the first afternoon, piqued by the grown-ups' lack of interest in him, he spotted to his delight the familiar figure of his brother Geoff coming back from a walk: 'Don', he called out with enthusiasm, 'it's brilliant down there. There are woods and fields that you can walk across.'

Life in Christ Church Lane soon settled down and Don found he was quite happy living with the Morleys. They had an upstairs bathroom with a washbasin and a lavatory, which greatly impressed both boys: 'My only knowledge of facilities was the party lavatory across the yard at home so this was something completely different.' Within a very short time of their arriving in Lichfield the children received visits from their mother. She would come up at the weekends and bring sweets and goodies and took the children for walks across the fields. They showed her their school and their secret haunts in the woods near Christ Church Lane. Phil used to look forward to these visits from their mother and Don remembers him crying whenever she left. 'But', he remarked, 'we didn't cry that much. I have always been aware how as children we were well adjusted. We barely cried, we didn't wet the beds and I can't remember any plans to run away. We seemed to accept the situation, which is remarkable really considering that Phil wasn't even five.'

As with many other evacuated children, schooling was shared with the local school and they started by having morning lessons while the local children had classes in the afternoon and vice versa the next week. As a result they did not mix with the Lichfield children and this inevitably led to some bad blood and the odd fight, some of which, Don recalled, were quite vicious. By Christmas a large number of the West Bromwich children had gone home but the Bayleys stayed in their three foster homes until the late summer of 1940. When considering why he and his siblings did not return Don came to the conclusion that either 'you had to shout and scream that you wanted to go home or your parents had to want you back'. As neither happened in the case of the Bayley boys they stayed put.

One day towards the autumn of 1940 Mrs Bayley turned up to visit Phil and Don and had a surprise in store. All their belongings had been packed up and she marched them down Christ Church Lane and into Walsall Road, stopping opposite number 107. 'Mom rang the bell and a grey-haired older lady let us into the house. When we entered she was ironing, which she continued to do whilst she talked to Mom. She frightened me and I was very fearful as to what would happen when Mom left us as she was going to do when evening arrived. How wrong I was.'

Mrs Coles turned out to be the mother that Don's own mother could never be for him. She was tender, loving, kind and from very early on the two boys sensed they were loved and needed. Twenty years later she wrote to Don that she felt the children 'had been sent to cheer us up'. Everything about Mrs Coles appealed to Don but most of all she gave him time; she talked to him and encouraged him.

114

I considered that this house was proper middle class whilst we were clearly working class. The main difference was that there were so many items around the house that we had never seen before. The first thing was the hunting trophies. These were the heads or horns of various animals that Mr Coles had hunted. The most noted one to us was the head of a fox that hung at the foot of the stairs. It was so low that we could put our fingers between its teeth. In the front room there was a full-size organ and on the walls were long school photographs taken of their boys at various stages of their lives at King Edward's Grammar School in Lichfield. And there were books. Many books on all different subjects and these fascinated me and sparked in me a lifelong interest in learning.

There were other items of interest in the house, including the various collections of stamps, cigarette cards and birds' eggs that the three Coles sons had built up over the years. Suddenly asking questions, being inquisitive and pursuing interests for their own sake was not only permitted, it was encouraged.

Mr Coles was different from his wife. The boys were frightened of him because he was very strict and would chastise them and on occasion beat them if he thought they had done something wrong. Don hated this treatment but he remarked later how strong Mrs Coles's influence must have been that she was able to keep her husband under control and continue to engender warm affection in the two Bayley boys.

During his years with the Coles family Don blossomed. He joined the local choir and became head choir boy, which he knew even then was something that he would not have done in West Bromwich.

I learned to appreciate all these different things from Mrs Coles. I learned how to talk to people and to address them properly and with confidence. I developed a different accent, dropping my Black Country slang. In fact I have to say that Mrs Coles changed me completely and she loved me, I'm ashamed to admit it, more than my mother ever did. She made me feel wanted. She called us 'My boys' and that really meant something to us.

At school Don began to do well and it was clear that he was clever enough to sit the scholarship examination, which he duly did and passed, although he was disappointed that he did not do as well in mathematics as he had in history, English and geography. Mrs Coles was delighted and Don knew that he owed his love of learning to her. All too soon and without warning, Don arrived at school to see Geoff standing at the fence with the unwelcome news that they were to return home that very day. This was a big shock for Don and he has no recollection of saying goodbye to Mrs Coles, which upset him at the time. He and Phil returned to West Bromwich where Geoff had been living for a few months and where there was now another baby. When Don told his parents that he had passed the scholarship his mother was horrified. 'Bloody big head!' she said to him. 'Him and them bloody books' was another refrain that Don heard all too often from her.

From then on I became 'bloody big head' in her eyes and she never really got the measure of me after I came back from living with Mrs Coles. She was always on at me 'you're in the way. Shift yer bloody books.' My dad, on the other hand, was so proud of me. He was a wonderful man, my dad. He was just as proud as could be. But the effect of my mother's negative attitude was that I didn't get on at school after I came home and I left at fourteen. I didn't get on with grammar school mathematics and I finished up at the bottom of the A stream which I didn't like. So I left.

Don went to the Junior Labour Exchange in Birmingham and got a job working in a steel factory. 'It was there that I learned skills for life but it was also where the lessons Mrs Coles had instilled in me came to the fore. I went to night school and there I met a teacher who took away my fear of mathematics and turned me round. I discovered I was really good with numbers and I even learned how to decimalise pounds, shillings and pence, which is no easy thing. In fact, at last, I believed in myself and accepted that I was very clever.'

Don trained as an accountant and ended up running a company pension scheme. He is in no doubt that he owes his determination to get on and educate himself out of his working-class background to Mrs Coles. She changed his life and

117

gave him the confidence to reach far higher than he would have done if he had not been evacuated in 1939. Don and Phil stayed in contact with Mrs Coles until she died in 1970 at the age of eighty-seven. 'She was a wonderful, wonderful lady. We were so lucky to live with her,' he concluded.

Although her influence was profound, Mrs Coles never completely supplanted Don's mother. For Norman Andrews the situation was different. As a direct result of the war he gained a new family and even though for some of his adolescence he found it difficult he acknowledged them as such. In dedicating his novel *The Dream, the Glass and the Firelight* to his foster parents in 2006 Norman wrote: 'For Florence Truda Lenton and Robert Henry Lenton, my foster parents, or rather my true parents, since they loved me when I was a child, and one has only one childhood.'[18]

When Norman thinks back over his childhood there is equally a combination of good and bad experiences. He explained: 'I can remember walking on my own across the fields near my foster home in Northamptonshire weeping out of sheer loneliness and wondering why my life was so difficult. I must have been eight or nine at the time.' Norman's life certainly had not got off to a promising start since his parents had separated in 1940 when he was five years old. He was sent to live with his maternal grandparents after his mother ran off with an actor and not long after that, probably about September 1940, he was evacuated to Peakirk near Peterborough without his parents. As divorce was seriously frowned upon and still unusual in those days, it did not make his life any easier when his foster mother told him that his mother was a wicked woman and that he would do best to forget all about her. Norman did not see his mother again until he was ten.

When he arrived in Peakirk from his grandparents' home in Walthamstow—his grandfather had been a customs officer in the London docks—he was so shocked by the primitive conditions that confronted him that he did not utter a word for the first seven days. The family he was sent to, the Lentons, lived in a two-bedroom cottage with no electricity or running water. Norman recalled water being fetched from a pump in the village, lighting by candles and lamps and an outside privy. It was a new way of life and one that it took him some time to adjust to.

The Lentons had little money and Norman knew that they relied on his father's contribution to his upkeep to help out. His father was an inspector of taxes in Hastings and he not only contributed to the Lentons' family budget but also paid Norman's school fees so that he could attend the same school, the King's School in Peterborough, where the Lentons' son, Tony, was in the senior school. 'Pop' Lenton, as Norman called him, was a railwayman. He had been shot through the thigh in the First World War so that as he got older he needed a more sedentary job and was put in charge of a crossing at Peakirk on the Peterborough to Spalding line. One of Norman's great pleasures was to join Pop in the hut at the crossing and there they would read together. Although he had left school at fourteen, Pop was an avid reader. He did not make any concessions to Norman's young age and fed him on a diet of philosophy and poetry. When Norman had finished all the books in the Lentons' house, Pop introduced him to the local library and encouraged him to read widely. 'I would say that Pop Lenton was a frustrated intellectual. His son did not follow his father's interests and wanted nothing but to be a farmer. He emigrated to Rhodesia at the first opportunity.'

Norman Andrews credits his foster father with helping him to shape his life. 'I am very much the person I am because of Pop Lenton. I didn't admit this until I was probably in my twenties but he certainly influenced my life and I think for him I was the son he really wanted. A son who could pursue his intellectual interests.'

Mrs Lenton was always known by Norman as Mummy and she took over the maternal role that his own mother had been unable to fulfil. She was small, with long hair that she wound up into a bun. He only once saw it loose and was surprised that it reached down to her waist. She had received more formal education than her husband and occasionally spoke to Norman in French. She was strict with him and as she was deeply religious he had to attend church twice on Sundays and behave respectably. 'She was critical of my wild ways when I got older. I do not think I was very wild but she was conservative and religious. I had great affection for her. I have a portrait of her in my office at home painted by her daughter, so I look at her every day.'

Living with the Lentons in Peakirk and attending the grammar school in Peterborough meant that Norman could stay at school until he was eighteen. Both his foster parents encouraged his studies and Pop Lenton took great pride in his academic achievements. For Norman the war was a distant event that did not impinge on his life until he went to Hastings in 1944 to see his father who lived in a hotel. Norman did not have the comfort of going to a familiar home and one night, not long after he had arrived, the hotel was severely damaged by a V1 flying bomb. This was the closest to the war that Norman had come and it was very nearly terminally close. The bomb had landed not on the hotel but between it and the next building but the force of the blast blew the wall out and the ceiling of the second floor came crashing down. Norman awoke to find himself covered in lath and plaster from the collapsed ceiling. The sturdy bed he was sleeping in had held up the debris so that Norman was covered in dust but otherwise unhurt. He managed to scramble to the stairs and eventually got down and outside, where he found his father sitting on the ground covered in blood due to cuts from flying glass.

This visit convinced him that life in Peakirk was safer for a ten-year-old boy than Hastings, so he went back to the Lentons. But before he returned he went to stay with his mother for the first time in five years. She was lodging in Ramsgate with her actor boyfriend. 'It was a very upsetting experience. My mother was a complete and utter stranger to me. I did not see her again until I was sixteen by which time she was separated from her boyfriend and looking after my grandfather since my grandmother had died.'

On his return to Cambridgeshire Norman sat the eleven-plus examination and was admitted to the senior school at King's which, after the 1944 Education Act, became one of the country's first state grammar schools. He did well at school and won an open scholarship to Christ Church College, Oxford, to read English.

I know Pop was really proud that I had got into Oxford. It must have fulfilled a dream for him which he knew his own son could never fulfil. My own father was not remotely pleased that I had got a place. I don't know why as he was a professional man, being a tax inspector. Nevertheless he refused to top up my scholarship so that I had to work hard during the holidays in order to make enough money to live on. I only lasted one and a half years at Oxford, then I left and decided I wanted to become a hotel manager. This was a bitter disappointment to Pop and he took it badly.

Norman found a job in Peterborough and continued to be a weekly visitor to Peakirk as he rose up the ranks of the hotel trade to become a manager. In the Lentons' twilight years he helped them out both practically and financially as they became more forgetful and unable to cope with the weekly bills. He was a son in all but the legal sense and he was devoted to them and grateful for the support and encouragement Pop had given him during his childhood and adolescence. 'It is quite clear in my mind that Pop Lenton was the most important influence on my life. It wasn't always easy and sometimes I hated him but I am very much the person I became because of him.' Though he loved her, Norman's relationship with his foster mother was more complex, as he

122

described in this excerpt from a poem he wrote in 1951:

And in the light, and by the firelight,
    steadfast, knitting,
knitting, Mother, not my mother, but she was
    my mother.

She made me her son, and I resented it.
She pulled me to her heart though I resisted
    it.
She rubbed my chest with ipecac.

She made my memories
as strange as old mythology.

Norman never went back to live with his father or mother, but he continued to visit them. With his father the relationship was formal rather than warm. 'I had nothing in common with my father but I realised I had quite a lot in common with my mother when I got to know her in my early twenties. Like Pop she was also frustrated. She was an intelligent woman in an era when being intelligent and independent counted for little.'

Norman's mother had worked alongside her own brother, who ran a garage, and had taught herself everything she needed to become a competent mechanic. When she married Norman's father she was twenty-one and he was forty. She could drive a car and knew how to fix it if it broke down. But this was a time when women were expected to run a home and have children, not drive cars and be independent, so she was forced to give up work and play the role of stepmother to her husband's eleven-year-old daughter by his first marriage and look after her baby boy.

My mother was never maternal, she did not want a baby but it was expected of her. After she ran away from home with the actor, Robbie Roberts, she got a job with Perkins Engines in Peterborough and became a first-class fitter of diesel engines and eventually a foreman. So my mother lived in Peterborough during the war but my father would not allow me to see her and the Lentons carried out his wishes. After the war was over she was told that she had to leave since the men were coming home and would need their jobs back. She found that very hard to take.

Although Norman never formed a close bond with his mother he became interested in her as a person in her own right. She died in her fifties and the mystery that was her background became the subject of Norman's novel. She represented a complicated strand for him as she engendered so much criticism, most especially from Mummy Lenton.

Nowadays no one would say to a child that it would be better off without its mother but Mummy did in those days. In fact I know that if my mother had tried to visit me, Mummy would have not have had her in the house. This left me with a feeling that there was something wrong with me on account of my wicked mother. Now I know that it is not as simple as that. She was just not cut out to fulfil the role that society expected of her and in the end I came to understand that and accept it.

4

HOSTELS TO FORTUNE

It was a memorable experience: neither a day school nor a formal boarding school, but an experiment, probably never done before and never repeated. I feel my life was enriched by the experience. Besides, you were away from your parents![1]

Tony Challis, schoolboy at Amber Valley Camp

Hostels, camps, even concentration camps were proposed as options for housing evacuee children from the cities after the initial rush to the countryside in 1939. Such accommodation, people argued, was far better suited to whole groups of children than were individual billets in family homes. However, this argument had more to do with the wishes of the private homeowners not wanting to have uninvited children billeted upon them than with the considered welfare of children. The government's problem was that even if it had found this idea preferable to private billeting, it had to be dismissed on practical grounds—there simply were not enough hostels in existence—and on cost grounds—it would have been prohibitively expensive to build enough camps and hostels to house the million-plus children. It was not until the spring of 1940, when lessons from the first wave of evacuation began to be learned, that the requirement for hostels rose up the agenda. As plans were made for a fresh wave that summer, the authorities realised that establishing hostels was going to be useful in dealing with the next mass movement of children from the towns. The hostels began as a convenient dumping ground for so-called 'difficult' children then were used for short-term stays for children between billets and even dealt with specific behavioural and psychiatric problems.

The need to take care of these children with services such as assistants with experience of social work, more school nurses and help to inspect and clean up the children prior to their being billeted, meant that interim accommodation had to be made available. The government could not afford to meet protests from householders about the state of incoming children this time. During the winter of 1940–41 many hostels were set up in great haste and generally in temporary or makeshift premises with mostly untrained and largely unsupported staff. Any child judged unbilletable by the council was placed there.

In July 1943 a survey of forty-eight hostels in England and Wales found that there were not only mixed sexes but also mixed ages, and the reasons given for admission could be anything from bed-wetting, running away or anxiety to stealing and general delinquency. It was not helped by the fact that the hostels were openly referred to as 'hostels for problem children', although this was condemned by the Ministry of Health's welfare officers. The numbers were always small. In early 1941 the percentage of children in hostels was about 3 per cent of the total number evacuated. By the end of 1941 over 10,000 children had been accommodated in some 660 hostels, with the total number of children in residential care, including camps and nurseries, reaching 22,000. This rose to about 12 per cent by March 1944, not because more children had become 'problems' but simply because the number of householders prepared to take evacuees dropped.

After the air raids of 1941, and in the lull that followed, the Ministry of Health set in train a reorganisation of the hostels so that the service better met the needs of the individual child. Throughout 1942 and 1943 the Ministry continued to push for reforms and improvements, encouraging councils to appoint, for the first time in their history, social welfare officers. All this, in conjunction with the energetic efforts of voluntary societies, did a great deal to raise the standard of care of 'difficult' children in hostels and promoted a better appreciation of the importance of mental health work in general. Staff were trained and the provision of psychiatric advice and treatment increased. Thus children who simply needed short-term hostel accommodation between billets, such as Doris Cox in Taunton, were properly catered for and felt cared for while they were there.

For many, the idea of children's homes and hostels conjures up bad images of neglected children and institutionalised bullying and deprivation. However, the experience of a large proportion of the children who were housed in these establishments appears to have been overwhelmingly positive. This was in part due to the success, in the later years of the war, of children being separated according to their needs and in part due to the ability of children to adapt to a structured environment.

There were some nurseries and children's hostels considered exceptional and which gave outstanding service to the children. Rommany Nursery School in West Norwood was run by a woman of great character, Mrs G. M. Goldsworthy. They had Ten Commandments in the staff bedrooms—but not the Ten Commandments that one might expect. The first was 'Let us remember not to herd.' Another was 'Let us remember that fun and laughter and a sense of security are as necessary as sunshine and milk and sleep to the growing child, who is not body only, but also mind and spirit.' The tenth commandment was 'Let us not think meanly of our job—the world moves forward on the feet of little children—shoe-buttons, blisters, elusive wellingtons, odd and un-darned socks; these are all the details in the building of tomorrow.'

Group billeting was deemed to be a success and its advantages were recorded not only by those involved but by inspectors and other interested neutral parties: 'The advantages of group billeting was confirmed in Berkshire by an HMI who wrote at length about the Cubbit Town Glengall School from Poplar. Originally dispersed among several villages, two units of the school were eventually brought together. One unit of 39 children was billeted at the residence of Lord Faringdon in Buscot Park, and another of 36 children was established at Coleshill House. Teachers and helpers lived with the children in what can only be described as an ideal setting.'[2]

A structure and some semblance of a system were quickly introduced and the children adapted

129

well to being part of a bustling school community with rules and regulations—with some freedom—so that they felt released of responsibilities to behave well at all times, as many of them had in their foster homes. 'It was just like being at boarding school,' one girl commented later. 'We very soon had routines going, lessons, homework, sport, evening activities. By the time the war was over I had left school and I went to college. Evacuation was disruptive only until we got established at Buscot Park and then I was very happy.'

The National Camps Corporation was set up in the late 1930s with a grant and loan of £1.2 million and assistance from the Campaign for the Protection of Rural England. Camp schools were formed by the government with the purpose of providing temporary educational establishments for children. The idea behind the project was to build fifty schools, each for up to 400 children, in remote areas where children from towns and cities could experience the countryside. Construction had begun in 1938 and the Camps Act was given royal assent in May 1939. Thirty-one schools were built to a formula designed by Thomas Smith Tait, a Scottish modernist architect who worked with Sir John Burnet on several of the Imperial War Graves Commission's memorials in the 1920s. The prefabricated dormitories, classrooms and ablution blocks were specified to be of Canadian cedar wood, heated by radiators, lighted by electricity and designed to give maximum light and fresh air. Many of the children who were housed in the camp schools could attest to the fresh air. Warm the dormitories were not, but they were on the whole clean and the facilities were up to date. The school hall had a stage for drama, the dining room had its own kitchens and the lavatory block had flushing water closets, showers, washbasins and baths with hot and cold running water. This was a luxury for many boys who had come from homes with poor facilities. There was even a small hospital block as well as accommodation for the masters and camp staff. The schools were government-funded but parents who could pay were expected to contribute up to six shillings a week for their maintenance. Although they were built primarily as residential schools first and holiday camps second, there was no doubt that the possibility of using the camps for evacuation purposes was very much alive in the government's mind. They were ideally situated in remote spots, away from the danger of air attack and could readily accommodate whole schools.

Tony Challis was at Amber Valley Camp School at Woolley Manor, between Alfreton and Tansley near Derby. The school appears to have been popular with most of the boys, who were particularly fond of their maths master, 'Pop' Burns, who was deeply respected by all the boys. He was in charge of the school's tent collection and took boys hiking during the holidays.

Peter Pollard, a boy at Amber Camp school for four years, remembered little of the academic work at the school but has strong memories of the outdoor activities, which included swimming, hiking and cross-country running. It had been a wonderful place to grow up, he said. The war hardly touched the boys, although they were aware that the local Rolls-Royce factory in Derby was a target for the German bombers. Their overwhelming sense of joie de vivre is palpable when reading their accounts of life at the school.

Pipewood Camp Boarding School in Blithbury took girls from the Dingle area of Birmingham from 1940 onwards. One girl wrote of her experiences with animals: 'We looked after hens, ducks and rabbits, gathering food in a bag on our walks. In Domestic Science we prepared chickens and ducks, plucking and cleaning them, also we were shown how to kill a chicken. I never did, but one of the girls did and we plucked it.'[3] If parents could afford to pay a little more there were shorthand lessons available on Saturday mornings in nearby Rugeley so that the girls left the school with useful qualifications as well as a grounding in domestic science and animal husbandry. Again, experiences seem to have been almost completely positive.

Ray Hewitt's father had not wanted his son to be evacuated at the beginning of the war and had resisted pressure from the school in Grove Park, south London, for him to go in the first wave in September 1939. He was a veteran of the First World War and had been in the medical corps in France and Belgium. On his return to Britain he had gone back to his job as a steward at the TB Hospital in south London and the family lived in a tied house on a new housing estate at Grove Park. Ray's older brother and sister had already left home so that by 1939 it was just Ray, aged eleven, and his parents living at home. His father, believing the hospital would be evacuated as soon as a new building could be found for the TB patients, kept Ray at home so that the family could remain together. It was not in fact until 1943 that the hospital was relocated to a former workhouse in York and by that time Ray's father had become convinced that the risk to his son remaining in London was so great that he would have to be moved. He was first evacuated to South Wales. It was a miserable experience and he lasted with his foster family for less than a month before he wrote to his father to say that he was planning to catch a bus back to London. Ray's father met him in Newport and after a few choice words with the billeting officer the two returned to London.

Ray's older sister had been bombed out of her house and the question of Ray's safety came up once again. This time he was sent, by the London County Council, to a camp school in Ewhurst in Surrey called Sayers Croft. Each dormitory, Ray recalled, had three radiators: one by each of the two doors at either end of the hut and one in the middle by the central door. What heat they gave in the winter was offset by the fact that the hut windows were kept open in all weathers.

Our two dormitory masters had been in the First World War and they were great believers in the benefits of fresh air. As a result we slept with the windows open all year round and I remember several times waking up with snow on my bed. I don't think it did me any harm, indeed it toughened me up but it was extremely unpleasant in the winter and we used to sleep in every stitch of clothing we could lay our hands upon. Once you got hardened, though, it's surprising what you could put up with.

133

The other problem at Sayers Croft was the lack of equipment. It housed a technical school from south London that taught typing and other practical disciplines, which took time to organise and initially classes were badly disrupted.

Despite the spartan accommodation and disrupted education, Sayers Croft provided a happy and secure base for many of the boys. 'Being in an institution was in many ways reassuring. It was like a boarding school with all the benefits of knowing that meals would be provided, laundry would be done, and order would be kept. We marched to meals, we marched to classes and we marched to church in the village every Sunday. There was little for us to worry about in that respect.' The boys were given a degree of freedom at the weekends and during the holiday months—they were discouraged from going back to London because of the dangers there, though many boys disobeyed and visited their families, if only for brief periods. During the summer months Ray learned to appreciate the countryside around Sayers Croft and he and his friends would go on long hikes. One of their favourite destinations was Friday Street, a good twelve-mile walk across the South Downs, to visit a widow one of his friends had known from his time as a Boy Scout in the pre-war years. In return for odd jobs around the house and garden, Mrs B. would give the boys lemonade and sometimes fresh bread sandwiches. Those treats were much prized.

Even more prized were the freshly baked cakes that Ray occasionally used to taste when he went into the local village to drop off his housemaster's washing. He would do the odd job in exchange for a treat or two. In addition to one-to-one help, the boys were also given work by the local farmers at harvest time. Paid 2½d per hour, of which ½d was kept back for industrial insurance, they had to work extremely hard. There was an element of exploitation, Ray felt, but with 10,000 extra square miles of land taken into agriculture and a large proportion of the farmhands away at the war, the 60,000 schoolchildren employed to work on the land in 1943, for example, were a vital addition to the workforce.

Ray stayed at Sayers Croft for eighteen months. At that time, he was fifteen and was concerned about the disruption caused to his education. In 1943 he wrote to his father to say that he intended to try to get into another camp school, Itchingfield, which housed Wilson's Grammar School. He sat the exam, was interviewed by the headmaster, and offered a place. Within a week he had left Sayers Croft and moved into the new school, run on the same lines but with a more academic focus. There were six houses at the school, with some sixty boys in each and the emphasis was on teamwork, sport and an encouragement to concentrate on academic work. 'Itchingfield was much better for my education. The staff were old-fashioned, many of the teachers called out of retirement to work with us, but by and large they were good and I enjoyed school.' One of the great joys of Itchingfield for Ray was that he could have a bicycle. He cycled all over the county and made visits to London to see his sister.

He stayed at Itchingfield until July 1945 when one day the boys were all told they were to go home. 'The government grant was terminated and there was no more money available to keep us at school so they more or less said to us "Cheerio, we'll see you back in London." So I got on my bike and, having sent two boxes of stuff on by post, I put the rest of my belongings into two home-made panniers and cycled home.'

Ray's return was difficult. His father had had an exhausting war and the pressures of running the TB hospital and coping with limits on medicines, the worries of air raids and the difficulties of keeping the patients safe, had taken their toll. His mother, too, was tired out by the war. She had had the constant worry over her daughter and granddaughter, who remained in London and were twice bombed out of their homes, once being buried for several hours under the stairs in a collapsed house. He explained:

Had I not been evacuated to Ewhurst I should have been living in that house when the air raid happened and 'my' bedroom was completely destroyed, so I should probably have been too. It was grim coming home, for one thing the house had been damaged as a result of several air raids and there were holes in the roof and no supplies available to make repairs. But it was the psychological damage that my father had suffered that made it hard for me. And then, when I went back to school, I found that the buildings had been badly damaged and our science laboratories were in a dreadful state.

The boys were expected to help clear the school buildings and over the next few months some form of order was restored and Ray was able to take his Higher Certificate in the summer of 1947. Three months later he had enrolled for national service and spent the next three and a half years training and, eventually, serving in Kenya. By the time he returned in 1951 his mother had died and his father was living on his own in the house at Grove Park. He says:

> The legacy of my evacuation was survival. I survived the war because I wasn't living with my sister in London. I survived the camp schools because I learned very quickly to put up with physical discomforts. I survived my education because I persuaded my father to let me try for the grammar school. I made some good friends at school and having been an only child, in effect, as my siblings were so much older than I was, I enjoyed the camaraderie, even though some of the school's population was transient as boys reached fourteen and had to leave. But the relationship with my family in the post-war years was almost non-existent and that is something that I regret. My father had wanted me to stay with him and my mother but it had not been possible as the hospital move took too long and my father felt he had to send me away.

Many of the boys who were at Sayers Croft and Itchingfield had similar experiences to Ray while they were at the schools. Then they went their own ways—to college, into jobs or most of them into national service. Some had no homes or families to go back to in 1945 and for these boys the return was difficult. It was only later, often many years later, that they began to think about their time in the camp schools.

Ray first went back to Ewhurst when his daughters were old enough to do long country walks. He took them first to Friday Street and then over the hills to Sayers Croft, which still existed as an educational establishment for children from the city of London, by this time under the auspices of the City of Westminster. He returned again and soon realised that other boys who had been at the school both during and after the war were visiting. He organised a Visitors' Book, which everyone who had been there signed. In 1998 he asked to borrow the book and sent a letter to everyone who had filled in their details suggesting a reunion. It was a success and there have been annual reunions ever since, where boys are able to go back and stay in the dormitories that were their home in the 1940s. Recently the school has upgraded one of the huts to provide adult accommodation with disabled facilities and this has proved ever more popular with former boys. 'At our first reunion it was very emotional. There was one of the original members of staff still alive and he attended the event. Now we don't have such large numbers of us still alive but people still want to go back and share the camp experience again and remember what they had had during the war.'

The Second World War offered a unique opportunity for members of the social welfare and medical professions to study the state of British families in a way that had never been possible before. In November 1946 a study was written up in the *British Medical Journal* comparing the state of health, nutrition, growth and absenteeism between 2,945 children aged five to fourteen in schools in Salford and 82 children who had been evacuated from the city to a residential camp called Whiteacre Boys Camp in Barrow, near Clitheroe in Lancashire in 1942–3. The study concluded that the boys who had been at the camp were on the whole better off on all measurements of weight, growth and nutrition and were likely to have on average two days a year off sick as compared with twelve days for their counterparts in Salford. This, the study concluded, was in part due to environmental factors such as clean air but also had to do with the worsening economic conditions in Salford as the war progressed. One young boy who felt he benefited from his time in Whiteacre Boys Camp was Arthur Taylor. His father, who had been gassed in the First World War, died during the Second World War. Arthur's mother was employed in war work, so he and his younger sister were sent to Lancaster as evacuees. In 1942 Arthur arrived at Whiteacre 'and I never looked back. I was extremely happy there. The school curriculum was wonderful and I went from being in a class with thirty or forty children to a structured system where I improved so that I ended up in the A stream and there I stayed for the rest of my time at Whiteacre.'

Arthur came from the back streets of Salford and was very poor. He said. 'I would never under normal circumstances have had the opportunity that Whiteacre offered me. Everything about the school worked for me. It was regimented and organised, with dormitories of fifty boys and competitions for everything. We were very well looked after and everything was done to make us organised and independent. We played sports and chess, table tennis and indoor sports in the winter.' In addition to the boys from Salford there were boys from other schools in the Lancaster area so that the school housed between 250 and 300 boys at any time during the war. 'When we left the school in April 1945 we were marched down from the camp to the railway station and I cried every step of the way. It had been such a wonderful experience for me and I knew that I was going to have to go back to my old school.'

Arthur was thirteen when he returned home. He went back to St Luke's School in Salford and was miserable. Academically he was at least two years ahead of the other children in the class and he felt that he was wasting his time at St Luke's so he took a part-time job in order to help his mother out. At fourteen he got a special dispensation to leave school so that he could become the main breadwinner for the family. Arthur said he was glad to be back with his family after the war but he regretted the ending of his education at Whiteacre Boys Camp. Nevertheless, the experience of Whiteacre gave him the determination to make the most of education on offer in later life and he got himself an adult apprenticeship. 'My family wasn't desperately affected by the war,' he concluded, 'but I did have my eyes opened by the experiences I had during evacuation and it made me determined to make something of myself.'

Another group of children accommodated in special schools were the disabled: children classed in 1939 as blind, deaf, epileptic, mentally defective

140

or physically defective. A glance in the index of any book on evacuation, indeed on the Second World War in general, will leave the reader with the impression that disabled children did not exist in the 1940s, or at least, if they did, they did not count sufficiently to be included in any official histories or in contemporary studies of the subject. Yet at the outbreak of the war there were 60,000 handicapped children in special schools throughout England and Wales. That figure does not included disabled children who were on the waiting lists for those schools nor children who were housebound, so that the real figure would be even higher. Plans for their evacuation were as carefully managed by the authorities as that of their able-bodied counterparts and there was even the trial run in September 1938.

However, it must be said that not everyone in Whitehall was wholly supportive of evacuation for children with physical and mental disabilities. There were those within the Board of Education who believed that disabled children were not capable of great achievements and thus they should be given vocational rather than academic training in their schools. There were others who held an even more extreme view and questioned the very idea that the children's lives had any value at all. One of the five principal assistant secretaries at the Board of Education, Cecil Maudsley wrote: 'Although it might be argued in cold blood that perhaps these handicapped children are not so much worth saving as the able-bodied, yet there is a good deal of sentiment for them on the part of the population, and the Ministry and Council might be in a very difficult position vis a vis the people of London if the evacuation plan were operated and these 450 blind, deaf, crippled or otherwise defective children were left behind in London.'[4]

Fortunately those officials and carers directly responsible for disabled children and adults did not subscribe to this view and made arrangements for the accommodation of as many disabled children as possible. Even so, the most severely handicapped were not included in the scheme and were left in the inner cities, a serious failure of a scheme that was otherwise well thought out.

Disability, either physical or mental, was seen by a large majority of the general public as embarrassing and something to be avoided by institutionalising children, getting them out of sight. Muscular Christianity, a movement popular in the Victorian era, espoused the idea of 'the Englishman going through the world with rifle in one hand and Bible in the other', slaying dragons and converting heathens in the more out of reach corners of the British Empire. The legacy of this movement fed into the early twentieth-century belief that a child needed to be strong to uphold the values of the Empire. Being crippled with rickets, polio or cerebral palsy did not inspire confidence. Author and film-maker Steve Humphries wrote: 'Producing a race that could dominate the waves and rule the Empire meant that children with disabilities were looked down upon, frowned upon, shunned even by their own families who could not admit they had given birth to children with disabilities.'[5] Over the first forty years of the twentieth century these children had been shut away in schools and institutions, and thrown back on their own abilities to establish friendships with children in the same position.

Humphries made a TV series for Channel 4 in the mid-1990s entitled *Out of Sight*. He examined the lives of hundreds of children who volunteered their stories to the research and found heartbreaking tales of misdiagnosis and mistreatment:

> Children with physical disabilities who were wrongly diagnosed as also being mentally disabled swelled the numbers who were locked up in asylums and mental handicap hospitals at this time (early 20th century). This increase (asylums numbered 2000 by 1914) was fuelled by a fear—strongly influenced by the new science of Eugenics— that the mentally disabled were undermining the health and strength of the British nation. They were closely associated in much official thinking with crime, poverty, physical degeneration and sexual immorality. The favoured solution was to segregate them from the rest of society to avoid further contamination. Right up to the 1950s children with physical disabilities continued to be wrongly incarcerated in mental handicap hospitals as a result of these attitudes.[6]

Ironically, when it came to evacuation this segregation quite possibly worked in their favour. It was not considered possible to evacuate children with disabilities to private homes as it would place undue burden on the householders, so arrangements were made to find places for

143

children in residential homes. This was settled in advance so that in contrast with their able-bodied counterparts, disabled evacuee children knew where they were going to be accommodated and their families were informed. The authorities, as Dr Sue Wheatcroft of Leicester University explained in her paper 'Children's Experiences of War: Handicapped Children in England During the Second World War' in 2008, went to great lengths to get the places ready with as little disruption as possible to the children and their carers. Some of the 600 disabled schools were run by religious charities or voluntary bodies but the large majority were local authority schools, some residential and others day schools.

In the first few days of September 1939 the evacuation ran smoothly with children and carers ferried to their new lodgings by ambulance and private cars. As with the able-bodied, evacuation of children at day schools was voluntary. 'Of the 8,000 handicapped children attending day special schools and eligible for evacuation in the special parties, only 3,200 registered. A further 2,200 attending open-air (OA) schools were deemed healthy enough to be billeted the same as elementary school children. The remaining 2,600 were either evacuated privately or stayed at home and, initially at least, were unable to attend school.'[7]

Sue Wheatcroft wrote: 'One reason for its success was the lessons learnt from the similar, although smaller, evacuation a year earlier during the Munich crisis.'[8] At the end of September 1938 a group of 2,100 physically disabled children were sent to St Mary's Bay Holiday Camp at Dymchurch in Kent. They were preceded by organising staff and teachers, as well as inspectors, who brought with them as much equipment as they could manage. The accommodation was in an old Army barracks, which leaked and had no heating. Another issue was the medical staff sent to the school. Rather than the school nurses there was a team of Red Cross nurses who had no experience of dealing with handicapped children at night and did not know the histories of individual children. After just over a week away these children and others—such as deaf children from another school evacuated to Margate—returned to London.

From this evacuation the authorities learned, for example, that their own school nurses with knowledge of the individual children were essential, and they had plenty to say about the state of accommodation on offer, in particular the need for adequate heating and the necessity for having some equipment required by the children in place before they arrived. Head teachers, inspectors and administration staff spent long days searching the reception areas for suitable accommodation for their schools. Although the buildings they found were often not ideal, and the lack of heating was a significant worry for the coming winter, the fact that such efforts were made meant that the overall experience for handicapped children was a less disruptive and difficult one than for many of their able-bodied counterparts: 'On the whole, the handicapped children were spared many of the distresses suffered by the other children. They were kept together with their friends and teachers rather than having to settle with a new family, and their accommodation and other essentials had been dealt with before their arrival.'[9]

It appears that the special schools benefited from community living. One example was the Manchester Lancastrian School for Cripples, which evacuated a hundred children to the stable block of a large country house in Shropshire. An official inspector praised the headmistress for holding together 'a willing, happy, hardworking team of domestics, nurses, and teachers'[10] in carrying on the normal activities of the school, in spite of their removal to a remote area.

The reaction of the local public to handicapped evacuees was on the whole compassionate and the children were treated with kindness and in some cases generosity. When Jessica Young (née Axford) arrived at Peckforton Castle in Cheshire, a neo-gothic nineteenth-century country house built for John Tollemache, a wealthy landowner and MP, she was given a pretty flower mug made by a local potter. The castle accommodated girls with 'physical defects' and she remembered it as a good experience. There were Christmas parties and festivals organised for the children and there were even visits from American and Polish forces stationed nearby. Jessica treasured the mug long after the war. It reminded her of a happy evacuation.

Similar stories came from all over the country. Ken Giles was an evacuee in West Sussex who suffered from hemiplegia or paralysis on one side of the body. He wrote about going out and about from Broadreeds camp at Selsey Point where he was housed: 'When we left the camp we tended to do so in groups. I cannot recall any adverse reaction to us as evacuees, nor as cripples. You must bear in mind that because we were housed at the holiday camp we were not forced into people's private homes; and the locals were used to the camp being occupied by outsiders because that is its function. So there were no tensions arising from invading other people's territories.'[11]

Barbara Booth had been struck by polio at the age of three and although she could walk with the aid of callipers she was not allowed to attend mainstream school in the 1930s. Initially she had been sent to a Chailey Heritage Craft School in East Sussex, which was a school and hospital for disabled children that believed in toughening them up. 'One of their most famous ex-pupils who attended the school in the 1950s was the pop singer Ian Dury,' Barbara pointed out. 'There was a sign in the boys' area that said "men were made here". It was a really tough education. You couldn't claim you couldn't do something until you were able to prove you couldn't do it. So if you were told to go across a field and you couldn't walk, then you had to crawl.' She was there for two years from the age of five until seven but then her parents moved to Tooting where there was a day school for disabled children and she was brought back home. As a result of her two years at Chailey she was extremely resilient and independent, so that when she was evacuated with the Franciscan Road PD (physically disabled) School in Tooting in September 1939 she saw it simply as the next stage.

Barbara was sent to the same camp as Ken Giles. Several London schools for physically handicapped children were evacuated to Broadreeds and over the autumn months

147

improvements were made to the conditions in the camp but when Barbara first arrived the huts they slept in were unheated and hopelessly insulated, since it had been designed for use during the summer holiday season. 'There was no heating and that was a big deal for me as a polio sufferer and I used to cry myself to sleep because my feet and hands were so painful, covered in chilblains.' Barbara's father was so upset by the conditions at the school, in particular the lack of heating in the huts where the children slept, that he came down to the school and smuggled her out, bringing her back home to London.

My mother came down first and reported back that my chilblains were bleeding and I couldn't sleep properly. I had nits and fleas too. She also told Dad that the camp was right next to an ack-ack station. We could chat to the soldiers through the chain-link fence. It was so close to our hut and when we first arrived and had no blackouts we were grateful for their searchlights so that we could read comics after dark. But it was a crazy place to put a school, let alone one for disabled children.

From the summer of 1940 the threat of invasion via the coasts rather than bombing of the cities meant that areas that had been deemed safe in 1939 were now suddenly vulnerable. Re-evacuating non-handicapped children away from the coastal towns and villages was a great deal easier than moving whole schools and camps of disabled children. Broadreeds was in a highly vulnerable area in West Sussex but insistence by the Board of Education to the Ministry of Health that the camp could be a target of German bombers—given its proximity to anti-aircraft guns and searchlights—and that it should be moved met with the remark in a letter on 8 July 1940 that 'we must be prepared to lose a certain number of parties.' Eventually arrangements were made to move the camp on 27 August but a week earlier a bomb dropped nearby. Three people in the camp were killed including a thirteen-year-old boy. It was not the only tragedy but it was without doubt more by good luck than good management that more children were not killed in the camps along the south coast.

When Barbara Booth came back to London with her father she remained at home and was not evacuated again.

I'd been sent away from home twice, first as a little girl to Chailey and then, as a ten-year-old, to the camp at Selsey Point and that was enough. I didn't want to go away again and feel that I was being got rid of. However, I don't think that evacuation affected me any more than being sent to the first residential school did and we had a very loving family so that I soon settled down at home when I got back. I think my parents hadn't wanted me to be evacuated in the first place but a lot of pressure was put on my mum because I was a disabled child and they said that a bomb might kill me. Well, if it had landed on the house it would have killed us all, not just me, wouldn't it?

It was not only disabled children who were accommodated in hostels and camps. Orphans and children who had, for one reason or another, been moved from their families into residential care, also had to be catered for. For some they became safe havens from dysfunctional family situations that were exacerbated by the war.

The legacy of abandonment had a strange effect on the life of Patrick Fitzgerald, an evacuee who had had a difficult childhood. However, it was his home situation rather than evacuation that shaped his life. Patrick was born in Brighton in September 1939 after his mother was evacuated from South Norwood as an expectant mother who qualified for the government scheme. His mother came from Rochester in Kent and appears to have been born into a relatively poor family in 1914. She was the third child born of nine and apart from the belief that she was once in service, Patrick knew nothing else about her life. Of his father he knew even less and they never met. His mother once told him that his father was a 'drunken sod' and he discovered, after investigating his family tree, that they were not married when he and his two siblings were born. Then, for some unexplained reason, the two of them married in 1942 just before Patrick's father went off to war.

Patrick had a brother born in 1934 and a sister in 1937. At the outbreak of war both these children had been sent to live in a terraced house with a Mrs Bowles in Bognor Regis. Patrick joined them some time in about 1942–3. He has no idea whether Mrs Bowles ran a foster home but he knows he lived there with his brother and sister until he was about five, after which he and his siblings lived in a children's home facing the sea in Bognor Regis. He recalls that the three of them were split up when it was deemed no longer acceptable for his sister, who was growing up fast, to live with boys and share bedrooms with them.

Although Bognor Regis was on the coast and therefore on the Luftwaffe's flight path to Portsmouth, 25 miles up the road, Patrick stayed in the town until 1945. As with the schools and camps for disabled children, moving a whole orphanage was far more difficult than rehousing individual children. After the war he was sent to a children's home in Guildford, then three or four years later to Camberley. In the immediate post-war years he was in the care of Surrey County Council. He said:

Although I have no memories of being unhappy in the various children's homes I was in, I have absolutely no recollection whatsoever of the names of the other children nor of any of the children I was at school with. That part of my life is completely blanked out. I remember learning that my mother had married my father in 1942 so that I was no longer illegitimate but that did not mean I could go and live with her. The flat in South Norwood was too small and, anyway, no sooner had my father gone off to war than she took up with another man, Charlie Edwards, and fairly quickly had more children, two girls.

So what effect had evacuation and the war had on Patrick Fitzgerald? He explained that the ties that might otherwise have held his family together were loosened. His mother lived in her flat in South Norwood for over sixty years but Patrick himself never lived there, other than his first eighteen months, of which he has no memory. He was institutionalised from the earliest days and the most unsettling period for him came in his mid-teens when he went to live with two foster families. He found he could not cope and soon ran away, preferring to live in a working boys' hostel in Woking until he was old enough to join the Army. 'The great thing about the Army', he said, 'was that I didn't have to think for myself. I hadn't had to think for myself in the children's homes either. The structures were there and so long as you followed the rules it was an easy way to live one's life.'

For Patrick the great sadness of the war was that he lost all contact with his siblings. He knew that his older brother, Len, went to live on a farm after the war and that the family had wanted to adopt him but his mother was set against it. Len lived briefly at 'home' but he did not get on well with his mother's new man, so he moved away and as far as Patrick knows he did not see his mother again.

His older sister faded out of his life but he made contact with her again in 2009. He met his two half-sisters in about 1957 when Angela, the older one, was ten. The two of them got on well and over the years became close. Patrick's mother died in 2006 at the age of ninety-two and Patrick contacted his brother Len via the Internet and found he was still living on the farm where he had worked since the war. A phone call was followed up by a visit but Len would not agree to see Patrick. In fact he told him to go away and never to contact him again as he reminded him of the worst part of his life. He went on to tell Patrick that he had written his family out of his life and told his children that they were all killed by a bomb during the Blitz. This, he told Patrick, was what the children's home had told him in 1944. The facts did not add up but Len was determined not to have any contact with the past.

Patrick said: 'The war destroyed our family. I think my mother was concerned for our safety, which is why she did not want us to come back to London to live with her. I cannot ask my sisters too much about their past and mine but there are gaps that I should love to fill but never will now.'

Although Patrick's family life was shattered as a result of the war, the treatment that he received at the hands of the authorities was good. He was adequately cared for, his needs were met at a School for Delicate Boys after he contracted TB aged eleven, and though he was given no parental warmth or affection, he was not abused nor was he unduly harshly treated during his childhood. As a result he was able to establish a happy family of his own when he married and had none of the attachment problems that many of the children evacuated to private billets spoke of. His life in the Army was busy and the three children, all born to him and his wife within thirty months of one another, were a great joy.

When Jessie Ritchie became the Mayor of Weymouth and Portland in 1989 it was a very far cry from her roots in Scotland where she was born in 1934. In fact it was so different that it is hard to imagine how the change might have come about without the dislocation provided by the war. Her humble beginnings in a tenement in Glasgow's east end were depressing in the extreme. Her mother found it difficult to cope with her five children and womanising husband who spent too much of his time in the pub, so she eventually ran away back home taking the twins and abandoning the three youngest infant girls in the tenement. Jessie's aunt found them alone in the one room, hungry, filthy and cold. They were sitting on a mattress screaming. Their father was summoned from the pub and put the children onto a handcart and pushed them to his parents' house where their grandmother took them in grudgingly.

Jessie and her sisters, one older, one younger, were brought up by their grandparents from then on and Jessie has only one memory of seeing her mother during her childhood. 'We were never loved in our lives,' Jessie stated simply. She recalled little of her early life except that she was permanently unhappy and afraid. The children were all made to feel that they were a burden to their grandparents and other relatives. They were told they had only been taken in on sufferance. Jessie pointed out that one reason for this was that her father, who she described as a ne'er-do-well, was the apple of his mother's eye. 'For all my early childhood I felt I was a nuisance. I never laughed or smiled. That was neither encouraged nor wanted. My life was full of fear. That is all I can remember. Fear of everything.'

Whatever the reason, Jessie and her sisters Joan and Georgina knew they were unwelcome in the family home. So they were not surprised when their grandparents took the opportunity to get them evacuated: 'In 1939 Joan and I were first billeted in a small cottage where we were practically starved. Georgina remained in Glasgow as she was too young to be evacuated. I remember gobbling leftovers from the family's empty plates and being utterly miserable.' Then in 1940, they were sent to live in a home for refugees, evacuees and abandoned children from Glasgow. The home was in a country house called Balendoch surrounded by woods and extensive grounds, situated outside the village of Alyth, about 7 miles east of Blairgowrie. It had been commandeered by the Perth Education Authority but run by three Christian Guiders, all spinsters, from Broadstairs in Kent. They had answered an advertisement in the *Guider*, the magazine for Girl Guides and their leaders, in the belief that they could do something for children displaced by the war. Miss Esther Reiss, who was the author of the Balendoch Evacuation Hostel diary from 1940–45, was officially the matron, Miss Ashby was cook and Miss Rutherford the housekeeper and general assistant. Miss Reiss wrote that despite the delineation of their jobs on paper they all mucked in and did whatever was required to make the house run smoothly.

When Jessie arrived in July 1940 she was typical of the children who came to Balendoch. Miss Reiss described them:

Most of the children come from the slums of Glasgow and have had no real training. They come dirty and underfed, and with practically no clothing. It is amazing to see how quickly they become part of the machinery here. Children who have had no possessions of

155

their own are thrilled to find they have a towel, flannel, toothbrush etc with their own number on it, a peg for their coats, a shelf for their boots, a locker for their clothes and so on. Their baths are a source of great joy, and so are their medicines—and if one needs a dose, so does everyone. If one child has to have his temperature taken, so does everyone in that bedroom, and even if one has a dirty head, everyone else manages to have 'an awful itchy head too, Miss'. Toothpaste is such a novelty that most children eat theirs— so much was eaten that we now have to keep it and put a little on everyone's brush for them.[12]

This was served up with a dose of castor oil to keep the children healthy. The oil always came before the sweet-tasting toothpaste. Jessie's first recollection of Miss Reiss was that she smiled at her. 'This was completely new. I don't recall anyone ever smiling at me before and here was this tall, portly woman smiling at me. Years later Miss Ashby described to me what Joan and I looked like when we arrived at Balendoch. "Stick thin," she said, "you looked like children out of Belsen." That is when I learned that the village schoolteacher had noticed our emaciation and had reported us to the Perth authorities and that is how we came to be at Balendoch with Miss Reiss smiling down on us.'

The home was run on 'Guide' lines, as Miss Reiss explained in a letter published in the *Kent Girl Guide Quarterly* leaflet not long after Balendoch had got going. The day was highly structured with each hour taken up with duties and

156

activities when the children were not at school. Breakfast on schooldays, she noted, was a silent meal 'owing to lack of time'. There was always porridge before school, whereas at weekends they had French toast made with dried eggs. School was in a village called Ruthven, a three-mile walk from Balendoch and the two classrooms in the school building were filled up by the Balendochers. Jessie recalled that they took their own packed lunches with them every day. 'Imagine making forty packed lunches for all those years.'

The routine seemed to suit the children and the three women organised the discipline in such a way that the children were rewarded for teamwork and cooperation rather than being punished for being unruly, though bad behaviour was not sanctioned. The results were impressive. Many of the children, and certainly Jessie Ritchie, had never known a structured day before, let alone one where praise and even rewards—gold and silver stars—were handed out for good or cooperative behaviour. It was a tremendous eye-opener for her. Jessie said:

It was a remarkable experience. Those three women—we called them 'our ladies'—kept control of us, about 44 children in total, and they taught us everything. We learned how to share, they encouraged us to think of others before ourselves. We learned to sing and dance, knit and sew, we learned to have fun and we were loved. That is something that had not happened to me before. Balendoch was the making of me in that respect. I learned what it was like to be loved. Their Christian ethos was an inspiration, though we didn't appreciate it at the time.

The Misses Reiss, Ashby and Rutherford were determined to do everything they could to give their charges as normal and full a life experience as was possible within the confines of living in a hostel. The children's education and daily discipline was structured and orderly, but they were encouraged to undertake projects that they might not have done at home. When the local farmers needed potato, apple and raspberry pickers the children were volunteered as all the men were at war. They were paid. Jessie remembers it was ten shillings a week and the farmer was very pleased with their work. Jessie was only six and this was the first time she had earned money in her life. The money was kept for the children so that if they needed something it could be bought for them but they were also encouraged to open bank accounts and one or two children bought savings certificates. All these things, explained Jessie, helped to form a discipline for life. 'We learned the essentials and it was all so useful later.'

All the festivals were celebrated and for Jessie many of these were for the first time. In October they had a Halloween party with bob apples and treacle buns. During November they made things that they could sell, such as purses, comb cases and handkerchief holders that could be sold to raise money for refugees in Hungary at Christmas. 'We were reminded that although we were poor there were others who were much worse off than we were.' Christmas 1940 was a first for many of the children who had never in their lives had a stocking before, and some of them had not ever received a present. That first Christmas the Guiders made the mistake of putting Christmas stockings on the children's beds and the unpacking had begun by 2 a.m. The next year they learned their lesson and the stockings were hung up in a line in the playroom. 'Generally a heavenly but very tiring day,' Miss Reiss concluded, after her 2 a.m. start in 1940.

Jessie learned to ride the bicycle at Balendoch (there was just the one), she learned to swim and play tennis and she learned to appreciate the world about her. At school they were taught to look at the birds and learn the different habits of the swallows and the robins. But it was not all educational. The Guiders were equally keen to allow the children to let their hair down. On one occasion the two stirrup pumps had to be cleaned out so the children were allowed to don their sou'westers and have a big water fight. In the school holidays they were taken camping to Gleneagles. Jessie remembers putting up the tents and then going for a walk. When they returned to the camp they found that the local cows had eaten their entire, enormous bowl of custard. It rained for the whole week but they had a marvellous time, the hostel diary recorded.

The war never really came close to Balendoch so that Jessie's only memory of the bombing was when a pilot dropped his unspent cargo on his return mission from Glasgow and it landed near Alyth. 'Miss Reiss took us to see the crater, which was impressively large. She showed it to us and explained that we were not to be afraid because they had not meant to hit us, they were just throwing their bombs away. That was as close as the danger came.'

Christmas 1944 was to be their last at Balendoch, though the children did not know it. Jessie was christened and confirmed by the Reverend Henry Reid and the Bishop of Glasgow that autumn and celebrated her first communion on Christmas Day in Alyth Church with her godmother, Miss Reiss. Two weeks later the hostel was closed down. Esther Reiss wrote in the diary: 'It took a good deal of careful manipulation to get everything and everyone packed in but eventually we were all waving goodbye and once more Balendoch was left in the sole possession of the three Broadstairs Guiders who had left the Sunny South in 1940.'[13]

When the home closed in January 1945 Jessie and her sister went back to live with their grandmother. It was as unpleasant an experience as she could possibly have feared. On the one hand she desperately missed the safety of Balendoch and the Misses Reiss, Ashby and Rutherford: 'And oh how we did miss them! It was like losing my mother.' And on the other hand she had the misery of life back with her grandparents and her aunts and uncles, all of whom appeared to dislike and resent Jessie and her sisters more than ever. She remembered going home and having to share a bed with Joan and her younger sister, Georgina, who had not been at Balendoch. All the colour, warmth and love disappeared from her life once again. It was replaced in her memory with rain and cold in Glasgow, people milling everywhere on the streets, no space around her and above all the rigid Victorian atmosphere in the home that was permeated by fear. Fear, she reiterated, was always present: 'I remember that my uncle particularly hated us because he had a daughter who was disabled and he resented the fact we were fit and strong. We were all told by him and our aunts that we had to go out to work at fourteen because we owed it to our grandparents. So, from the age of eleven I started working on Saturdays in a fruit shop.'

Jessie loved senior school. It was a safe haven. 'I cried when I had to leave aged fifteen but fate dealt me a wonderful hand. One evening there was a knock at the door and I heard the voice of my English teacher, Mr McLaughlan. I was listening upstairs and I heard him say to my grandmother: "Don't send Jessie into a shop or a factory. There is a special secretarial course being run at Langside College and Jessie has been chosen from Whitehill School."' The bursary was £200 for nine months. 'My grandparents leapt at the bursary and I leapt at the chance!' It offered her a way out that she thought had been barred when her grandfather had told her that a university education would be wasted on a 'lassie who will just get married and have bairns'. When Jessie finished the course she got a job as a shorthand typist in an office in Glasgow and would perhaps have carried on but for the fact that her grandmother, who was dying, told the three girls that they would have to join the services. 'You'll have a job, food and a bed if you join the services because when I die you won't have a home. My two sisters joined the WRNS and I joined the WRAF and was posted to Egypt.' Jessie met her first husband while she was in the forces and they had three children, a boy and twin girls.

161

In 1963 Jessie moved to Weymouth and has lived there ever since.

What became of the extraordinary women who changed her life? Jessie kept in touch with them all until the end of their lives. None of them married but they were all very active in various charitable ways. Miss Rutherford died of cancer in the early 1960s. She and Jessie had exchanged Christmas cards but they never met up after the war. Esther Reiss died in 1982. She was living at the time in Wolverhampton and when Jessie visited her before she died she took her to the Town Hall on a civic visit as a Visiting Borough Councillor and told the Mayor how wonderful she had been to the children of Balendoch during the war. 'It meant a lot to me to do that, to tell people what she had done for me, for all of us. Out of earshot I then asked the Mayor if he would recommend Auntie Esther to the Queen for all her good works. He made the recommendation and she received the Silver Jubilee Medal. To the day she died she never knew who the recommendation came from.'

Miss Ashby moved back to live in Broadstairs and worked tirelessly for Save the Children for the latter part of her life. Jessie had the satisfaction of being able to help 'Ash' financially in her old age. 'She lived to the age of ninety-five and when she was ninety I took her back to Balendoch for a visit down memory lane and we both cried.' It was a minor contribution, she felt, to the very great debt of gratitude she felt towards the old lady. 'Ash was so private,' Jessie explained, 'that no one knew her Christian name until she died. She was Ada Edith Ashby.'

Jessie Ritchie was given the Balendoch diary by

Miss Ashby and in 1998 eventually decided to place it with the Imperial War Museum. So how did it feel reading the diary again over fifty years after the war? Jessie wrote an appendix note when she reached the last pages and it reads: 'I'm crying as I write this bit because we all cried and cried at leaving Balendoch. It was years before we realised just what these three wonderful ladies had done for us, and what a life-giving example they had set for all of us underprivileged children.'

Evacuation for Jessie was not typical of the stereotype often portrayed. For her it was a wholly positive experience that informed the rest of her life and turned her into the person she is today. The basic tenets of kindness, loyalty, putting others first, working hard and expecting nothing were born at Balendoch with the Christian example set by their 'three ladies' but it was Jessie's personal strength of character that allowed her to hold fast to those when life turned against her on her return to Glasgow after the war. Life has not always been easy for her and she admits that she found it difficult to lavish affection on her own children since she had not known that in her childhood. She brought them up firmly, to understand discipline and she was always anxious that they should want for nothing, so she worked hard to put food on the table. Perhaps the example of the upbringing in the hostel was more influential on the way she brought her children up than she realises, since she continues to have good relationships with them and is devoted to her grandchildren.

One other aspect of Jessie's evacuation continued as a theme through her life and that was her gratitude towards the American Red Cross. At Balendoch they had received huge boxes of toys, clothes, girls' dresses and material as well as dried eggs and, best of all, dried chocolate. When she moved to Dorset she joined the county Red Cross but it was only in 2001 that she really had the opportunity to show her appreciation for the gifts and food the Americans had sent over during the war. 'I always felt I needed to say thank you to the Red Cross in the USA and when the 9/11 tragedy struck I went out with a big begging bowl. Sitting outside Tesco in Weymouth I raised £2,000 which I sent to the American Embassy in London.'

When Jessie became involved with local government she was able to empathise with those people who were not well off in society, either financially or for other reasons. She knew that her background stood her in good stead and the experiences of her childhood, both good and bad, informed much of what she did. In the end, she concluded, she would not have had the life she has enjoyed had she not been an evacuee sent to the hostel in 1940: 'They were the happiest days of my life as a child, those years spent at Balendoch being cared for by those saints. I always felt I wanted to write to the Queen and tell her that if anyone deserves a Victoria Cross it is those three women who looked after us.'

5

OVER THE SEAS AND FAR AWAY

Our contemporary horror at the idea of parting children from their parents is a post-war development and although it is often tempting to use that early 'trauma' as the excuse for all my deficiencies, I have the impression that the majority of the evacuees survived intact and were even enriched.

Jessica Mann, Out of Harm's Way

Domestic evacuation was at the forefront of the government's planning for children's safety in 1939 and 1940 but the threat of invasion in the early summer of 1940 led to a large number of parents opting to send their family abroad. Many of these children went on privately organised schemes, some just on a one-to-one basis between family, friends or contacts, others were set up to take groups of children. People came forward from companies, universities, church organisations or schools, keen to offer the children of Britain safety in the English-speaking Dominions as well as America. More than 13,000 children are estimated to have taken up places offered in countries as far away as New Zealand and Australia.

Ann Spokes Symonds was evacuated as one of a group of over a hundred children of Oxford University academics and affiliated families who were offered homes by fellow academics at Yale

165

University in the United States. A group was set up with the descriptive title: 'The Yale Faculty Committee for receiving Oxford and Cambridge University Children'. A general invitation had been issued to both universities to send their children to Yale; then John Fulton, Professor of Physiology at Yale, who had been a Rhodes Scholar and later a Fellow of Magdalen College, Oxford, cabled friends and colleagues at both universities on 6 June 1940. This two-pronged approach received a particularly warm response from Oxford and a group of 125 children and 25 mothers were booked on the SS *Antonia* due to sail in early July.

Once the decision had been taken to put the children beyond the reach of the feared German invasion it could not happen quickly enough. Dr Maude Royden, writing in the *Christian Century* in April 1941, tried to sum up the mood of June 1940: 'To many British people, the fear that their children could be brought up Nazis was worse even than the fear of death. Will you Americans, vowed as you are to freedom . . . look for a moment at your children and ask . . . what so dreadful a threat would mean to them?'

Ann and her twelve-year-old brother, Peter, were fostered by a couple in New Haven called C.C. and Beecher Hogan. He was a Fellow at one of the colleges at Yale and she was a very competent pianist. Ann in fact completed her school education in America although she had been keen to get home before the war was over. In her book *Havens across the Sea*, published in 1990 at the time of the fiftieth anniversary of their evacuation, she wrote: 'As one of the older girls—I was fourteen when we left England in 1940—it was perhaps natural that I would suffer a sense of guilt because in wartime I had left my country for another. But I was intensely happy with my foster-parents and hated the idea of leaving my school before graduation. However I was equally anxious to return to England before the war was over.'[1]

Ann wrote to her mother and said that she would like to join the Wrens (WRNS), something she had always wanted to do. Her mother wrote back to say that there were now no vacancies in the Wrens so the only thing she could do is join the ATS (Auxiliary Territorial Service) as a cook or a nurse. Ann wrote back in despair: 'Isn't there anything else? The reply came informing me that if I were to obtain entrance to the university I could escape the horrors of cooking or nursing.' This meant staying on at school until June 1944 and getting good grades. Entrance to Oxford for the children in America was not decided by the usual examination but on evidence that they had obtained a place at a reputable college or university in the United States. Ann was accepted at Vassar so the only thing left for her to do on returning to Oxford was to pass her college exams for St Anne's.

She returned to Oxford in August 1944 where she met, for the first time, her baby brother, who had been born while she was away. She needed to bond with her younger siblings as well as settle in Oxford once again. Her sister, who had been very close to her brother Peter—they were just eighteen months apart and people often thought they were twins—was very disappointed that he hadn't returned with Ann but stayed in the United States.

He was eventually adopted by the Hogans in New Haven. 'Peter was twelve when we left Britain and sixteen when I came home. He became American soon after he set foot on US soil and settled very quickly. He has remained there ever since and now lives in Minneapolis. I think my parents were very sad he chose not to come home. It must have been very hard for them to accept.'

Ann described her life after her return as one big adventure. Within about six weeks she learned that she had been offered a place at St Anne's College to read PPE. 'I was so thrilled, I just hugged myself when I heard that I had got a place there. It was a fantastic time and we girls who had been in America were so much more fortunate than the girls who had been left in this country. We had the latest fashion in mid-calf length skirts and high heels and were quite the belles of the ball at all the dances that autumn. It was such fun.'

Ann is certain that one of the reasons she did so well on her return was because she had gone willingly, she understood that it was a temporary solution to get her out of harm's way and it was a fantastic opportunity which she should not waste. She was also impressed by the fact that the academics in Yale had taken the trouble to match the right sort of children to the right sort of home. Before joining their foster families the Oxford children had spent time in the Yale Divinity School waiting to be allocated to the most suitable hosts. 'Hardly any of us children were aware that Mr Byron Hacker, the director of the Children's Center, and his staff of assistants were undertaking their investigations during this time, matching up children with the most suitable hosts. During their time at the Divinity School, children were observed and sensitively interviewed to make sure that placements were as successful as possible.'[2] In Ann's case this was wholly successful. She and her brother were very happy with the Hogans, who had no children of their own but had a niece and a nephew of the same age as Ann and Peter. The Hogans sent them to good schools and took them on wonderful holidays.

Another reason she felt comfortable coming home was her age when she went to the United States. To leave on an adventure at fourteen was, she felt, perfect timing. She was young enough to be moulded to some extent by the experiences of her time in America and she readily absorbed the culture and the traditions as well as the academic work on offer. When she returned aged eighteen she was wholly independent, an adult in all but definition (the age of consent then was twenty-one) but still close enough to her family to be able to slot back in to their life and routine with real pleasure. The fact that she went more or less straight to university meant that there was no need for her to readjust to the English school system, which younger friends had to do, and often did with considerable difficulty.

The only thing that troubled me in all those four years was a feeling of guilt that I had been lucky enough to get away from the war to safety while my younger siblings, my family and all my friends who stayed in Oxford had to put up with wartime deprivations. Luckily Oxford was not bombed and of course the invasion that my parents and other adults so feared never happened either but no one could have foreseen that. However, I was intensely happy in America and equally happy to be home, so the outcome of the whole experience was a very good one indeed for me.

Shirley Williams, who spent two and a half years in Minnesota, did not share the same feelings of guilt that Ann Spokes Symonds had felt, since her parents brought her home in 1943 so that she and her brother, John, could experience the war when the threat of invasion had all but disappeared. Already at boarding school in 1939, Shirley found the prospect of war exciting rather than terrifying: 'war was heroism, adventure, excitement' but for her mother, Vera Brittain, the war brought back terrible memories of the loss of her fiancé, her brother and many close friends in the First World War. As the rescue of the British Expeditionary Force was under way at Dunkirk in May 1940, she wrote in her diary: 'Feel sick at heart when I think of John and Shirley, and can only pray that the tide of war will roll over their heads without harming them.' Weeks later a telegram arrived from a couple in America known slightly to Shirley's mother saying, 'Send us your children'.

My mother was coincidentally wrestling with the moral dilemma of whether she had any right to risk us being orphaned in Britain, should the Germans invade. [My parents] were never worried about German bombing—indeed they would bring us back from the United States as soon as they could after the threat of an invasion faded. They wanted us to share the experience of the war that would shape our country's future. But the consequences of an invasion for us were different. My parents had reason to believe—which was later justified by the fact that their names appeared on the Gestapo blacklist—that if the Germans conquered Britain they would both be among the earliest people to be eliminated.[3]

Vera Brittain's best-selling autobiography *Testament of Youth*, published in 1933, with its message of peace was anathema to the Nazis.

The Colby family in Minnesota were acquaintances of Vera Brittain. She had met them whilst on a lecture tour in the United States in the 1930s and they had immediately offered to take her children when the threat from the Nazis became ever closer. They also tried to encourage the parents to come. They both refused and Shirley acknowledged in her autobiography that the decision for her mother must have been acutely difficult but her sense of duty to her country, as a leading pacifist and sponsor of the Peace Pledge Union, made it impossible for her to abandon Britain. In 2000 Shirley Williams reflected on her parents' decision. They were right, she was sure, to send her and John away given the circumstances: 'I wouldn't have respected them less if they had kept us but I would certainly have respected them less if they had come themselves. I had a lot of respect for their decision not to do that.'[4]

Apart from a week or two at the beginning of

her stay when she admitted to feeling a little homesick, Shirley's three years in Saint Paul, Minnesota were full to the brim with activities, experiences, thrills and near stardom. In 1940 she was chosen to take part in screen tests to find a child star for the film *National Velvet* and was only beaten in the final round by 'a beautiful English child living with her mother in California. Her name was Elizabeth Taylor.'[5] She revelled in a society where the walls between the social classes were porous. 'Money and talent would enable one to traverse them. The absence of accent as a defining feature enabled Americans to present themselves as whatever they wanted to be.'[6] So absorbing was her new life that her parents' letters began to feel 'like echoes from a distant place, visited a long time ago'.

After almost three years Shirley's parents decided it was time for the family to be reunited. Her brother John had already returned, in a naval convoy, and was back at school by the time she sailed in August 1943. Her voyage home was fraught with excitement, drama and very near disaster but at the end of September she was met by her father at an RAF airport near Bristol. 'Although he was a man of deep emotions, his upbringing . . . had instilled in him a very English reserve. So, on the slow train journey to London we talked about the war, the United States, John's return and my voyage home, but not about our feelings at this reunion. For me this was a relief. I knew I was supposed to be ecstatic at being home, but I didn't actually know how I felt.'[7]

Her relationship with her mother was more distant and it took her, she wrote, several years to learn to love her 'and then it was to love her as an adult, a beloved friend, rather than as a child loves its mother'.[8] Vera Brittain understood, and regretted the passing of that affection. She wrote in her memoir: 'The carnation pressed in my diary from the parting bouquet which John and Shirley gave me remains a poignant relic, for the lost years of their childhood are lost to me still. The small gallant figures which disappeared behind the flapping tarpaulin of the grey-painted *Duchess of Atholl* have never grown up in my mind, for the children who returned and eventually took their places were not the same; the break in continuity made them rather appear as an elder brother and sister of the vanished pair.'[9]

England's drab shabbiness did not bother Shirley Williams anything like as much as the rigid formality of the school and examination system after the easy-going Minnesotan equivalent. Back at St Paul's School for Girls in London—she had refused to return to boarding school—she gradually found friendships and accepted some of the discipline foisted upon her, but as a tomboy, a daredevil and carelessly untidy, especially about her personal appearance, she was constantly being ticked off. Nevertheless there was plenty to keep her enthralled and she found, as she wrote later, wartime London a fascinating place to be. 'I felt I had an exciting war,' she said in an interview in 2000. 'I hadn't sort of sat comfortably in a little cotton-wool place and then been returned at the end of the war to Trafalgar Square and victory celebrations, so that when people said to me "What was the war like?" I could say "I had a good war." '[10]

In 1944 Shirley spent a year in the New Forest. Her school had been evacuated to Bournemouth after the buildings in London were badly damaged in an air raid. 'My year in the New Forest brought cohesion to my life. It was as if a shaken kaleidoscope of experience settled back into a new and pleasing pattern. My relationship with my mother had become an easy, loving friendship. I had found a home in which I was able to be free.'

In 1990 Ann Spokes Symonds held a half-century reunion for children of the Oxford and Cambridge exchange to which some seventy former evacuees who had sailed on the SS *Antonia* in July 1940 attended. This was a high proportion of the original 120 or so who had gone to the United States and Ann was surprised by the take-up. As they all chatted about their varied experiences, both of their stay in America and of their returns home, it struck many of them how very hard they had found readjusting to Britain. It was often the relationship with their parents that was the most difficult and this reunion was frequently the first time the former evacuees had been able to talk about it at all.

She realised how ill-prepared many parents had been for the reunion when it came. 'Settling in was not always the happy time parents had looked forward to for so long. Some younger children did not recognise or even remember their real parents, and yearned for the "mother" they had left behind; and no one thought of preparing parents for this. It was not easy for the "strange" child to settle back into a family as if they had never been away.' For those children, such as Ann, who had been unaccompanied, the only contact they had had with their families in the four or, in some cases, five years they had been away was by letter, the occasional broadcast or rare telephone calls. Thus the children who came back to Britain after the war had strong American accents, a view of the world shaped by their recent experiences and, above all, no intrinsic knowledge or understanding of the war and what it had meant for their families in terms of rationing, rules, damaged homes and, for some, tragedy. Bombed-out, war-torn Britain looked very tawdry to their American eyes. Where were the short skirts and the bobby socks?

Elizabeth Symon wrote to Ann:

We were met by our parents in London. They had last seen us as young British children; we returned to them as American-style teenagers. It must have been quite a shock . . . London was blacked out, and so was the train that took us back to Oxford. It was back to black-outs, yes, to rations of food and clothing and petrol, to 'make do and mend', to an all-girls school and uniform (I had to dye my American plain coat navy blue, and startled the gym teacher—I was fifteen—by having painted toenails), back to Latin and air raids. I had a tin helmet, which I used as a door stop in my room.[11]

Helen Lock agreed: 'It was good to be home, but England looked shabby and the people, especially the women, tired and anxious. My American accent faded, and I learnt about rationing and English pounds, shillings and pence, as I settled down as an undergraduate.'[12]

175

'By and large,' Ann concluded, 'the children who were inherently unhappy, for whatever reason, were unhappy when they were sent abroad and they were equally unhappy when they got home. The experience did me the world of good and I would not have missed it for anything. I was fourteen when I left England so completely in agreement with the decision to go out to the USA and I benefited from every aspect of my life out there and indeed from my life at university when I came home in 1944.'

How children settled down at home depended on a variety of factors, any one of which could affect the way they judged their return. First there was the question of age. To a child who had gone to America at the age of ten or twelve, the whole experience had been one of living in a different country, learning about another way of life and, on return, working out how to weave those experiences into their own narrative. For children who had been sent abroad before they were old enough to have formed proper memories, say at four or five, America had very quickly become 'home', the 'familiar', the 'place where I really belong' and coming back to England was as strange at nine or ten as it had been for the older children leaving in 1940. Many of these younger ones regarded their American foster mothers as 'Mummy' and their natural mothers were someone different, someone they had to get to know. Bridie Luis Fuentes said that the most difficult thing for her was leaving a loving foster family to live with parents who were strangers. She told fellow evacuee Michael Henderson that she had to learn all over again to be someone else's child.

Children who had left siblings behind found that there was adjustment on both sides. Little brothers or sisters who might have been too young to travel abroad felt anything from delight at seeing their more grown-up siblings return to intense jealousy at having to share their parents. Sometimes these emotions came all at once, on top of one another, and made for a stormy ride but in most cases the waves were soon calmed. One girl said: 'My parents loved the fact I had made so much of my time abroad, and I think my younger siblings were secretly rather jealous of me but they were pleased I was back.'

Returning to school in Britain caused dismay amongst former American evacuees. Single-sex schools, uniforms, English history, Latin, French and school rules seemed so strict and parochial in comparison to the freedom and relaxed atmosphere of the American schools. The children's memories took on ever rosier hues as autumn turned to winter and drab colours, food rationing and queuing added to the discomfort. Diana Deane-Jones, then aged fourteen, wrote in a letter in 1944: 'It is more like a reform school than anything else, terribly formal, ugh! A lot of people who were in my grade (form) when I left are still there. At first they treated me like a museum piece, now they have actually condescended to speak to me.'[13] Some were taunted for their American accents and quickly learned to adopt an English one: 'My brother's first words on my return to Oxford in September 1943: "He's a little Yankee." The taunt of "Yank! Yank! Yank!" at the Dragon School made me adopt an Oxford accent pretty quickly.'[14] Michael Henderson, in his book

177

See You after the Duration, was rather more measured in his appraisal of the difference between American and British education than Diana Deane-Jones. Writing nearly sixty years later he concluded:

> All of us returnees had to contend with an educational syllabus that was different. Coping with English money sums was particularly challenging. But it was not so much the niggles about rules, regulations and rugby that troubled returning children in the long run but somehow the implication—either expressed or implicit—that they had returned just in the nick of time to be saved from full Americanisation in terms of dress, manners, accent and, above all, education. This rankled with many children.[15]

Others found their lack of knowledge of English history, literature and Latin was a problem. Knowing the names of the American presidents, the words of the Oath of Allegiance, or the heights of America's peaks was of no use for the English curriculum.

The question of accent was a big topic for the children who were evacuated abroad: whether to keep their English accent or adopt a new one to fit in with their new world. It appears to have been a particularly big issue for children going to the United States. Some over-emphasised their speech and manners to become super-British whereas others, good at mimicry, picked up the local accent in no time and blended in well.

Many children spoke, and later wrote, about

feeling guilty that they had ducked out of the war. They were reminded of it by their peers, most especially when they compared post-war Britain unfavourably with America. The author Lynne Reid Banks came back to England from Canada at the age of fifteen. She wrote:

At last the war in Europe ended and we sailed home. It was early summer of 1945. London was in ruins. My father's hair had turned white. My aunts looked much more than five years older. We came back into a poverty-stricken, ration-blighted, war-torn country, licking its still-open wounds. Our loved ones welcomed us with utmost warmth and helped us, as far as they could, to fit back into our places. They never let us feel like deserters. But that's what I knew I was.[16]

American hosts were aware that there would be adjustment problems for children returning after years away and some warned the natural parents discreetly in letters what to expect. The New York correspondent of the *Evening Standard* interviewed several children who had been evacuated through the Actors' Orphanage Scheme and wrote: 'They are bringing some shocks with them for parents who probably do not realise what four years and America have done for them. . . . I would not be a truthful reporter if I did not straight away warn their parents that not all of them are in the least enthusiastic about the idea of going home.'[17]

Muriel Parsons had been in Canada for four years when, in September 1944, a letter arrived for her out of the blue to say that Britain was now safe and she could return home. The ship she was to sail on left New York within the week, so she had two days to make preparations to leave after four years of a happy life as a guest of the Canadians. 'It all happened so quickly that it just felt like another adventure. But there was a desperate sense of something precious being taken away from me as I left Edmonton.' The passage home was exciting but her overwhelming sense on her return was one of sadness. She missed her Canadian friends, she missed the wide open spaces and the countryside.

Muriel was not alone in feeling that she had lost something treasured. Children were removed often with as little warning from their host families as they had been from their homes in 1940. She summed it up:

It was good to be home, but England looked shabby, and the people, especially the women, tired and anxious. We had carried framed photos of our parents with us like icons all the time we were away. I can remember the shock when I saw my father again. His hair was white and he was stooped. I think the main thing is that, had I not gone away, I should have had a very different relationship with my parents. My parents were old when I was born, my father fifty-one and my mother over forty, so that was already a gap. But I think they did what they felt was the right thing to do for us. They had two children and they 'lost' us too early. When I returned—my brother Roger never lived at home again—I was like a stranger in the house. Although I lived at home until I qualified as a doctor I was never really their daughter again. I had had my own life in Canada.

Muriel Parsons never had children of her own.

In addition to the private evacuations arranged through universities, companies, churches or to relatives abroad, there were a handful of private schemes that catered for more than one family. One such was started in Boston by a formidable organiser and wholly impressive spinster called Sylvia Warren. A horse breeder, she had contacts with families on the west coast of Ireland and as the threat of invasion grew she offered to find families for children of friends. Her contact in London was Betty Coghill, whose two children, Toby and Faith, went out to America in the summer of 1940 to stay with Sylvia's neighbours, Isabel and Mike Farley. In total the Warren Committee, as it became known, placed over fifty children in private homes in the Boston area and helped with advice for several hundred others.

Tim Sturgis was fifteen when he, his sister and his mother sailed to America under the auspices of the Warren Committee. He was invited to stay with relatives, the grandmother of the family having written to say that they would be prepared to look after 'any common ancestors'. The experiences of the children who were part of this small, private scheme seems to have been almost wholly positive. Tim explained his situation:

Life in England for the middle and upper-middle classes in the 1930s was one of nannies and boarding school with relatively little contact with our parents. Now, for the

181

first time, my mother was wholly involved in my life and I loved that. I also thoroughly enjoyed school in America and found it more imaginative and wider-ranging in the topics we covered than the British system. There was a good social life with girls and a real excitement about education which I had not felt before.

Tim returned to Britain in 1942 as his sister was old enough to join the forces. Although he found public school in Britain formal and lonely when he got back, and no one was quite sure about 'Tim the Yank', he eventually found his feet. He spent two years at Oundle School and then joined up, aged seventeen, at the very end of the war, spending eighteen months in Palestine after a six-month engineering course at Cambridge University. Evacuation was for him a relatively small part of his overall experience during the war but it left him with a great affection for America and enormous gratitude towards the families who opened their homes with such unstinting generosity to British children:

I therefore came back to England a more open and less conventional young man, for which I am grateful. Also it made one far less parochial; things could be done differently, policemen didn't have to have funny hats, you didn't have to drive on the left, there was baseball as well as cricket. So one was able to become far more critical of one's own country, which was I am sure good for it and for me. But perhaps the greatest reward was having an American family who had become friends, who visited us in England and whom we visited in America. And this trans-Atlantic social traffic has continued with our children.[18]

Faith Coghill was equally happy with her family in Needham, Massachusetts. She remained in the United States until the summer of 1944 when eventually a permit to travel was issued and she managed to get a passage home. Her foster mother had not wanted her to go back to Britain as the war was still on but Faith's mother was keen for her, and her brother Toby, to return, so they boarded a ship in New York and had an exciting journey back across the Atlantic with a group of very mixed passengers.

For Faith and Toby the homecoming was more difficult than for Tim Sturgis and his family since Betty Coghill had no home and was living, initially, at the vicarage in Charlbury in Oxfordshire. Faith said:

I had had the most wonderful time in America and had been indulged by my foster family who sent me on summer camps, took me skiing and sent me to excellent schools where I made many good friends. I did not really want to leave America but I was very glad to see my mother again. I was used to being independent and there were a few difficulties as I settled down but I knew how hard it was for my mother, so being young I just got on with it.

Moving from considerable luxury in Boston to the vicarage in Charlbury and then to a two-bedroom service flat in Oxford was a big change, as was going back to school. Faith explained that one piece of good fortune was that she was able to spend the whole of the summer of 1944 cycling around Oxfordshire with her friend, Barbara, who had also been in the USA. This helped both girls to get to know the countryside as well as giving them plenty of exercise and the opportunity to acclimatise before they started back at school in the autumn. 'The one thing I regret is that we were never grateful enough for all the kindness and generosity shown to us by Aunt Izzy and Uncle Mike. They did so much for us, far more I expect than we will ever know, and I am not sure we really showed our gratitude at the time.' Tim Sturgis felt the same: 'Those of us who came were only children, and we took it all very much as it came, amazingly unquestioning. The overwhelming feeling of us all was the unbelievable, open-ended and endless generosity of our American hosts, so often given without our knowing, in the hope we would never know. They were memorable years, and a bond had been forged, which has lasted these fifty years.'

Although small in scale, the Warren Committee evacuation played a significant role in the lives of the families who were involved and they were delighted when Sylvia Warren was awarded the King's Medal for Service in the Cause of Freedom in 1947.

In 1940, 125 girls aged between six and sixteen, including girls from Sherborne School in Dorset, were sent to Branksome Hall School in Toronto. A captivating snapshot of this evacuation is compiled under the title 'A Very Hard Decision' and published in privately printed manuscript, a copy of which is lodged at the Imperial War Museum in London. In the introduction the compiler, Elva Carey, wrote: 'It seemed to us that being evacuated abroad was not just a minute part of the history of the war. It raised questions about separation, about growing up in a different culture, about adapting *twice*, the second time to parents and a country changed by war. How had we fared? What had the influences been? What links with Canada still remained? Had it been, for us, personally, a mistake or a liberation?'[19]

The girls who went to Branksome were fortunate because their families had not had to wait for the government-funded evacuation scheme. Their parents had been able to afford to pay for their passage to safety. As with the other groups, the fear of invasion was the overriding reason for sending the girls. Asked afterwards whether there were other reasons that might have influenced their parents the girls gave a variety of replies. Some suggested personal excuses such as family deaths, illness, rocky marriages and the desire to be free to do war work. However the underlying factor seems to have been the parents' experiences of the previous war. Many of the girls have fond memories of their time at Branksome, although a significant number were homesick and a few felt they had been abandoned by their parents.

The larger shock came for them when they returned to Britain. Having been part of a tightly knit group at school they all went their separate ways on arriving home and for some it was very lonely. Clare returned to London where her widowed mother was out on war work from dawn until dusk. She felt bitterly alone and missed Canada so much that she would go to Piccadilly Circus and stand at the stop of an escalator and listen out for Canadians or Americans just to hear the accent.

The physical discomforts of returning to Britain dominated the thoughts of many of the girls and they were highly critical when asked to give their first impressions for the school book in 1990:

'1943—Drabness, drabness, drabness—and darkness. Dark trains; women doing heavy work; uniforms; no signposts; masses of poor-looking, ill-looking people waiting in queues for everything.'

'Everything was grey, from people's clothes to their faces; the streets were grim and grimy and there was no colour. Vast bomb sites and aching spaces and endless queues for fish, liver, or cigarettes—and the cold was ghastly.'

'I returned in 1944 and my first surprise was that everyone spoke with an English accent. Also, I had not expected my parents to be unfamiliar.'

'The general drabness of life for those in Britain in 1944 had to be seen to be believed. I remember being stunned to see my sister painstakingly mending her cami-knickers so she could spend her precious coupon on outer clothing.'

Some girls expressed mixed feelings: 'It all seemed rather grey and dirty in London but the country was as lovely as ever. I remember feeling torn as England was where my roots were, yet nothing was the same as it had been and in some ways I felt alienated and wanting to go back to Canada. I found it difficult to feel close to people in England and I felt sad at that.'

A few were delighted:

Beautiful! Trains were tiny of course after the big high-stepped Canadian ones. The weather was warm and sunny, and what impressed me almost above all else were the flowering trees, especially the golden laburnum. London seemed vibrantly alive, swarming with Allied soldiers. I think I was impressed by the *normality* of things. I felt excited at coming back and attracted by all the handsome young men in uniform and became deeply attached, especially, to a charming flight lieutenant—a pilot. It was like a romance from the movies! My father sounded very la-di-dah.

For some the initial shock of seeing their parents for the first time in four or five years, worse still if they didn't recognise them, wore off only gradually. 'I think I just retreated into my shell and looked out on life slowly,' said one girl. Another felt embarrassed and unable to know how to react after such a long absence, feeling shy and awkward as a gawky seventeen-year-old but another was more defiant: 'Mother was very surprised to meet a daughter with permed hair, high heels, lipstick and nail varnish and persisted in referring to me as her "little girl". I was 5' 8" and thirteen years old.'

For others it was pure delight. 'I adored being back with my marvellous mother who treated me as a trusted adult, companion and friend.' Another was 'overjoyed to be home. No reservations, no hang-ups, just plain glad'. For some it was such a welcome relief to feel they could indulge in unbridled affection and love. 'It was a joy and a delight. They listened to me and we talked about everything under the sun. They cared so much. I was amazed and loved it.'

But for the girls at Sherborne School in England who watched their compatriots coming back from Branksome Hall School it was an eye-opening experience. As the returning girls felt the keen and critical eye of housemistresses and games teachers disapproving of their attitudes, manners, lack of Latin and inability to win house points in hockey, so the younger girls admired these incomers from the brave new world. They had arrived home as the first teenagers in Britain. Shirley Byles was at school at Sherborne when the girls returned from Branksome Hall School. A contemporary of Elva Carey, she explained fifty years later what an impact it had made on her and the others who had remained in Britain:

You lot from Canada . . . were still technically schoolgirls. Of course you had caught the teenage bug yet to infect Britain. This we found both fascinating and unsettling. We had curlers, ankle socks and prim utility blouses. You talked of 'bobby pins' and 'bobby socks' and said you 'couldn't care less' whenever possible and wore loose sloppy Joes to prove it.

You were ready to stand up for what you thought and (almost) confront the adult word as an equal group. We did as we were told and waited obediently to join the magic circle. Perhaps *we* would suddenly find all that breezy self-confidence.

Elva Carey had left England at eleven and was sixteen on her return and found school very restrictive. The headmistress at Sherborne was understanding and she used to invite the returnees to supper on Sunday evenings so that they could tell her what they thought was wrong with the school. 'Sometimes my friend used to kick me under the table if she felt I had gone too far,' explained Elva, 'but the headmistress was sympathetic and I think she was interested in how confident and outspoken we were.' It certainly helped the girls to feel they were being listened to.

Once the excitement of the return had worn off and the good or bad impressions had begun to meld with the everyday impressions of life in Britain, so the real cost of living away from home for four or five years showed through. For many of the former evacuees their horizons had been broadened and they had learned about other cultures but they realised also that it had changed their lives for ever and the relationship with their parents and siblings had altered. Not always negatively, but changed nevertheless. Sandra did not feel comfortable in Britain so she went back out to Canada in 1947 and married the following year: 'My family were most supportive. They had written twice a week. I had written home without constraint, and I felt that they had kept pace with the ways I was changing: they had both been to North America and were well travelled.' She goes on: 'I consider myself Canadian, British Columbian, but my roots are still British. My mother, brother's family, aunt, husband's family are still there. In retrospect I feel I had the best of both worlds and was exceptionally lucky to come to Canada. Because of the age I came out [fourteen], I do not feel that I was adversely affected; maybe my attitudes were already formed. I feel it made me more self-reliant.'

Diana came back to England after four and a half years abroad, fifteen years old and with plenty of confidence but also a strong sense of her own family. She and her parents had communicated every week by letter, numbering them so as to know that they were getting every one that was sent. 'I never worried that I would not see my parents again. I knew of the developments of the war but I think in a detached way. I think I was too young to worry about England. I have no recollection of being unhappy or homesick. I missed my family, but I did not pine for them. I think having my older sister with me made all the difference.'

She returned in 1945 and her parents knew enough about the difficulties she would have adjusting to life in Britain that they took every precaution they could to ease her homecoming. Her father went out to Canada to collect her,

The first deliberate targeting of civilians: Guernica, 1937

31 August 1939: London children ready for evacuation

Nigel Bromage on the farm at Llandeilo where he was so happy during his evacuation

Doris Cox's greatest regret after evacuation was the loss of her Cockney accent

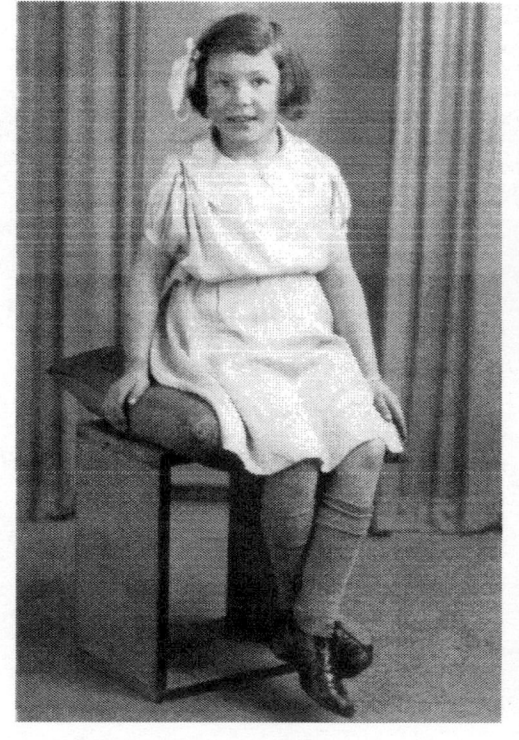

'Uncle' Harry Mayo and Sheila Ripps (later Shear) on a family holiday in Bournemouth, 1946

Joan Risley aged seven

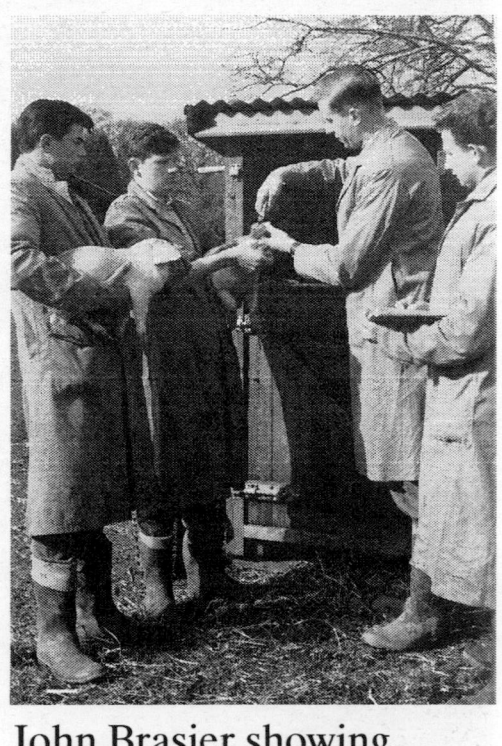

Robert and Florence
Lenton who became 'Pop'
and 'Mummy' to
Norman Andrews

John Brasier showing
students at Bicton College
how to notch piglets' ears

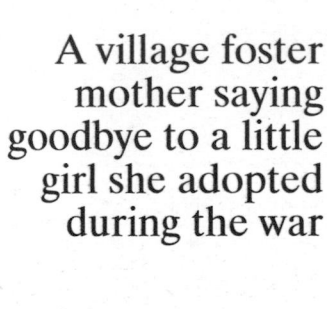

A village foster
mother saying
goodbye to a little
girl she adopted
during the war

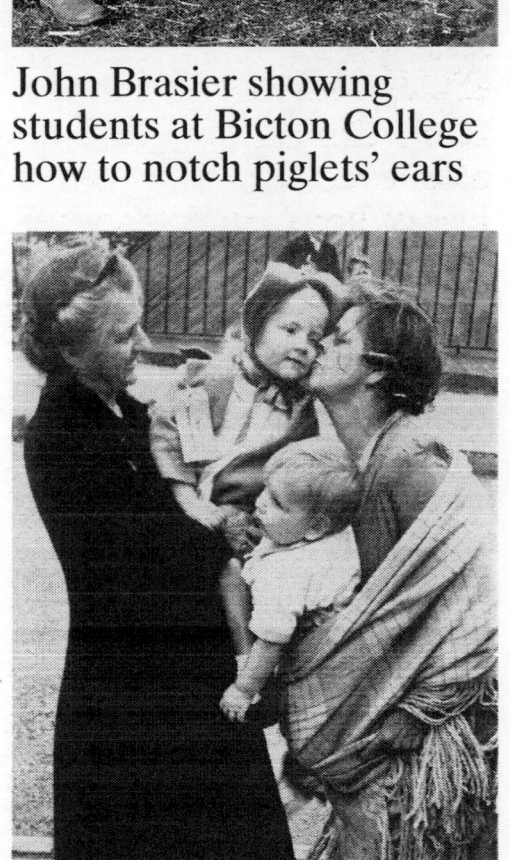

The large
dome of St
Paul's
Cathedral
wreathed in
smoke from
burning
buildings
after a
German
air raid

Amber
Valley
Camp,
Derbyshire,
in the snow

Bathing pool in
the River
Amber, summer
1943

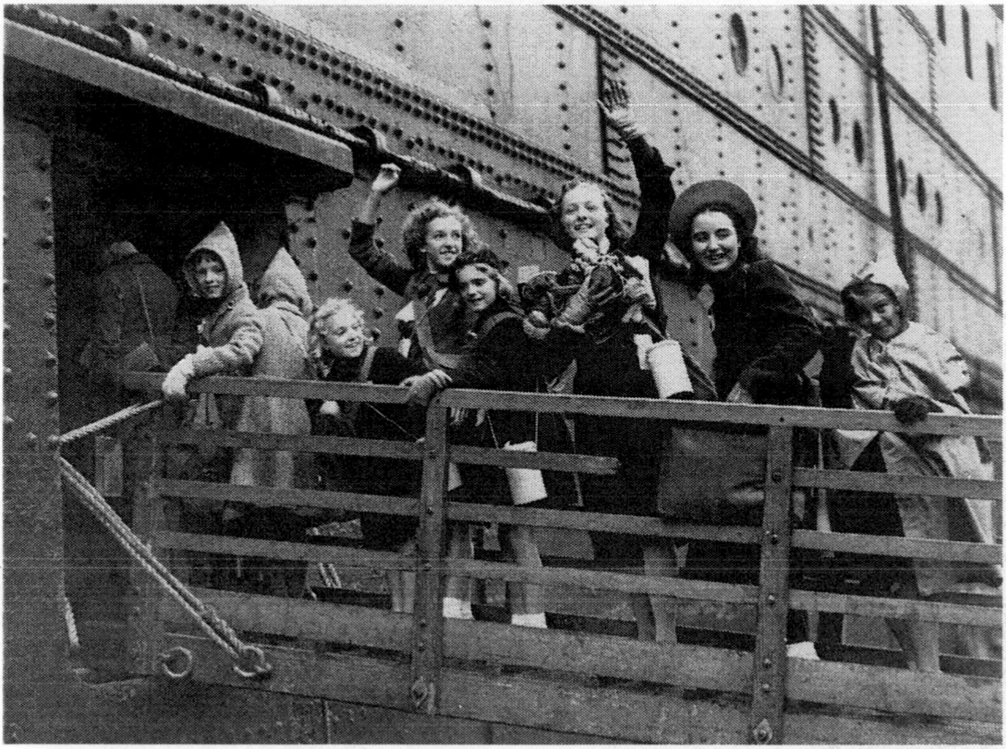

British evacuee children leaving for Canada

Faith Coghill standing beside her brother, Toby, with Michael Henderson and his younger brother, Gerald, on arrival in Boston

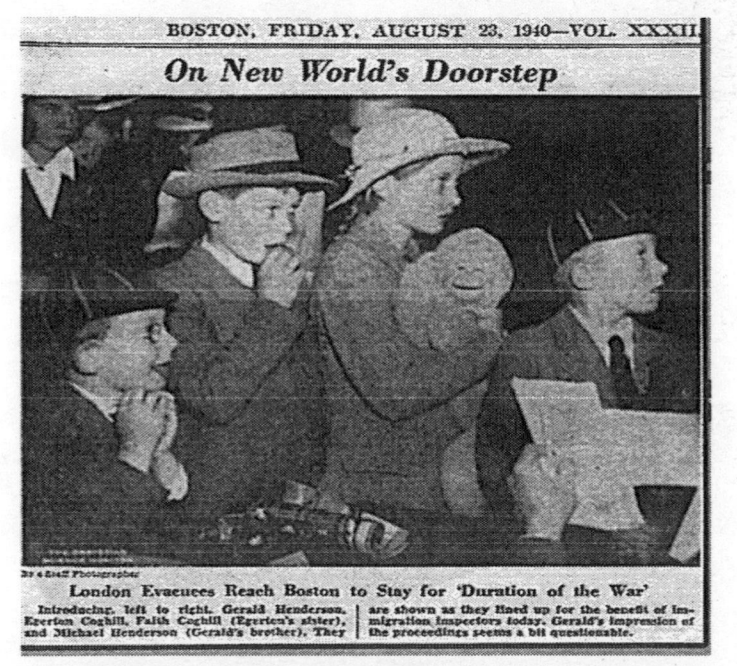

BOSTON, FRIDAY, AUGUST 23, 1940—VOL. XXXII

On New World's Doorstep

By a Staff Photographer

London Evacuees Reach Boston to Stay for 'Duration of the War'

Introducing, left to right, Gerald Henderson, Egerton Coghill, Faith Coghill (Egerton's sister), and Michael Henderson (Gerald's brother). They are shown as they lined up for the benefit of immigration inspectors today. Gerald's impression of the proceedings seems a bit questionable.

Louise Milbourn sitting on her foster mother's knee, surrounded by her American family. Sister Blanche is second from right

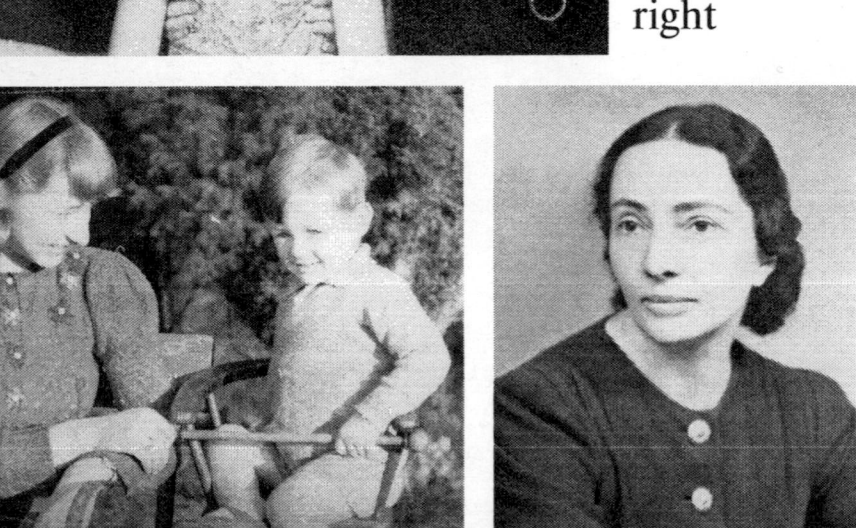

Ann Spokes Symonds met her baby brother Rodney only after she returned from America in 1944

Mary Cornish, unwilling heroine of the *City of Benares*

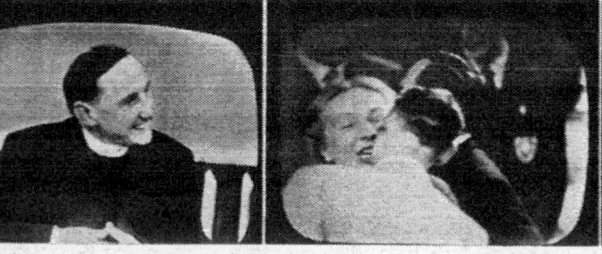

Padre O'Sullivan looks on as Mary Cornish is embraced by one of 'her' boys live on the *Wilfred Pickles Show* in March 1956

Dr Cuthbert Stanley, 1940.
Dr Stanley was known as the
most handsome doctor in the
Malayan Medical Service

Nigel Stanley beside
the River Dee in
Scotland, mid-1950s

Nigel and Elizabeth Stanley with Dorothy and
James Fisher in 1978

Joan Zilva at Killiney, near Dublin, September 1949

Ann Daly on her wedding day, 31 January 1953. 'For the first time in years I had something to look forward to that I could really believe would last'

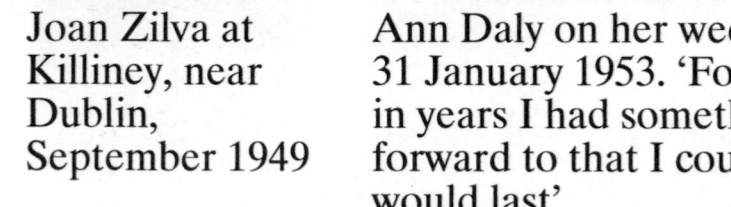

Evacuees return home to London after a wartime stay in Leicester

spending a few months living there so that he could absorb some of the life that had become hers and thus have an understanding of it when she talked about it later. Her mother was anxious that Diana would find her much aged by the time she came home; she knew that the war years had taken their toll on her. However, she need not have worried. 'We adapted very easily,' Diana wrote. 'I found that one could be very close to one's family without any contact for nearly five years. I was amazed by how well we ate on such poor rations. I was intrigued by clothing coupons, liked making clothes out of parachutes and silk maps. I enjoyed the attention I received from my peers, who thought I was very grown-up, well dressed and interesting.'[20] Diana's parents took the trouble to find her a small school where she did not feel constrained by petty rules and regulations. Some of the girls found her rather awe-inspiring but she found she fitted in and did well.

After studying orthoptics at college, Diana applied for and got a job in the United States, a country she had always wanted to visit. There she remained. 'I had five years in Canada being different, then nine years being different in England, and still enjoy being different here,' she concluded.

And the long-term effects of all these experiences? Some felt it matured them. Others were toughened up and rue the fact that they later found it difficult to show their true feelings. 'Until I had children of my own I don't think I realised what had been missing in my relationship with my parents. Our relationship normalised after marriage and children.' While more still saw the enormous advantages they had enjoyed in being free from the fears of wartime Britain and being exposed to fascinating and exciting activities, cultures and friendships. In summing up the effect of evacuation of Sherborne School to Branksome Hall School in Canada, Elva Carey wrote: 'A majority feel the experience was broadening or stimulating, and that it made them self-reliant, independent, more tolerant, better able to mix and keen to travel. A sizeable minority feel that, for them, this was largely illusory; underneath they were insecure, lacking in confidence, driven into a shell. A few still have to steel themselves to travel abroad.'[21]

Analysing why some girls did better than others in Canada, Elva Carey concluded that certain factors made a substantial difference. Age and stage was important, as was the presence of siblings. Girls who had older sisters with them had someone to look up to and rely upon, those with younger sisters had someone to care for and worry about. But it was the strength of home-life back in Britain that seems to have played the greatest role. Keeping in touch, communicating regularly and openly with mothers and fathers, maintained this bond while the girls were away and reinforced it when they returned. Temperament certainly mattered but that would have been a key factor in evacuation whether domestically or internationally. The final element that girls cited was their attitude towards their evacuation experience while they were away. If they had decided to make the best of it, then by and large it worked and was a success.

Conversely, the combination of a timid child, an

unloving (if kind) foster family and unforeseen tragedies in Britain such as deaths or separations could swing the pendulum in the opposite direction. Sometimes two sisters in the same family with the same foster parents gave completely different answers to questions about how they got on.

If generalisations can be made, then two opposing reactions seem to persist as a result of overseas evacuation. The first was the overwhelming feeling that returning children never wanted to leave home again. Travel became an issue for hundreds of former evacuees who found their reaction to going away, some even for short stretches not far from home, fraught with anxieties and concern. 'I am inclined to think that my time in Canada made me more nervous and pessimistic, and left me with a strong dislike of leaving England,' wrote one girl. Another said: 'Even today packing to leave reminds me of sitting on my bed watching my mother squeezing my precious few things into a little brown suitcase. I can smell the leather and it hits me like a punch in the stomach. It takes a lot of strength to make me leave and I spend my time away longing to be home again.'

The other end of the spectrum was wanderlust. Some never settled on their return to Britain and felt the need either to go back to the country where they had lived during the war or simply to travel. Stability had been so effectively disturbed that 'home' was no longer a single place in the world. Jane Carter found that life abroad had given her a wider vision of what was possible. It had opened up her horizons and made her more ambitious: 'I was no longer satisfied with my life in England as my friends were. I now had desires and goals and saw no reason why I couldn't carry them out. Most of them wanted marriage. I wanted to become a nurse—to train in Canada.'[22]

Louise Milbourn returned from America in August 1945 and felt an outsider, much as she had done when she first went to America five years earlier. Her mother found it extremely difficult to adjust to life with her two daughters back home and she appeared jealous of the affection Louise and her sister clearly felt for their American foster mother. Louise concluded, in her warm and affectionate book about her experiences, *A Very Different War*: 'There is no doubt that the greatest loser in this whole story was my mother. She missed out on seeing her daughters grow and develop at a critical time. Sadly she was not able to accept my sister and me as we were when we returned as my father and Aunty Helen did and thence gradually establish a new relationship with us.'[23]

Louise and her older sister, Blanche, had been evacuated on the *Duchess of Atholl* to America in August 1940 as part of the Quaker exchange that was an extension of the hospitality that Quakers had been extending one another for over two hundred years. The links between the New World and the Old stretch back as far as the seventeenth and eighteenth centuries when Friends travelled across the Atlantic in both directions, and quite frequently. A Quaker tradition is that when Friends travel abroad they take with them an 'epistle' of greeting from their home meeting to the new Friends they are visiting. As with an extended family, hospitality often includes overnight accommodation as well as a convivial meal.

The decision to send the girls had been taken by both parents because of the turmoil in Europe. They had been helping refugees who were fleeing from occupied Europe: 'It is difficult to explain, today, how real this fear was. Country after country across Europe had fallen to the advancing jackbooted army of Nazi Germany. Czechoslovakia, Poland, Norway, Holland, Belgium and even France had crumbled before Hitler's troops. Did this mean that my parents would have been persecuted for this activity should the Germans arrive in Britain?'[24]

As an eight-year-old, Louise was of course blissfully unaware of the war. She was living a happy, carefree life in Devon with her older sister and younger brother before everything changed in the summer of 1940: 'I wonder if my mother and father realised the impact of the decisions they were making then. Our relationship to one another would also change for ever. It would affect all of us but probably my mother more than most.'[25]

Louise's father, Francis Lawson, was well aware that if he sent the girls to America he would incur a debt to the people who gave them shelter and kindness that he would never be able to repay. Yet he also understood there were people who had sought his help who felt the same and he wrote that the experience of helping refugees from Central Europe during the previous year had convinced him that 'their friendship has been the best repayment for our trouble'.[26]

Like so many other children who were heading

for the United States, the parting from their parents took place in the Grosvenor House ballroom, the temporary extension to the US Embassy in London, and Louise's last sight of her mother for five years was from the floor of the ballroom in a sea of orphaned children up to her on the balcony. 'Later Mother said she had no idea our separation would be for such a very long time. She wondered many times if she and my father would have made the same decision and have had to sacrifice seeing their daughters grow up had they known it was to be so very long. The heartbreak of saying goodbye would have compounded the distress if she had known this then.'[27]

Among the memories of the journey Louise remembers the ship as being full of corridors and passageways: 'As an adult I have this recurring nightmare: I am trying to find my way through a large building with many rooms, more staircases and more corridors and I can never find my way out. The buildings of my dreams are very varied and rarely the same but always that lost feeling in long corridors. Does this stem from that lost feeling below decks on the *Duchess of Atholl*, dragging my orange lifebelt behind me?'[28]

The Quaker family Louise went to in Moorestown, New Jersey, lived in a modest, chaotic house quite different in many ways from her home in Devon. Mrs Wood, who quickly became Aunt Nancy, was acutely aware, from the outset, that although she was responsible for the two little girls *in loco parentis* she had to reassure their mother that she was not trying to take over her emotional role. In the more than two hundred letters that Nancy wrote to the Lawsons she went out of her way to reassure them that the children loved their natural parents and not her:

It seems to me that they put all their love of home and you in a very precious box and have almost consciously put it carefully away where they won't see it so often that it would make them unhappy and dissatisfied here . . . The children are fond of us and entirely affectionately accept our jurisdiction but they do not love us. That is kept entirely for you which is as it should be. Only, I sometimes feel that if I could reach down a little deeper into their hearts I could help them grow more easily. However, I don't think they are unhappy at all. They laugh and sing and work and play, and eat, like the most well-adjusted children in the world and I think they are really happy.[29]

Louise disputed this assertion on the part of Aunt Nancy and was sure that it was written, and continued to be written, to reassure her mother. There was no question in Louise's mind but that she loved Aunt Nancy and her uncle deeply. For five years the girls enjoyed a whole American life full of love, affection, friendship with other children, humour and a good, rounded education. The vivid letters from Aunt Nancy gave the Lawsons back in Devon a wonderful and sometimes too clear a picture of what the girls had been up to, so that Mrs Lawson would respond by return that she did not approve of Blanche going to the cinema with a boy or staying out late. Aunt

Nancy wrote gently: 'I think you have missed a great deal by not having your children to grow up with because it means you have not had touch with early adolescent people during these years and they have grown through stages you will have to bridge in imagination.'[30]

Blanche was much more straightforward with her mother and wrote:

Aunt Nancy said that in a letter you wrote to her that you were shocked to hear that I was coming home from the movies at 9:30. Well, you just don't know your thirteen-year-old daughter. You will have to realise that I am older than I was when I left England. I go to bed at 9:00pm every night so 9:30pm is really not very late, you know. After all in America we have fun especially our crowd. In America we go out with boys as Aunt Nancy has probably told you. We have fun. Don't get poor ideas about me please.[31]

By now the gulf between the children and their mother had grown to such an extent that the children realised it was not going to be easy to readjust to life back home. Another problem for Louise was that her memories of England faded as her life in America took new and exciting turns. It was a subject of much greater importance for the parents, both natural and foster, and it took up their correspondence for much of 1944. The value of this correspondence, and Louise Milbourn's account of her life in America, lies not only in its unusual detail, but also in the glimpse it offers us of what must have occupied the minds of thousands of parents whose children were abroad for years.

Already in 1942 Aunt Nancy was wondering in her letters whether it would be better, for the sake of the children and for family unity, if they were to return. It was not to be. She then began to hatch the idea of getting Joan Lawson out to America to spend time with the children before she took them back to Britain 'to grow into their background here so their Americanisms would not jolt you too much'.[32] She added, in that same letter, that their return to Britain would be a great loss 'for they feel like our children now and we would miss them fearfully'.[33]

By 1943 the plan to get Joan Lawson out to America was gaining momentum. As it did, so did the anxiety on both sides of the Atlantic: 'I think you will be pleased with both girls when you get them back, but don't expect little children or treat them as such. I have grieved all along that you should miss the transition years for it is so hard to realise it has happened unless you have lived it with them.'[34]

The following year Blanche wrote: 'On August 29th Lou and I will have been in Moorestown FOUR years. Do you THINK we will EVER get HOME?'

Eight months later, on 3rd June, just five days before the end of the war in Europe, Louise was called to the phone. It was a call from Montreal. Her mother had come to fetch them.

The voice I heard was in this very precise English of which I had no memory at all. Was this my mother? My emotions were all mixed

207

up. I disappeared upstairs to be on my own and have a quiet weep. I was excited and very apprehensive at the prospect of meeting my mother. I had lived all my time in America knowing where I really belonged was in England with my parents. After all, I had written and received letters all during this time which kept this fact alive in my mind. However, I was very happy where I was, I loved the Wood family as if they were my own, I had no recognition of this foreign English voice from the woman who was my mother, and she was going to arrive tomorrow, oh dear. My mind was saying one thing and my heart another.[35]

The Woods took Louise to meet her mother at Philadelphia Station. Louise did not immediately recognise her: 'Was this my mother? If it was she had definitely shrunk.'[36] After the initial surprise at hearing her mother's clipped English consonants and seeing in front of them a much smaller woman than she had in her recollection, both the girls began to wonder privately how they were going to get used to her and whether they would ever be able to establish a mother–daughter relationship again.

For Joan the shock was immense. She wrote to her husband of her first impressions of the girls: 'It was really impossible to get any scrap of likeness into her [Louise] voice that I could recognise, just incredibly impossible . . . Blanche is bottled down and scared, watching me like a cat and mouse, Lou's eyes are full of affection and Blanche is lovely. We shall get on well when she can learn to open up to me and some of her excessive accent wears off.'[37] She added: 'I am a complete stranger to them, someone who has to be sized up and learnt and understood in just the same sort of way. For Blanche, poor darling, that is going to be a much harder task than for Louise who seems to accept me without question.'[38]

The relationship between Nancy Wood and Joan Lawson was cool. There appeared to be mutual suspicion on both sides and Joan was very critical in her letters home about the way Nancy ran her household, likening it to one run by an extremely chaotic relative. What surprised Louise most when she read the letters that her mother had written during the two months she had spent in Moorestown in 1945 was her apparent inability to accept that the children's stay in America had added to their life experience.

As time went on, Louise realised that rather than accepting their 'Americanism', as Joan described it, she resented it. Even a few weeks after her arrival in Moorestown, Joan wrote home: 'Their Americanism is so complete that it would be both foolish and unkind to restrain and alter it. Much the best, and I should think the only way, is for it to drop off naturally in England and for them to mould themselves to the English pattern by the sheer force of example of English behaviour which they will see around them there. Their mannerisms and modes of dress, more than almost the methods of living and thinking, are other planetary.'[39] This ingrained sense of superiority of all things English over things American was unfortunately prevalent in this era and it was something that troubled many of the children who had spent time as guests of

209

American hosts.

As Louise discovered her mother's side of the story over sixty years after the war she found herself asking whether it had been sensible, let alone beneficial, for her to come to America to collect the children. Her mother had never travelled before, had never left her husband and was of course missing her little 'English' son she had left behind. She was perplexed by her two American daughters and she was overwhelmed by the household and the life they had led. Louise had still one week of school to complete while her mother was there and she was proud that she could show off her teachers, her education and her friends. All the mistresses told Joan how much they were going to miss Louise when she went back to England. She never knew what her mother made of those warm remarks.

Blanche was at boarding school when her mother arrived in Moorestown and told Louise years later how alarmed she was that Joan had now actually arrived to take her home. That year at Westtown School was the very happiest of her whole time in America and the last thing she wanted to do was to leave a school she loved and say goodbye to her close friends: 'The next five years were to prove extremely difficult for me school-wise and getting to know our parents again, especially Mother, which was the most difficult. I really did not enjoy myself very much until I got to university.'[40]

The last few days of the girls' stay in America were hard for them all, including Joan. She was aware of how they were torn by the thought of going home and the terrible sadness they would feel at leaving their lovely, familiar, settled life behind. Joan wrote:

> Our biggest task is to gain their love and respect and oh, it's going to be hard. They have received me as an unpleasant necessity, poor darlings, and quite frankly and uncompromisingly prefer Aunt Nancy. It is hard to keep a festering jealousy from rising up inside me. Perhaps it is not jealousy but just a new sort of heartbreak that has gone with this whole business over these five years. But it is not only our own heartbreak but theirs as well. Theirs that I do not come up to their expectations, that I do not identify myself here and that modes and manners here are so obviously not ours at home.[41]

On her return Louise felt out of place both at home and back at school. To her shock she found herself sent to a Friends' boarding school in Sidcot, Somerset, just a fortnight after she came back from America. She hated the uniform and the hat but most of all she could not understand why her parents, who had been without her for five long years, would send her away to boarding school rather than let her enjoy life at a local school and allow her, gradually, to readjust to her home. At the time she felt rejected but she wondered later whether it was her mother's determination to get her 'Americanism' stamped out of her and thought that the British boarding school system would be the quickest and most effective way of doing so. What was even more bewildering to the girls was that Blanche was also sent to boarding school, but

211

to a different one, in the north of England, where 'their efforts to bring her into line were quite unimaginably severe'.[42]

Louise felt uncomfortable at school. She found the syllabus different and difficult, particularly English and history, and she discovered she loathed French. But the biggest sadness for her was that she felt once again like an outsider, only this time she was more aware of the differences between herself and the other pupils. Two impressive women saved her. The first was the school's headmistress who reminded her of Aunt Nancy and the second was Joan's sister, Aunt Helen, who she also compared favourably with Aunt Nancy. Aunt Helen lived locally and Louise was able to visit her regularly. She came to respect her aunt who never commented on her accent or mannerisms but rather accepted her 'for who I was, not what I might have been'.[43]

In her account of her return from America, Louise wrote with great understanding about the difficulties her mother had in readjusting to life with her two American teenage daughters. She seldom mentioned her father but whenever she did it was in the context of his trying to bridge the gap, generally by doing something kind, thoughtful or practical. In December 1945 he bought Louise a Dartmoor pony as a Christmas present. The pony was trained to pull a trap but it was also big enough to ride and she was thrilled. It helped to dull a lot of the pain she had felt when she left her good life with the Wood family.

Louise Milbourn's story is not unusual but it is singular in that she was able to draw on such a rich vein of wartime correspondence to reconstruct the story of her life in America and her return. She remains convinced that her experience of living in Moorestown had a very beneficial impact on her life and made her into a more rounded and interesting person than had she not spent those years away from home. She is in no doubt, however, that her relationship with her mother suffered for the rest of her life as a result of the separation. Her mother never recovered from the loss of her two little girls.

BEYOND HARM'S REACH

This story it is not just a strange slice of social history, with rather quirky political undertones and overtones, but a story about real people, most of them very sensitive human beings, whose lives have been touched by CORB, for better or worse.

Michael Fethney, The Absurd and the Brave

It was one thing for private individuals or small groups to organise overseas evacuation for children but for the government such a scheme was an altogether different undertaking. More than anything it showed just how strong public feeling was that children should be put beyond harm's reach but it also had the suggestion for many of an acceptance that Britain would not be able to hold the Germans at bay and, for a variety of reasons, it would be better to have children out of the country. A leader in *The Times* on 1 June 1940 suggested: 'it would be a small price to pay for escape for children from the sort of ruthless bombing which Poland, Norway, Holland, Belgium and France have all experienced.' The main reason cited was one of safety but there was also a sense that these children were the fruit of the future and they would keep alive the patriotic British spirit and bring it back to the mother country when times improved. One mother, who applied for her seven-year-old daughter to go to Australia, wrote after the war: 'Only having one child I was very concerned for her safety, and when I read in the paper that quite a number of prominent people wanted their children overseas, I thought it must be very serious.'[1]

The idea of sending children abroad on an officially organised scheme had not been give any serious consideration in the planning for civilian evacuation in the 1930s. There is no reference to anything about overseas evacuation in government papers until the early summer of 1940. Nevertheless, the government had received offers of help from the Dominions as early as January 1939 when Miss Evelyn Mitchell had written to the governor of Southern Rhodesia outlining plans to take 200 children from danger zones in Britain and send them to the colony where farming families had already expressed a willingness to have them. The governor thought the plan a good one and Miss Mitchell was encouraged to write to Prime Minister Neville Chamberlain with full details. This letter was passed quickly to the Migration Section of the Dominions Office where it was dismissed as 'good hearted but impracticable' and duly filed. Miss Mitchell received a polite note from Chamberlain's secretary saying that the practical difficulties made the scheme impossible.

Over the summer of 1939 various other suggestions of help from the Dominions, notably Canada, came to the notice of the Dominions Office. Interest grew on both sides of the Atlantic and there was even a question in the House of Commons in August 1939 about what the government's attitude was. The official reply was

215

that the difficulties of getting the children safely overseas 'were insuperable'. And with that the subject was dropped. By December 1939 the whole subject of evacuation had become unfashionable and the government was having enough trouble with its domestic policy of keeping children in the countryside without having to worry about sending them abroad.

In May 1940 Germany launched the Blitzkrieg, invading Holland and attacking Belgium and France. The British Expeditionary Force was engaged for the first time and after less than three weeks of fighting was forced to retreat from Dunkirk. The seaborne rescue of 338,226 men was hailed in the press as a great triumph for the little ships involved in bringing the troops home but for many of the soldiers it was an ignominious retreat. The war had reached the Channel and the Germans looked unstoppable. The question of what to do about the civilian population, and in particular children, in the face of the stark realisation that a mere 22 miles of sea stood between Britain and the advancing Germans concentrated the minds of politicians and general public alike. From mid-May until the end of July 1940 the government ran a second phase of domestic evacuation, sending some 213,000 unaccompanied children from the coastal towns to safer regions in the UK. At the same time a serious discussion took place at the highest levels of government about the possibility of taking up the offers of help from the Dominions.

Geoffrey Shakespeare, in charge of looking into the viability of the scheme, had served under Chamberlain as parliamentary and financial secretary to the Admiralty and had seen first-hand Britain's unpreparedness for war. He was moved, by Churchill, in May 1940 to become parliamentary Undersecretary of State for the Dominions. At first he was not convinced by the sense of evacuating children abroad but once appointed as Chairman of CORB in June he became a convert to the cause and embraced the task with enthusiasm. Churchill was implacably opposed to the evacuation but on 17 June when the subject was discussed in the War Cabinet he was clearly distracted by events in France, which came to a head at 1 p.m. and all talk about CORB ceased. As Shakespeare left the Cabinet Office he saw 'Winston Churchill . . . now only present in the sense that his body was sunk in the Prime Minister's chair. His spirit was far away—soaring over the battlefields of France . . .'[2] Two days later the scheme was given Cabinet approval and plans to send children, unaccompanied by their parents and paid for by the government, to the Dominions, took immediate shape.

There was a precedent for sending children abroad to put them out of harm's way. Recently the Basque government had requested sanctuary for its children during the Spanish Civil War. In 1937, 33,000 Basque children were sent to Britain, France, Belgium and Russia. Nearly 4,000 sailed to Britain from Spain arriving towards the end of May at Southampton. The British government had accepted the evacuees on the condition that there would be no public funds called upon to assist. It was also agreed in advance that the children would be returned to Spain once it was safe. The Basque Children's Committee was set up to administer the

217

evacuation and housing, and to care for the children. So that the children would maintain their Basque identity the Basque government insisted that the children should remain together in groups, known eventually as 'colonies'. A great deal of care was taken of these children who had fled from a war zone. All over Europe the images and descriptions of the aerial attacks on Guernica had caught public attention. As a result, no foghorns were to be sounded when the children arrived in Southampton and air traffic was asked to give the largest camp at Eastleigh a wide berth, so as not to disturb the children more than was necessary given the ordeal they had fled from.

The evacuation of the Basque children was judged, by and large, to have been a success. The colonies, each with about seventy children, were set up all over the country—as far apart as Old Colwyn in North Wales and Wickham Market in Suffolk. Large houses, palaces and estates in the countryside were made available. Some colonies had to move more frequently than others, which was particularly disruptive for the children's education, but the experience of staying together in groups seemed to help them to feel secure. They maintained their own language, they socialised together and identified themselves as 'the Basque children'. Coming from a war zone to the safety of Britain gave the children back their childhoods. 'I have three families,' one former Basque evacuee who remained in Britain explained, 'there is my family in Spain; there is my family here and there is another family—our friends in London, the Basque brothers and sisters.'[3]

When many children were repatriated in 1938

the Spain they had left no longer existed and their families had been scattered during the Civil War. Some were so young when they came to Britain that they did not remember their families and found strangers on their return. A small number—420—were still in Britain in 1940 and British families were encouraged to adopt these children who could no longer be repatriated. This was not easy as few of them spoke English, having lived in the colonies for the past three years. Thereafter they learned English and when they finally returned home some found they had forgotten their mother tongue. 'By the end of the war some of the adopted children had become so linguistically assimilated that they could only understand letters from their natural parents with the help of a translator.' Over 250 stayed permanently in Britain, preferring to remain with their adopted parents rather than going back to Spain. The story of the Basque children's evacuation, described by one newspaper of the time as 'a beautiful incident in these evil times' is an illustration of how a group of children quickly formed a collective identity, becoming the 'Basque children in Britain'.

There were valuable lessons that could have been learned from the Spanish experience for the British domestic scheme yet little seems to have been drawn from the event. One difference was that the children who arrived in Britain from the Basque Country in May 1937 were fleeing from a war zone. The children who were to be evacuated to the Dominions from Britain were being sent away from a very serious threat but without the horror of bombs falling around them, although as the evacuation got under way there were air raids occurring all over Britain. The other difference was that the children were going to countries where English was the first language. It is not clear that anyone considered the question of cultural differences when making plans for CORB.

One overwhelming concern of the government when embarking on the CORB scheme was to ensure that it was not seen as a programme that favoured the rich. As already mentioned, the private evacuation of around 13,000 children overseas took place over the summer of 1940 and this was well known to those in Whitehall who were responsible for kick-starting CORB. The public reaction was clear on this, as expressed later by the journalist and author Elspeth Huxley: 'Why should the son of the rich man sleep in security in New York's gay lighted towers, the roar of traffic bound on peaceful errands in his ears, while the son of the poor man dozed in crowded shelters below our dangerous cities, menaced by the bomber's drone? It was unfair; and something ought to be done.'[4]

CORB was set up in answer to such questions and it was intended from the outset that the majority of children would be from families who could never have afforded to send them overseas privately. In the end 90 per cent of those who went on the CORB scheme were from non-fee-paying schools. Interest was immense. The press caught the mood and followed the first few days of the scheme with enthusiasm. 'First Seavacuation by 20,000 Children Going to Empire Homes' cheered the *Daily Express* on 20 June. A week later it announced: 'US Ready to Welcome 50,000

Children'. Over half the children eligible for CORB had been registered within ten days of the scheme being made public. This totalled over 211,000, almost the same number again as those sent to the country in the second wave of domestic evacuation.

By August the first batches of children had been selected. Escorts, who were volunteers drawn from all walks of life, would accompany the children and then return to Britain. They had applied in their thousands and were eager to take on their duties. One escort would be responsible for a group of approximately eight children. As with the earlier domestic evacuation, the need for secrecy meant that children and parents were forbidden from telling friends and relatives that they were going abroad. Parents had to see the children off at stations and were not allowed to the ports to wave goodbye. This was the moment for many when the stark reality of separation dawned and there are heartbreaking accounts from both sides of bitterly sad farewells. Julie Smith and her brother left Doncaster by train bound for Australia. Within hours of their departure their parents realised they had done the wrong thing in allowing the children to be sent away but despite making desperate enquiries they were unable to stop the passage of their two children to the other side of the world. When the children finally came home they were strangers to their parents. Julie soon found her feet with her mother but she never again had a close relationship with her father. Her brother, she explained in 2009, 'went off the rails'. She felt that her parents lost out badly as a result of their evacuation.

Margaret Jones was a twelve-year-old CORB evacuee from Cromwell Road School in Manchester. Although she was excited that she would be travelling with friends and that their escort was her class teacher, she was very disturbed by the idea of leaving her family once the crunch came: 'My parents tried to be very brave, but as the train pulled out I saw them break down through my own tears and I thought my heart would break.'[5] Margaret wept all the way to Liverpool and nothing that her teacher, Miss Redfern, or her younger sister, said could cheer her up.

Another little girl remembered feeling bewildered and excited as she left Wimbledon station for Liverpool. She was destined for Australia but it was only when she was sitting on the train that she realised what her journey really meant: 'I was a little unsure, but found the situation of being with others challenging, especially in such a novel setting. I wondered whether I would ever see my parents again. I was shocked at the thought. I will always remember their brave smiles as they looked through the carriage window. Then all was blotted out by dismay once the train moved from the platform.'[6]

Complaints about the state of evacuees arriving from the cities a year earlier were still echoing so efforts were made to ensure that the children were fit to travel and clothing lists had been supplied to the families. Medical checks were made before the children sailed and, as agreed between the Dominions Office and the High Commissioners, the checks had to be sufficiently rigorous so that there was no risk of children being sent home again once they had arrived at their destinations.

About 330 children were turned back at the two ports, some 11 per cent of the total number, since they failed to meet the medical standards laid down by CORB. These stipulated that any sign of mental defect or feeble-mindedness could be a sufficient reason to refuse them passage, as could epilepsy, blindness or partial blindness, or severe deafness. It was also requested that every endeavour should be made to exclude enuretics (bed wetters). There were other complaints that could not be countenanced and meant immediate exclusion including TB, congenital syphilis, ringworm and acute homesickness.

And so they left. Some went from Liverpool, others from Glasgow. There were no parents to wave them off as they boarded the ships but Geoffrey Shakespeare made an effort to attend as many send-offs as he could and gave each departing group a lecture about keeping a stiff upper lip now that they were acting as ambassadors for Britain. Often there was a song as the ship left harbour and these farewells proved to be more emotional than he and others had expected. Shakespeare wrote in his autobiography *Let Candles Be Brought In*: 'Mr Graham Cunningham, who joined the (Overseas Reception) Board . . . came as a hard-headed businessman, with little respect for politicians, and with less for civil servants! . . . I thought he was devoid of feelings until, on final farewells to a crowd of CORB children, singing, as usual, "There'll always be an England". I turned to pass a remark to Graham Cunningham and, to my surprise, the tears were coursing down his cheeks.'[7]

In total, nineteen batches of CORB children set

sail in August and September 1940. Eleven went to Canada, three to Australia, three to New Zealand and two to South Africa. Sixteen of the ships arrived safely at their destinations. Of the three that did not, one, the *Volendam*, was torpedoed but without loss of children, the second, the *City of Benares*, lost all but thirteen of the CORB children aboard (and is dealt with in the next chapter) and the third, the *Rangitata*, returned her contingent of children to Britain only hours after sailing as a result of the *City of Benares* incident. The dangers were evident and the ships, sailing in convoy, were not immune from submarine attack. As proposed at the outset, the vast majority of the children who arrived safely overseas were from state schools: 2,606 out of the total 2,664. The remaining 58 were from independent schools but of those a further 15 had parents whose income was so low that they were required only to pay the basic evacuation fee of six shillings.

As the children made their uncertain voyage across the world's seas, foster families in Australia, New Zealand, South Africa and Canada were coming forward to offer homes and hospitality to the 'seavacs'. The various governments tried to engender interest for the scheme and with some success. Reasons given for agreeing to host a child were varied, from fulfilling a sense of public duty to repaying a kindness from the past. One Australian soldier had convalesced in Manchester after being wounded at Gallipoli in 1915 so a quarter of a century on his children decided they would take a child from Britain. Other couples were childless and wanted young children, so volunteered. Others still were keen to support their own religious groups. Mrs Rose Gofsky in Edmonton explained that she knew there were two Jewish children coming to the town so she and her husband agreed to take one of them, Bernie, and another local Jewish family took the other boy, Ivan, so that they could be comfortable with their familiar customs.

The success or failure of relations between host families and CORB children depended on a number of factors, not least how far individual governments were prepared to go to ensure a smooth transition and thus establish the roots of a good relationship. Advice was available to the families but it was not always followed. Aware that there might be difficulties when the children first arrived abroad, the CORB Advisory Council commissioned a senior civil servant, Mr W. J. Garnett in the Dominions Office, to write guidelines for CORB representatives overseas. Mr Garnett sailed with a batch of CORB children to Australia in August 1940 to become the first liaison officer in Australia.

Garnett's guidelines were simple and practical but they were not always followed. He advised that homes should be inspected prior to placement; that family members should be kept together and, if not possible in one home, then in the same locality; that those children who had made friendships on board ship should be kept together where possible, as this would help them to feel not so alone in the new country; also that children should be sent to homes of the same social strata from which they had come, a lesson clearly learned from the domestic experience. Finally Garnett suggested that religious beliefs should be taken into consideration. An article written by Marion Gutman in New York in 1940 was full of excellent advice about how families might help an evacuee child adapt to their new situation and warning that it would take plenty of time and a considerable amount of determination on the part of the hosts to make sure it worked well. A small case history accompanied each child but in most cases it was scanty and inadequate. Although Garnett had recommended children be sent to families with similar backgrounds to their homes, the reality on the ground was that since the CORB board refused to contribute towards their upkeep abroad until 1942 it was only wealthier families who could afford to take a child.

Understandably but disappointingly, the Advisory Council agreed that the supervision of evacuees and their hosts would be left to the local authorities in each Dominion. The CORB liaison officer should 'remain in the background, letting the local machinery operate'.[8] No vetting of homes or families took place and later this was considered by critics of the scheme as one of its greatest shortcomings. From today's perspective it is almost impossible to imagine sending a child to the other side of the world to live with an unknown family for an unspecified length of time with no assurances whatsoever about the household they would end up in. And it was in direct opposition to what happened on the majority of the private schemes to the United States and Canada where families were screened and, as seen in the case of the Oxford University children, psychological testing was undertaken to ensure a good match. Even then, it must be said, placements were not always successful.

In New Zealand the Garnett advice was followed and it would appear from stories told later that those children who went to New Zealand felt welcomed and wanted, which greatly eased their assimilation into the families. Placement and aftercare was organised centrally by the welfare division of the government's Department of Education, meaning that there was a single body responsible for the families and children. The advantage for New Zealand was that as a small country the distances were as nothing compared to Canada and Australia, where children were separated by hundreds and often thousands of miles. In South Africa things were organised at the most local level, with the neighbourhood magistrates being designated the legal guardians of all the evacuees in their judicial area. Without the overview of a single guardian it was difficult for the CORB liaison officers to keep an eye on what was going on. Thus, in a number of cases, things did not go smoothly and serious problems of misunderstanding and worse arose.

One boy who went to South Africa had such a difficult start that it affected him for the rest of his life. He wrote: 'The five years of evacuation left scars on my soul. I was billeted at first with a middle-aged, eccentric English couple who hated everything South African. As a ten-year-old, I was terrified of them and hated them as only a child can, especially as I took to the South African way of life like a duck to water.'[9] He eventually moved to live with a kindly, older couple who had a farm and there he settled down and was happier. However, those first months had such a strong impact on him that he never recovered his equilibrium.

He was not the only child who suffered from an initial bad experience. A twelve-year-old, Ronald, was sent to Australia with his younger brother. The children were separated, with Ronald's brother going to live with his host's son and daughter-in-law: 'so I lived with people much older than my mother and father, whilst he was lavished with a bike and a pony and holidays at the summer cottage; and I was expected to work at my foster-parents' grocery story after school and at weekends in the summer. So, I had some feelings of unfairness. I yearned for room for self-discovery, room to make some mistakes without feeling I had committed the unforgiveable sin.'[10] Later Ronald was moved to another foster family so that he was away from his brother and the comparisons that made him jealous faded. But this time he caused concern for his new foster parents, also older than his own mother and father, when he formed a completely innocent friendship with a local girl with whom he went skating and to the cinema. His foster parents left copies of Salvation Army tracts lying around that warned him about what happened to girls and boys if they became too familiar. Ronald was upset by the lack of trust but eventually over the next few years he developed such a love of Australia that he returned to settle there after the war. Looking back he could see that the concerns that his second foster family had had were born out of kindness and concern not prurience. Many children said that they understood only later why certain actions were taken on their behalf and at the time what seemed like restrictive rules were simply put in place to protect children who were not their own and for whom the foster parents felt an extra sense of responsibility.

Michael Fethney, himself evacuated with the scheme to Australia, wrote in his authoritative book on CORB, *The Absurd and the Brave*, published in 1990:

> Many of the CORB children, with their restlessness and difficult behaviour, illustrate, in rather extreme forms, the emotional disturbance created by being uprooted from home, travelling across the high seas in wartime; and also the difficulties of adapting to a totally new environment. Some of the older boys tried very hard to join the forces under age, or showed a particularly strong urge to go back to sea. Perhaps the care authorities took little account of the fact that many evacuees were bound to be disturbed, rebellious, high-spirited young people.[11]

The major problem for both the host families and the children evacuated abroad was the absolute nature of their evacuation. Unlike the situation within Britain where families could sometimes intervene to collect unhappy children or foster families could be in touch with some hope of resolving the situation, the sheer distances and length of time for communications to be exchanged meant that the children were effectively cut off from their families for the whole period they were away. For many this meant that they shelved any thoughts of life back home and got on with their new lives for the duration. For others it meant a permanent, rumbling sense of worry and homesickness and for a few it meant having to resort to desperate measures. Two boys, Ian Hamilton and Dennis Furnish, ran away from their foster homes in Canada and, after hitchhiking to Halifax, managed to get on ships to Britain. Dennis Furnish signed on as a mess boy aboard a Norwegian vessel and arrived back in Darlington just as his parents received a letter to say that he had run away from his foster home but that they were not to worry as he would not be able to leave Canada owing to restrictions on wartime shipping.

Dennis was embarrassed in later life about the inconvenience he must have caused his Canadian hosts. He was not unhappy in Canada, he explained, indeed the family had introduced him to culture and made him feel welcome. He simply saw that the war situation was getting more serious as time went on and he wanted to be at home and to take a more active part. Looking back he feels he failed his foster parents but at the time such thoughts did not enter his head. His only desire was to get home.

Going home was on everyone's mind from the end of 1944 onwards but for some the return to Britain did not happen until early 1946. On 22 February, Miss Maxse, of the CORB office in London, was able to report at the last advisory meeting that 1,809 of the 2,664 children who were evacuated had either returned or were due to return. That left nearly 900 children in the host countries.

As we have seen with domestic evacuation, the return could be as difficult as the going away and equally for the foster parents it was a sad event. One girl said: 'It was as traumatic as the parting from my parents had been carefree! I was five years older, had more idea of what the parting meant, and had transferred all my love and affection to my aunt and uncle whom I thought of as my parents. My uncle and aunt, too, were terribly upset to part with us. It was awful.' Her aunt described going home after seeing the children off at the docks. She went into their empty bedrooms, one by one, realising that her precious children had gone for ever. She sat down on one of the beds and wept. A little part of her had died at this bitter parting for those who were no longer 'her' children. They belonged to their own family. What remained for her was a void to be filled with memories.

Another foster mother, who had been childless until she took an evacuee in 1940, was equally bereft: 'I watched that ship and Bob until he was only a speck. I remember being numb with sadness. We were trying to adopt a baby, and the Welfare Department gave us a two-year-old to mind two weeks before Bob sailed. So, after returning from the ship, I tried to concentrate on making her a frock. But even though we got the new baby, it took me months to get over Bob going away.'[12] Often foster parents and children had developed very close relationships over the years and the partings were achingly sad, but for the foster parents perhaps in some ways the more so because they had nothing to fill that gap. They had dipped in and out of the children's lives but few could hope—or indeed want—to replace the child's natural parents. The great warmth of bonds that criss-crossed the globe lasted a lifetime for many families and former evacuees and went on to the next generation.

Other children coming home had mixed feelings. They had made good friends at school as well as becoming close to their foster families. Unhappy to be leaving, they were at the same time excited at the prospect of seeing their parents again and eager to see Britain. As they were transported home they noticed some changes from their passage out. They travelled in smaller batches and had more freedom than on the outward voyage. Two of the ships sailed over VE and VJ Days and the children joined in the celebrations when five German U-boats surfaced and surrendered in the Atlantic.

Aboard the ships the escorts briefed the children about changes they would notice in Britain. There were food shortages and bomb damage. They warned the children that people might feel they had run away from the war and had an easy time. This was sound advice and many of the children found that this accusation was one that was levelled at them on their return.

For some the intense emotion of the moment of homecoming is as raw now as it was in 1945. Rita Patterson had spent five years in Australia and had only childlike memories of her home in the North East: 'In the dusk, we rolled across the Tyne Bridge. Through the window of the train, I saw Mum and aunts start running alongside the train as they caught sight of me. As we stood there, embracing and crying, I looked over their heads and saw my father at the gate. And, as I write this, I'm crying again—I will never forget that meeting as long as I live.'[13]

After the initial shock of the immediate homecoming—mothers with grey hair, fathers who appeared to have shrunk, siblings who had grown and houses that were familiar but strange—the stage of settling in took time. One girl described the syndrome, as she saw it, as 'Fallen Idol Shock'. Here was her father, 'just a deaf, little old man' whereas her image of her beloved father had grown in her mind over the years to something completely divorced from reality. It took her time to see that it was not her father who had changed, but the image she had constructed of him in her mind while she was away. For other children the change was soon absorbed as they got used to being home. 'Inevitably, my family all appeared smaller to my fourteen-year-old eyes—as did "Home". But this feeling soon passed, along with my broad Aussie accent!'[14]

Others developed a certain restlessness.

Living in Australia from the age of nine to fourteen helped enormously to broaden my mind. I learned very quickly to take people for who they were rather than for what street they lived in or what school they went to. Out there that didn't seem to matter nearly as much. I found that very refreshing and it taught me a valuable lesson for life which I have continued to draw on in the course of my career, which has involved a great deal of travel in foreign countries. I never left Britain again permanently like some CORB children did but I found my ties with it were loosened and though I love coming back and chose to retire here, I was very happy to live abroad for stretches. I don't think my parents found that at all easy to adjust to but they had to. They had to accept the person I had become. Looking back on it now I find it sad to think how hard that must have been for them, losing me as a little girl and getting back a headstrong adolescent who knew her mind and did not want to be told.

The one thing that no one who was evacuated on the CORB scheme had any doubt about was that the experience changed their life. There are those who talk about the advantages in encountering a different philosophy of life. They felt they had gained a broader understanding of the world, of the ways of different peoples. And they gained independence, self-reliance, the ability to mix with others, to adapt. At the same time they talk about the lost years for their parents and the fact that relationships between parents and children, or other siblings never recovered from the total severing of relations at such a tender age. 'It certainly destroyed a true relationship with my mother, and God knows what it did for her, poor woman,'[15] said one girl in 1988.

For a small number of children evacuated on the CORB scheme the move became permanent and they never came home. They were so happy in their adopted countries that they had no desire to return at the end of the war. Emigration from Britain in the late 1940s reached an all-time high and a few families jumped at the opportunity to leave and join their happy offspring. A girl evacuated to Australia wrote: 'The evacuation scheme changed my whole life—and that of my family, after my brother, parents and married sister joined me here. It was very much to our benefit. I know I wouldn't have wanted things to be otherwise.'[16]

Another child was so happy in New Zealand that she persuaded her parents to join her. They did so in 1951 but it was not a success. Her father felt comfortable and was willing to stay but her mother was permanently unhappy and eventually, in 1967, decided to return to Britain with her husband. By that time, however, the other children had become settled in New Zealand so that when the parents returned to live in Britain they had only one of their original four children living with them. 'As such,' she wrote, 'I still feel that my evacuation is affecting our lives.'[17]

Some never returned at all. Tom Willis was born in Maidstone in 1929 and evacuated to Quebec via Montreal. His father had died in 1936 when Tom was seven years old and he was the youngest of four brothers, two of whom were in the forces. After two years working on a farm in Quebec, where life was basic and tough, he took a diploma in agriculture, funded by his foster family, and graduated in 1948. That year he applied for a job with the Carnation milk company in Sherbrooke and was still working for them in 1990 when he answered a questionnaire about his evacuation. His first visit 'home' was in 1971 when he was pleased to note that 'very little had changed, especially on [my] visit to London. Tower Bridge still intact, as were St Paul's and Buckingham Palace.'[18] When asked why he had remained in Canada rather than returning to Britain he replied

235

simply that there had been more opportunities on offer for a young man of his age and with his qualifications.

In 1952, Tom married and had nine children. The one thing, he said, that really affected him was when each of his children reached the age of ten as he had been when he left England in 1940: 'I tried to put myself in my mother's position and ask myself if I could let my youngsters go to another country in similar circumstances. I really think if it came to that I couldn't do it, but I am glad that my mother decided for it.'[19] Tom is not alone in wondering what decision he would have taken in similar circumstances and he comes to the same conclusion as the majority of former evacuees, which is that they would not be able to part with their children. Few hold it against their parents and most acknowledge the very difficult decisions that they had to make, often at short notice and under enormous emotional and governmental pressure. And yet many wonder whether their parents would have done it if they had known how long their children would be away.

For Barbara Wood the return home in 1945 was a jolt. The daughter of a railway signalman from York, she was evacuated with the CORB scheme to Canada in August 1940 at the age of fourteen along with her three siblings. They were separated and sent to different families on arrival. Barbara's first experience in Canada was in the wealthy home of a family that owned a business school. That did not work out because the daughter of the family, who was three years older than Barbara, was jealous of her. In 1941 she went to live with a doctor and his family in a mining village in

Thorburn, Nova Scotia. What really struck her were the lack of class structure and the strong sense of community and family spirit in Thorburn. In some ways, she said, she might have expected her stay there to be strange because there were no children of her own age in the family, and at first she was a bit put-out at being surrounded entirely by adults.

In 1944 the doctor's wife died but Barbara stayed on and continued to live as part of the family, now with the doctor and his housekeeper. Although, in her words, 'most of the people were in the lower class and didn't extend their education beyond high school' there was a great deal of social interaction and no sense that those with education or money were 'above' the mining families. 'Perhaps this is why I found the British so stiff and withdrawn when I went back. My parents had moved from one side of the city to the other just before I arrived home—a nicer neighbourhood—but I think I missed going back to a familiar house and finding out if things and people were the same. None of the people I knew before I left were around and it seemed as if I were coming back to a strange place . . . I still found a great deal of snobbery in evidence.'[20]

For Barbara the most insidious snobbery was about her accent. She wanted to become a teacher but her tutor told her in no uncertain terms that she could not be allowed to teach 'with that dreadful Canadian accent'. This reaction made her miss her friends in Canada and the easy-going way of life perhaps more than she might have done. Having her whole education belittled by her tutor undermined her confidence. She graduated from

Leeds University and after teaching at an English grammar school for a year she went back to Canada. Her parents were very much against her returning to live there but Barbara felt that only by getting away from the snobbery and prejudice could she find perspective in her life. She wanted, she said, to concentrate not on material possessions but on the things that really mattered to her such as the children she was teaching and, later, her own children. She reflected ruefully that her sister, who returned to Britain and stayed, seemed perhaps to be more concerned with status and less with the values that the two girls had learned about in Canada.

In 1991 an American undergraduate, Miss P Y Lin, wrote a BA thesis about CORB. She had conducted a survey of over a hundred former evacuees and asked them to fill out a questionnaire about their experiences. Although all described their evacuation as a major change in their lives, a surprising number wrote about the positive impact they felt it had had on them after the war. One of them, Ivy Streatham, wrote about her experiences of being sent from her working-class home in Kent to a middle-class foster home in Perth, Australia. Ivy's father was a gas-fitter on the railways and her mother had worked in a sweet factory until the children, seven of them, came along. 'We had a lovely childhood,' she wrote, 'we younger siblings were like a second family and were looked after by the older ones. Our home was small. We had three bedrooms with an outside flush toilet, no bath and no electricity.'[21]

As she was already fourteen her parents consulted her about going to Australia and she decided it was a great opportunity. The family that fostered her were childless. They had asked for a ten-year-old boy but got a fourteen-year-old girl, which caused a few problems to start with: 'I did find things a bit constricting and confining as I had had such a carefree life at home. It took me a while to understand what a big responsibility I was and really at an awkward age, I suppose. But we sorted it out and I stayed with them for all of my evacuation period.'

Her foster parents saw her through school and helped her to train as a shorthand typist. Although her parents sent out seven shillings and sixpence a week for her upkeep her foster parents had saved it up for Ivy and gave it to her when she was due to return to Britain after the war. She sailed back in 1945 and was thrilled to be home in Kent.

> After two months it was like I had never been away. My fiancé—we got engaged in 1946—and I had been writing to one another all the time I was in Australia. He had been in the Navy in the Far East and got back soon after I did. We were married in 1948 and had four children. I think in my case evacuation overseas was the most marvellous experience and I am so glad I was able to go. I was just about the right age. Not too young to understand what was happening and not too old to worry about it too much. It must have broadened my understanding of other people and races and the way they lived. But I am not a person who really digs deeply into things.

Another Ivy came from the other end of the

239

country. Ivy Lee was eleven when she was sent from Glasgow to Cobar in New South Wales on 5 August 1940 to stay with her mother's brother, who was married with two children. 'I came from a working-class suburb of Glasgow but we were well educated in our state school. I was the youngest of the family and the only one still at school in 1940. I was not asked whether I wanted to be evacuated, it was not a topic for discussion. I just went. My uncle lived in a bush town and worked for the New Occidental Gold Mines. He drove the cage that took the miners up and down the shafts to the mine.'

After adjusting to the heat and mosquitoes, Ivy loved her life in the bush. She enjoyed the freedom of the outdoor life and took huge pleasure in hiking in the hills. A half-day drive from Sydney there was not a lot of opportunity for secondary education in Cobar so after leaving school at fifteen she worked in the offices at the gold mine until she was sent home in November 1945. Her first complaint on getting back was the cold and the second was that her neighbourhood seemed very crowded and built up after living in Cobar for five years. She missed the relaxed way of life and her friends but she settled down in Britain and married. A quarter of a century later she visited her family in Australia and realised how enormously her stay there had influenced her and how happy she had been:

I would say overall, the experience was very good for me and gave me a broader outlook in every way. It was great to see other countries and the way other people live. It has convinced me that people going abroad can do better for themselves than if they remain here . . . I think going to Australia taught me to be tolerant of other people's races and religions and I like the way working-class people can do well there and be on equal terms with the upper classes. I think the experience came into the way I brought my children up, by teaching them to have open minds . . .

Thirteen-year-old Colin Hill was also evacuated to Australia on the CORB scheme. His parents lived in a back-to-back house in working-class Bradford and he described their lifestyle as 'pretty hard'. 'My father was a builder and slater by trade and had to work outside in all inclement weathers. My mother worked in a very large mill doing various jobs making knitting wools and yarns. My parents set great store by education.' When the question of evacuation arose Colin's parents decided it would be a chance to send him to safety. As they had a sister and brother-in-law in Merredin, 160 miles from Perth, that seemed sensible and Colin recalled being very excited at the opportunity to go out to stay with them. 'My parents wisely thought that going to Australia would be a new life for me and broaden my outlook, hopefully make an easier life for me than that to which they were accustomed.' It worked. He loved Australia and he relished the opportunities on offer.

I lived in a wholly different world for four years. In our garden in Merredin there were apple trees, grape vines, apricot trees, fig trees, passion fruit vines, orange and lemon trees all waiting for the fruit to be picked when it was ripe. We didn't learn French but I was taught how to divine water, which came in very useful when camping out in the bush with boy scouts. I loved the outdoor life, the sports, the activities on offer all year round, and I enjoyed the working opportunities too. When I returned to Britain in November 1944—I was missing my parents so I got a passage with the Merchant Navy—I found it difficult to readjust at first. My parents had moved to Sheffield and so I had to get used to a new neighbourhood as well as the smog, fog and cold, damp wintry weather. Seldom did we have a summer we could call such. But the overall experience of my evacuation enriched my life. Ever since the first day we travelled by train to Liverpool my life changed completely. First there was the travel out to Australia, then four years packed with experiences, followed by two years in Austria after the war when I was sent with the Royal Corps of Signals to Graz. This, once again, was almost a lifetime of experiences. Thanks to my evacuation I have a much broader outlook on life, far in excess of any of my friends who remained in England. And my related experiences have been magnificent as well.

In 1983 one of the women involved in CORB from the beginning, Miss Elspeth Davies, was asked to evaluate the scheme's outcome. Perhaps surprisingly she was unequivocal in her criticism, saying that in her opinion it was a mistake from the start, born out of desperation at a time when something 'so absurd' could be considered as the best route to take. She reserved her most trenchant criticism, however, for those at the Board of Education who refused the suggestion in 1945 that there should be an inquiry into the effects of the scheme upon the evacuees and their families. This, she felt, was one of the greatest missed opportunities because not only were valuable lessons lost but the children involved in the scheme felt a sense of abandonment on their return home as they, like other returning folk—servicemen and women, domestic and private evacuees—were just expected to put up, shut up and get on with life. Some, but by no means all, CORB evacuees would agree with her.

CHILDREN OF THE *CITY OF BENARES*

I have nightmares when I wake up screaming
and I'm just back on the lifeboat, back into
some part of the story. They have that saying
'Lest we forget'—well, you don't forget, you
never forget.

Colin Ryder Richardson

Of the nineteen CORB vessels that left the United
Kingdom in 1940, sixteen arrived safely at their
destinations. Three did not and it was the fate of
one of these three ships, the *City of Benares*, that
changed the government's attitude towards the
whole scheme. The story of this tragedy is
extraordinary and some of the children cannot
speak of it even seventy years later. Others are
happy to tell their tale. Since the first reunion of
the children of the *City of Benares* they have met
every five years and, as one survivor, Derek Bech
said: 'It has become a family. We are all linked by
this one terrible event and have it as our common
experience.'
By and large when things went awry with
evacuees it was on an individual basis and although
each was a trauma or even tragedy for those
involved, it did not become headline news. They
were disasters on a human scale and the public
took little notice. That was until the sinking of the
City of Benares. The ship, carrying ninety children

on their way to Canada under the auspices of the Children's Overseas Reception Board, as well as ten children who were private passengers, was hit by a 500-pound German torpedo at 10.05 p.m. on 17 September 1940 when she was 253 miles west-south-west of Rockall. She sank without trace within forty minutes of the torpedo strike. Twenty sets of parents lost more than one child and one family lost five of their ten children in the disaster. It was one of the worst civilian tragedies of the war.

Of those ninety children, thirty were killed instantly by the force of the explosion, which was immediately below the cabins where they were sleeping. Most of those CORB children who survived the torpedo strike were so near to the heart of the explosion that they were thrown from their bunks. As they scrambled their way towards the lifeboats in the darkness—the lights in their cabins had temporarily failed—they did not think in their desperate confusion to lay their hands on coats, shoes or the emergency blankets that were folded at the ends of their beds.

The ten CORB escorts had survived and did what they could to reassure the children and lead them gently but firmly towards the lifeboats, putting into practice the drill they had followed every day for just such an eventuality. In an attempt to calm them down, one of the escorts, Mary Cornish, found herself repeating in soothing tones: ' "It's all right, it's only a torpedo", rather as she might have said to a child nervous of bulls, "Don't worry, it's only a cow"—until it occurred to her that this was, perhaps, rather an odd form of reassurance'.[1] Another of the escorts was Miss M

245

E 'Daisy' Day, a fifty-three-year-old housemistress from Wycombe Abbey School in Buckinghamshire. She took overall charge of the CORB group. Huxley explained: 'Miss Day already knew which of her escorts had complete groups of children with them, and which children had not survived the explosion. But, alas, much worse was to come, and the real anguish started with the attempts to launch the lifeboats. Miss Day watched helplessly as the boat containing Miss Gilliat-Smith, with her entire group of evacuees, was tipped into the water. All had survived the attack but none survived the cold of the sea.'[2]

In the confusion following the explosion some lifeboats were lowered before they were full, so that survivors had to climb down the slippery ropes trailing from the davits. A number fell into the icy, choppy seas with little chance of recovery. Others waited until the lifeboats had settled on the water and then attempted to jump onto them as they were tossed about on the waves. The situation was desperate but all the while the survivors knew that time was against them and the ship was going down fast.

When Miss Day finally left the sinking ship and got into her lifeboat she had with her one very seriously injured child, the child's sister and several others. As it was lowered the boat hit the waves and filled with water to the gunwales. The children were drenched and in their hopelessly inadequate clothing they began to shake uncontrollably. The injured girl died, then her sister died not long afterwards. Miss Day later described how 'the little ones faded out, quite unable to stand up to the awful conditions . . . All we could do was to hold them above the water till they were gone . . . We gave them what comfort we could. A few children grew a whole lifetime during that dreadful night.'[3]

The first ship to arrive and help with the rescue was HMS *Hurricane*, which eventually encountered the first survivors at 2.15 p.m. the following day, a full fourteen hours after the torpedo had hit the *City of Benares*. By that time many more had died. The *Hurricane* passed several lifeboats that were fully occupied, each one waterlogged, with not a survivor amongst them. Only one lifeboat they came across had more than six survivors and, significantly, this was the only lifeboat that had not taken on water. 'Too often, they found bodies with hands still tightly clenched, still seeming to cling for life to a raft, a plank of wood, a float or anything that promised buoyancy. Too often, the bodies were those of small children, faces sometimes tilted upwards, as though still hoping for rescue.'[4]

HMS *Hurricane* picked up 105 survivors in total, all but 3 of whom were revived though many were unconscious upon rescue. They were suffering from hypothermia, 'immersion foot', a condition brought on by immersion in seawater, and shock. Derek Bech was one of the first to be rescued. He, one of his two older sisters, Sonia, and his mother, Marguerite, had succeeded in getting onto a life raft, which was pulled back from being sucked under the ship by a man in the water who spotted the danger to the soaking, frightened family. They spent most of the night on the raft and Sonia recalled falling off the raft and feeling a great sense of peace as her head went under the water. 'Then I was hauled back onto the raft by the sailor

247

and felt very shivery. After many hours Mummy said "Sonia, let us take off our life belts and go to sleep in the water." And I was very insistent that we waited a little longer.' Eventually they were spotted by another of the lifeboats and were dragged into it and spent the rest of the day in relative safety, if great discomfort.

The next thing the children remember was hours later being hauled up into the ship and to safety. Marguerite Bech was distracted with worry about her older daughter, Barbara, who was not in their lifeboat, nor was she on the first, second or third boats to be picked up by the *Hurricane*. The children coming onto the ship were in a piteous condition and Marguerite welcomed each one that she could, helped to bath them and to console them. Every time a boatload came in she asked the sailors if Barbara was amongst them and every time the answer came back, 'No, not in this batch.' And then, as the very last boat came alongside the *Hurricane* she heard the joyous news that Barbara was on board and had been rescued.

A total of 365 people were aboard the *City of Benares* when she sailed from Liverpool on Friday 13 September, 177 crew and 188 passengers, of whom 90 were CORB evacuees with their 10 escorts. In addition to the 77 children who perished, 171 other passengers and crew, including the master and commodore, died either in the explosion or in the icy seas of the Atlantic.

As the battered survivors returned to Gourock in Scotland, the press, the BBC and Geoffrey Shakespeare descended on them to hear their tales. Shakespeare was outspoken in his condemnation of the Nazi atrocity:

I am full of horror and indignation that any German submarine captain could be found to torpedo a ship over 600 miles from land in a tempestuous sea. The conditions were such that there was little chance for passengers, whether adult or children, to survive. This deed will shock the world. It is another example of the barbarous methods of warfare associated with Nazi Germany and it is only comparable with their present brutal and indiscriminate bombing of women and children in London.[5]

Whilst it is not possible to single out one family as having suffered more than another, it is impossible to overlook the tragedy of the Grimmond family from south London. Five of their ten children had been selected to go to Canada. After their home in the East End had been demolished on the third night of the Blitz a special effort was made by CORB to get them away as quickly as possible. Officials moved with great speed, formalities were waived, and three days after they had been bombed out, the five small Grimmonds—two boys and three girls— found themselves on board the *City of Benares*. None survived. Less than a week after the sinking their father was interviewed by the press. He told them that the day he had received the letter telling him that his children were dead he also received their first letters written from aboard the *City of Benares* as she sailed. Aged forty-two and a veteran of the Great War he announced that he would join up again and fight. 'Hitler is not going to break our

249

spirit,' said his wife, 'we are going to see it through.'

Beth Cummings was fourteen when she left Liverpool aboard the *City of Benares*. One of the older girls on the CORB scheme, she said she had the strange impression, even as she was leaving, that she was not really going for long. After the ship was hit and the lifeboat Beth was in had been lowered it turned turtle and everyone was thrown into the sea. Beth and her friend Bess Walder managed to keep swimming and scrambled onto the upturned lifeboat where they remained, clinging on for their lives, 'With just bare hands— child's hands, not big strong hands at all, but that's all I had', explained Bess. Shortly after Bess had grabbed the keel she saw Beth crawling up the lifeboat beside her. They looked at one another and nodded. All around them people were falling into the sea and drowning: 'Beth and I said nothing, but bit by bit as other people let themselves go, we realised that we were the only children left holding on.'[6] Of all the friends Beth had made on board in the short time the children had been together not one had survived. At one point Beth slipped off the upturned boat but she managed to catch a rope and pull herself back up. She shouted to Bess to grab the rope, which was less slippery than the keel. They were now opposite each other hanging on. They clung to it through an atrocious Atlantic storm: 'The wind was terrible and the rain and hail lashing your face. The boat hull was moving backwards and forwards, up and down, so we were being thrown away and bumped back all the time. All we could do was to shout to each other, "Are you all right, Beth? You

250

all right, Bess?" That was all we did most of the night. We couldn't say much because it was impossible to talk properly, if you opened your mouth it got full of seawater.'[7]

Thoughts of home kept the girls going, and for Bess the overriding need to get home to tell her parents what had happened to her brother, Louis, and how she had tried to look after him. For Beth getting home to her widowed mother mattered just as much. Both her brothers were abroad and she did not want her mother to have to spend the rest of the war alone. As dawn broke the hoped-for scene of other lifeboats, rescue vessels perhaps, failed to appear. They were completely alone on their upturned lifeboat in the middle of the Atlantic with one other person, a seaman, 'nothing alive except us', Bess said. However, the girls had been spotted and help finally came nineteen hours after the torpedo attack when they were rescued by Albert Gorman, the coxswain in a 'whaler' rowing boat. Gorman had to be very careful as they came alongside the upturned boat so as not to capsize it. He succeeded in climbing onto the keel and ran along it to where the girls were clinging on. He could see that they were only an hour or so away from death. He picked Bess up first: 'Come on, darling, let go,' he said to her but she could not. Her hands were tight around the rope and Gorman had to prise them off the rope gently so he could pick her up. He ran back along the keel and put her in the whaler before returning to collect Beth.

Gorman got the girls to the *Hurricane* and went back to rescue other survivors. The next time he saw them they were sitting up in bed. The captain came with him and had a little surprise for Bess:

251

'You thought you'd lost your little brother? Well, here he is, we found him in the boiler room, charging all over the place.' Gorman described the look on Bess's face 'as though you'd switched a light on. That's the memory to hold onto.'[8]

After their joyous homecomings both the girls, and many of the other survivors, had to learn to come to terms with the lasting impact of their ordeal. A lifelong sadness for Bess was that she was unable to have children as a result of her eighteen hours exposed to the Atlantic storm. For Beth there were quite serious problems with her hands as a result of clinging onto the rope for nineteen hours. She developed arthritis and also began to go deaf in her late thirties, possibly because of the exposure. But she was very philosophical about the psychological side of her ordeal, telling a journalist that the one thing that always reminded her of that night is violent wind, rain and hailstorms—'they all remind me of that day. It never leaves you', she said. She and Bess remained the closest of friends and Bess eventually married Beth's older brother, Geoff. The girls agreed that the fact that they could talk about their ordeal meant that the long-term psychological effects were less damaging for them than for some of the other children who survived but who had lost their brothers or sisters.

There was one more twist to this tale and it was a story of heroism, survival and outstanding bravery. The unwilling heroine was a forty-one-year-old unmarried music teacher from London who was briefly catapulted to fame by her actions after the sinking of the ship and retreated into obscurity afterwards. Her name was Mary Cornish.

252

She had become separated from her group of charges soon after the explosion, having gone back down to the cabins to see if there were any more survivors. When she got back on the deck her two fellow escorts had gone, presumably into a lifeboat and Mary Cornish was directed to a boat full of crew members and a handful of small boys. She was ordered into the boat and obeyed. The boat was one of the last to be lowered so that it continued to fill up with escaping passengers. Another CORB escort in the lifeboat was Padre Rory O'Sullivan. He had recently made a dramatic escape from occupied France where he had been teaching in a school since 1930. On arriving in Britain he had offered his services as a chaplain to the Army, Navy and RAF but there was a waiting list, so, anxious to do something for the war effort, he had volunteered as an escort and was put in charge of fifteen boys. He had suffered badly from influenza aboard the *City of Benares* and had that night been given a sleeping tablet by the doctor. When the torpedo struck the ship he had been fast asleep in his cabin opposite the berths of the boys he was in charge of. After the explosion and a lucky escape from his cabin he mustered as many boys as he could find from his group and made his way to the lifeboat point. He had carried one small boy and shepherded the other six towards the lifeboat. The youngest boy was taken away from him by a sailor and he and the six remaining clambered into lifeboat 12.

By the time the boat was lowered into the heaving seas there were over thirty passengers including six CORB boys, Ken Sparks, Derek Capel, Freddie Steels, Howard Claytor, Billy Short

253

and Paul Shearing, aged between eight and thirteen. Eventually there were also thirty-two Indian seamen, five British crew and a Polish shipping magnate, Bohdan Nagorski, making a total of forty-six in the lifeboat, which Mary Cornish described as '30 feet of timber, about four feet longer than a London bus'. 'As it was lowered the boat dropped with a violent jerk, leaving the stern tilted at a dangerous angle, and forcing the passengers to cling on like monkeys. The sea was very rough. Waves slapped the hull viciously, and the boat rocked like a tub as it rode beside the *City of Benares*, attached to the liner by a rope.'[9]

As they drew away from the ship they were tossed about on the waves: 'From the troughs Mary Cornish could discern nothing save black walls towering high overhead, lipped with foam; but from the crests, in fitful moonlight, she could see other lifeboats dotted around, and brief signals flashed from torches, and sometimes the speck of a head or a tossing raft whirling by. Now and again a shout would rise above the wind's screaming, to be quickly drowned again. During the night, four or five dripping, half-conscious figures were hauled over the side of her boat, rescued from an ice-cold sea.'[10]

Mary Cornish was a classically trained musician from the Royal Academy in Vienna. The sea, she told her biographer, Elspeth Huxley, meant little more to her than a stretch of water to be crossed before reaching France. Yet she had volunteered as a CORB escort and now found herself adrift on a lifeboat in the middle of the inhospitable Atlantic Ocean wearing a short-sleeved silk blouse, a thin skirt, a jacket and silk stockings with sandals. The boys in the boat had fortunately all slept in their kapok life jackets but only one of them had a coat and two of them were wearing shoes. They were hopelessly inadequately dressed for survival at sea.

When dawn broke the next morning grey, sullen and cold they were completely alone. There was no sign of the other lifeboats or of any rescue vessel. Just miles and miles of ocean whipped up by a gale into a storming, heaving sea. During the first day the fourth officer, Ron Cooper, organised the paltry accommodation in the lifeboat so that Mary Cornish, Padre O'Sullivan and the six boys were in the bows and all together. He later told a friend that he was an uncertified fourth mate at the time as he had sat his second mate exams and failed the oral on lifeboat sailing.

Fortunately for them the ship's steward was in the lifeboat and he took charge of rations, so that their first meal was a sardine on a ship's biscuit and a dipperful of water: 'The dipper was a small cylinder of about the diameter of a penny; it held something less than a quarter of a pint.' Padre O'Sullivan had suffered badly from seasickness in the first twenty-four hours which had exacerbated his influenza and was lying at the bottom of the boat wrapped in a coat. Apart from thirst, the main problem for the boys was boredom and Mary Cornish realised that her greatest challenge was to keep them occupied. They were cramped, uncomfortable, cold and at times frightened. She organised sing-songs, games of I-spy, though she observed ruefully that there was not a lot to spy in the middle of the Atlantic Ocean. But the favourite diversion was the stories she invented of Captain Drummond, a square-jawed hero of whose exploits

255

she told ever more fantastical tales as the days went by. 'Only in tales of action,' wrote Huxley, 'could they altogether forget their thirst and hunger, their cramp and cold, and the sea.'[11]

Mary Cornish had to alternate between being reassuring and kind and being brusque with the boys. If she heard one of them whimpering she had to stop it immediately so that it would not spread to the others: 'Don't you realise that you're the heroes of a *real* adventure story?' she would ask the boy. 'There isn't a boy in England who wouldn't give his eyes to be in your shoes! Did you ever hear of a hero who *snivelled*?' It worked every time, she said. She knew she could not allow the boys to begin to feel self-pity.

By the fourth day the whole boat had become despondent. There were early symptoms of exposure which could so easily lead to death. Legs and feet were the worst affected, swollen and painful through cold, exposure to seawater and immobility. The boys suffered as badly as the adults. She massaged their feet and legs before they went to sleep to prevent the sluggish blood from leaving the extremities altogether. For her own feet she could do nothing. They felt like lumps of wood on which she could barely stand. That night there was a terrifying storm. Great waves crashed over the boat, filling it with freezing cold seawater, soaking everything and chilling them all to the bone. By morning the storm had abated but the passengers were more despondent than ever. Then on the afternoon of the fifth day, a Sunday, they spotted a steamer on the horizon. Mary Cornish's petticoat, already requisitioned on the first day as a signal of distress, was run up to the mast-head. They watched eagerly while Padre O'Sullivan called on the boys to pray that it would spot them and come to their rescue.

Curiously enough, Mary Cornish had dreamed repeatedly of a similar scene in her childhood, and now the dream came back to her in all its vividness. She had been shipwrecked, and was adrift in a crowded boat, weak from exhaustion, when a steamer was sighted. The vessel came closer, intent on rescue, and the lifeboat was made fast to her side. Mary Cornish had to leap across a gap, and upwards, to safety, but in her weakness she could not span the distance; she dropped down between the steamer and the lifeboat into the sea and lay on the bed of the ocean.[12]

The steamer made towards them, then turned slowly until she was broadside on. There was tremendous excitement amongst the boys and relief among the crew. They talked of how they would slake their thirst and straighten their backs after five cramped days at sea. Then, without warning, the steamer turned away. 'They saw the water churning behind her screw. Then—slowly, inexorably, incredibly—she steamed away. This was their darkest hour.'[13]

Two days later one of the boys became delirious and the following day another. He was in so much pain that he could not bear to allow anyone to touch his feet and he kept shouting out: 'I'm mad, I'm going mad, I *know* I'm going mad.'[14] He had to be quietened as his screams might drive others over the edge. Padre O'Sullivan knew that the

257

child was dying of thirst so he asked the steward for some drops of water. They were down to one ration of water a day now. Lips were swollen and cracked, throats sore and swollen. Several of the Lascars were lying semi-conscious in the bottom of the boat. They had been adrift at sea for a whole week. Their situation was desperate.

The next day the steward issued only tinned salmon at noon. There was no water that lunchtime. He had taught the boys to suck on their buttons to ease their thirst but the effect did not last for long. Soon after their meal a boy spotted a Sunderland flying boat. A dozen had been spotted over the last week, only to resolve themselves into seagulls, but this time there could be no doubt. The Sunderland had seen the lifeboat and swooped low over them. The pilot leant out of the window and waved at them. They waved back wildly. The pilot circled a couple more times and flew off. Not long after another Sunderland came and dropped a parcel containing food—beans in tomato sauce, cans of salmon and peaches—and a note to say a destroyer was coming and that she was only 40 miles away. Rescue! At last. The steward refused to issue the remainder of the water. But at four thirty that afternoon, eight days after the *City of Benares* had sunk without trace, the Royal Navy in the shape of HMS *Anthony* hove into view.

The sailors boarded the lifeboat and helped the boys and semi-conscious Lascars onto the ship. Mary Cornish, too weak to climb the rope ladder on her own, was helped aboard and carried below to a cabin where she was put into a comfy chair which, the commissioned engineer told her kindly, was kept for the reception of human wrecks. There she was served with a tray of bread and butter and a cup of tea, but she could not drink because the liquid was too hot and her throat too sore. When the engineer brought her water to wash and a fresh toothbrush and pyjamas she found herself unable to undress, so stiff was she and so unfamiliar with the act of taking off her clothes. She was confused and anxious to see the boys, who had been in her charge for the last eight days. The engineer was not having any of it. He lifted her onto her bunk and when she tried to protest he said gently: 'You've handed them over to the Navy now.' The following day she was reunited with the boys, five of whom were up and about in the highest of spirits, wearing clothes borrowed from the sailors. They were rushing about the ship announcing they would join the Navy or fly Sunderlands when they grew up. Mary Cornish learned that Padre O'Sullivan was in the sick bay but would make a full recovery. One of the Lascars had died in the night, following the rescue.

That evening, at about 7.30 p.m., the *Anthony* sailed up the Clyde and berthed at the port of Gourock. It was 26 September. As they disembarked Mary Cornish was eager to hear about the safety of the little girls who had been in her charge. Then came what she described as the greatest blow of all. Of the fifteen girls she had been responsible for only one was still alive. Of the ten escorts, six had perished. Mary Cornish could hardly grasp the horror of the *City of Benares* story before she was faced by an eager press who wanted a slice of the newest British heroine. It was almost too much for her to take. As she walked out onto the street the following day she was surrounded by a crowd of well-wishers and sightseeing locals, all of them wanting to get as close as they could to this legendary woman.

At night she found she could not sleep. The minute she dropped off her nightmares would throw and pitch her around in a lifeboat tossing on heavy seas while she worried about the boys. Then she would awaken in a panic and grasp at the glass of water by her bedside, sweating with terror that it would not be there and the thirst that had racked her body would return.

The boys appeared to be in the best of health and to have shrugged off their ordeal. When they came to say goodbye to 'Auntie' they looked to be in high spirits. Each of them had had his treasured pocket money doubled, as promised by the Polish passenger, Mr Nagorski, and each had a gold brooch of the City of Glasgow, an armful of adventure books and a kilt. Appearances were misleading. Within a few weeks each boy had suffered some form of collapse and several were in hospital where they remained for months. For two of the boys, Derek Capel and Billy Short, the delights of the return were no consolation. Their brothers had not survived.

The public reaction to the disaster was one of outrage and indignation but there was also inspiration derived from the bravery of those who had survived the sinking. Far from being put off sending their children across the Atlantic, parents seemed more anxious than ever to get them passage abroad. The staff reporter on the *Daily Express* wrote on 24 September 'Not one cancellation of passage was made yesterday.

Instead many parents called or telephoned the Children's Overseas Evacuation Board to ask if, in the event of cancellations due to the tragedy, their children might be moved up on the waiting list, so that they might sail sooner.'[15] On 2 October 1940 the government announced publicly the suspension of the CORB scheme, at least for the coming winter. The overall losses to shipping were more than the UK could hope to replace and the Admiralty was against the scheme. This marked the end of the large-scale movement of children overseas although a few hundred left Britain privately during the autumn of 1940.

Some survivors of the sinking of the *City of Benares* shrugged off the experience and got on with the rest of their lives. Anthony Quinton, later Lord Quinton, was a private passenger sailing with his mother to stay in Canada. He was flung into the water but hauled into a lifeboat where he and his mother sat with twenty-three others waiting for rescue. One by one their fellow passengers died so that when they were finally picked up by the *Hurricane* there were just eight of them still alive. 'I don't think the ordeal affected me in any lasting way,' he said, 'but I was a bit of a nuisance at school as I used to have nightmares and shout a lot in my sleep. The incident became known as the T.E., the "Terrible Experience". I did not have survivors' guilt, as some of the other children did whose siblings died and I think the only real impact it had on my life is that I remained in England whereas if I had got to Canada—my mother was Canadian and widowed—I think I should have stayed there.' Others claimed it had little impact on them but they could never quite get the image

261

of the sinking ship out of their minds. For a few the disaster has remained with them. John Baker, whose older brother Bobby gave him his life jacket so that he could be saved, spent years trying to forget the memories of that night: 'I spent 40 years forgetting and putting it into a little box in my mind. It's only at moments—like the reunions— that I open the door, and open the box, and . . . and I don't always like what I see inside.'[16]

Derek Capel was one of the six boys who survived the eight-day ordeal in the lifeboat with Mary Cornish and Padre O'Sullivan. 'When we were first picked up we didn't feel too bad. We were living on adrenalin, I suppose. My father came up from Middlesex to collect me and that was at about the time I found out that my brother, Alan, had died. I was so worried that they would blame me for losing him but they never did, at least they never showed me they did.' In the sick bay in Glasgow the day after they were brought back to Gourock the six boys received a cursory medical inspection from the Army doctor who had spent the last months dealing with victims from Dunkirk. 'I can remember that visit from the doctor so clearly. He came in and he said: "You boys have had a rough time. Now you must pull yourselves together." And that was it. We had to do just that.'

After a few days Derek's father took him back home by train. As they arrived in London, Derek's legs gave way and he could no longer walk. His father struggled to carry him but when they got to Hounslow and discovered the tube wasn't working he became despondent. So he enquired of a greengrocer where he might get a taxi from. The greengrocer recognised Derek from the papers

262

and said that there was no need for a taxi, which they would not find anyway, he would take them in his vegetable lorry. 'So that is how I got home! In the back of a vegetable lorry. And then I heard that I'd missed my own memorial service. Two in fact, one at the local church and one at the school where the headmaster had said nice things about me.'

The Atlantic ordeal had taken its physical toll on Derek and the other boys and they all spent time in hospital in various stages of painful recovery. While Derek was in hospital Lady Seaton came forward and offered his family her cottage in Cornwall, which they accepted. 'That was where the real healing began. It was so lovely and quiet there and even though I was still in a wheelchair I could really enjoy myself for the first time.'

The effect of his experiences from the sinking of the *City of Benares* was that Derek had nightmares and anxiety attacks into his forties. He found it difficult to settle and the feeling that he should somehow have saved his brother, Alan, was always hanging over him. At the age of eighteen he volunteered for the Navy and spent seven years sailing round the world. 'The great thing about the Navy was its structured life. That really suited me. And funnily enough some of the others joined the Navy too, even Padre O'Sullivan. . . . [In the Navy] you were never the worst off. There was always someone who had had worse problems than you and there was usually someone luckier. That really helped me to get a perspective on things. That, and getting married at twenty-one.'

At a reunion of the survivors of the sinking of the *City of Benares* fifty years on Derek was

263

standing chatting to another survivor when a man in his fifties walked up to him and said: 'Are you Derek Capel?' Derek replied that he was, whereupon the man said: 'Ah, at last. My father has been looking for you for years. He was the coxswain on the *Hurricane*.' That was when Derek learned that his brother, Alan, had been alive when he was picked up from the sea by sailors aboard the rescue ship. He died on board the ship. Derek later met the South African doctor who had attended Alan.

I asked him if he remembered my brother and I found I didn't even have to say his name. He said to me: 'Alan Capel? I have thought of him all my life. He came on board like a sleeping angel and I just couldn't wake him.' Well, that really shook me. My parents never knew this story. Sadly, they were already dead. But for me, when I understood what this meant, well it was a huge release from the guilt I had harboured all my life that I could have or should have done more to save him.

Once the truth about his brother Alan came out it changed his perspective and he made up his mind he would enjoy life even more than before. 'I think the net result of our terrible experience is that it made us better people. It also made the six of us boys very close. We all stuck together after the war and even if we did not see each other for months or even years, the bond was there and we were, are and always will be "the six boys".'

And what of Mary Cornish? Like the others aboard the lifeboat she was assumed at first to have perished. Her niece, Elizabeth Patterson, remembers her mother's distress when the news first came through. 'There was a week of misery at home. My mother and Mary were just a year apart and very close. It was so sad to see her weeping on my father's shoulder and I remember being told not to slam doors or make any noise. Then we heard she had survived and my father went straight up to Glasgow to see her.' Mary Cornish came back to Midhurst, where her sister lived, and worked for a short time as a Land Girl before having a nervous breakdown. The loss of the girls affected her deeply, as did the ordeal of the eight days in the lifeboat. However, she recovered and went back to teaching music. In March 1941 she was invested with the British Empire Medal.

Elizabeth Patterson remembers her aunt as a very strong character who seldom spoke about her Atlantic ordeal. 'It wasn't that she found it difficult to talk about, I think, but rather that we had been told by our parents not to ask her about it. I think she would probably have liked to have spoken about it more often. I know she felt terribly guilty about the little girls she was in charge of but could not save. That certainly bothered her but she used to bring out her British Empire Medal to show her music pupils.'

Mary Cornish went to live in West Lavington near Midhurst in a wooden house on the corner of Church Lane and Selham Road, opposite her sister and brother-in-law. She had a very wide circle of musical friends and Elizabeth remembers her as a dramatic personality who always had stories to tell. Even a train trip from London to Midhurst could turn into an adventure. 'My aunt was anything but

265

a hopeless spinster. She was loving, generous, a great gardener, a brilliant teacher and good with children and an excellent story-teller. She was also proud of "her boys" and I know she went to as many of their weddings as she could.'

Padre O'Sullivan was taken from the ship to hospital where he remained for several weeks. He lost his toe- and fingernails, as well as the skin off his tongue and gums. It was there that he learned that nine of the fifteen boys in his care had died. In addition to nightmares about rolling and pitching on the sea, of terrible thirst and hunger, he suffered from anguished dreams of guilt about the loss of the children entrusted to him. Five weeks after arriving back on land he was told that, subject to being passed fit, he was appointed a chaplain to the Royal Navy at war. Four months later he was back on board ship and continued as a naval chaplain for six years before being demobbed in 1946 and returning to teaching in Annecy.

On 21 March 1956 Padre O'Sullivan received a telephone call from the BBC asking him to come to London the following day. He assumed it was a prank but it was not. The BBC planned to stage a reunion of the surviving members of the CORB contingent who had been aboard the lifeboat. Paul Shearing, one of the boys, had written to the BBC to suggest this and the corporation had agreed and organised for them—that is to say, himself, Mary Cornish and the six boys—to appear on the Wilfred Pickles show in front of a live audience. Mary Cornish had only agreed to appear if the Padre came too. He did and twenty-four hours later he was in London. When he arrived at the television studios he was told he would not be meeting any of the survivors until they were on camera, to maintain the spontaneity. There was chaos all around him, band members practising clumsily and falling over chairs, a man with an orangutan sitting next to him and another with hundred-day-old chicks. It all seemed surreal. Then, he wrote:

Suddenly I saw Miss Cornish on the monitor; it was her voice that I recognised, so venerable was her appearance with her hair turned white. The presenter was asking questions and in reply she was telling him about being torpedoed five hundred miles out to sea, the dark night, the storm and how she had been unable to locate her fifteen little girls and so had got into one of the lifeboats with my boys; she recounted the awful launching and then, how our ship disappeared beneath the waves.[17]

Mary Cornish was visibly moved as she told her tale and it was only thanks to the presenter's gentle questioning that she did not collapse in tears when she spoke about the seventy-seven children who had died that night. It occurred to Padre O'Sullivan that members of the girls' families, and of the other children who had not survived, might be watching the programme and he felt for them as the pain of the event sixteen years earlier would come flooding back.

Then Padre O'Sullivan himself was called onto the set to talk about the ordeal in the lifeboat. It was the first time he had seen Mary Cornish in sixteen years and he stood shaking her warmly by

267

the hand for a good long time. He spoke about the bleakness of their situation on the boat and how she had been so courageous with the boys, how she had not minded giving up her petticoat to run it up the mast as a distress signal, and then of course their dramatic rescue.

Both Mary Cornish and Padre O'Sullivan told the presenter they were impatient to see the boys again. 'Look towards the band,' he told them.

> Then we saw, camouflaged behind the music stands, three young men who could scarcely contain their impatience. We stood up and they rushed towards us, kissing and hugging their 'Auntie' as they used to call her, during which time three others came onto the set. Nothing could have been more spontaneous or more moving. One of the six, speaking on behalf of them all, publicly thanked the two people to whom they owed their lives, because sixteen years earlier they had been too young to know how to.[18]

Soon they were ushered off the stage and the BBC stood them a round of whiskies in the bar while they carried on their excited exchanges. It was a wonderful, moving event for them all and the warmth of the thanks to Mary Cornish and Padre O'Sullivan was deeply felt. Mary Cornish died six years later of cancer, but Paul Shearing kept in regular touch with Padre O'Sullivan who lived well into his nineties.

The story of the sinking of the *City of Benares* is one of the most moving of all the civilian disasters of the Second World War. John Baker, who survived in the lifeboat for eight days, summed up the tragedy by paying tribute to his older brother: 'I'm here because of what Bobby did for me. Bobby gave a great gift to me and I shall forever be grateful . . . he gave me his lifejacket and he has given me sixty-five years of life, which he didn't have.'[19]

ORPHANS OF EMPIRE

That week, the week of Christmas 1941, was the end of my childhood. I was eleven years old. From then on our life was a waiting game. We felt in transit.

Ann Daly

Thousands of expatriates living in the Far East watched with anxiety as the war in Europe progressed. They worried about their families back in Britain but in Hong Kong and Singapore, hugely important Imperial outposts, they felt relatively secure. Only a small handful of far-sighted British Malayans saw the Japanese takeover of the rest of Indochina as the threat that it was, since it meant they came one step closer to Malaya. A few succeeded in getting their families out at that stage but the majority did not. There was no war in the Far East and the peacetime atmosphere reigned. The 'China Incident', which had rumbled on for four years, was the only cloud on the horizon and few took it as portentous. The result was that the colonies were not only unprepared militarily for the Japanese invasion but planning for the safety of the thousands of women and children had not been thought through.

When Churchill was on his way to meet Roosevelt at Placentia Bay in August 1941 and was asked whether he thought the Japanese would attack Malaya, he replied: 'No, I don't think so. And if they do they will find they have bitten off more than they can chew.'[1] Such was the confidence in the collective minds of Whitehall and Singapore that the threat from Japan was dismissed almost with a wave of a hand. In Hong Kong, with its proximity to the Chinese mainland, there was greater concern. Various defence studies had concluded that the colony would be extremely hard to defend under a Japanese attack. Thus the decision was taken in June 1940 to evacuate what the Governor of Hong Kong, Sir Mark Young, at the time described as *bouches inutiles*, or useless mouths. In July 1940, 1,500 service families and at least as many wives and children of European civilians left Hong Kong, many of them making for the Philippines where, unfortunately, they were rounded up by the Japanese in 1941 and sent to internment camps for the rest of the war.

Daphne Bird was a civilian internee in the Philippines for four years. She was imprisoned with her little boy Derek, while her husband, she later learned, was a prisoner of war in Hong Kong. Daphne made a set of watercolour drawings of her life in the camp, which give a frightening portrayal of the physical deprivations they endured. What these do not convey is the mental anguish she and her fellow internees suffered in their anxious wait for news from the outside world. In the letter she wrote on her release to her husband there is a hint, however, of the long-term damage that their separation and detention might cause, of their two lives running parallel under extreme circumstances and all the while the underlying feelings of guilt that she and her little boy had survived when others had succumbed to starvation and disease and died. And finally, the worry about how she would adjust to seeing her much-missed husband after three and a half years apart and how they would start again to live as a family after their world had been shattered. For the children, the evacuation from Hong Kong in July 1940 was less traumatic than for their mothers. The immediate impact on their lives was that they had to leave their homes and their fathers but as their mothers went with them they did not suffer the extreme sense of separation that the domestic evacuees in Britain had to endure.

Ian McNay was nine when he and his mother sailed to Manila and then on to Sydney, where he spent the war at school waiting for news of his father who became a prisoner of war when Hong Kong surrendered on 25 December 1941. Ian and his mother returned to the colony in March 1946. His strongest and clearest memory as they entered Hong Kong harbour was seeing the masts of scores of ships which had been sunk or scuttled in the harbour. Although many families who had been evacuated to Australia chose to remain there once they had been reunited, Ian's family felt differently. Hong Kong was their home and they wanted to return. 'I adjusted to life back there very quickly. I seemed to have lost very little schooling during the war and when the Central British School reopened in July or August 1946 I went back there. Strangely I do not recall any of my friends from the pre-war era returning to the school. My fellow pupils were all new.' Ian took the Cambridge School Certificate in 1947 and was awarded a Hong Kong government grant which he took up to study at Edinburgh University. 'There were no strings attached but it was hoped that I would return to Hong Kong after my studies and work, probably in the government service. That would also have been my preferred choice. But my father had been a POW and was not in good health so my parents retired to Sydney in 1952. So I decided to return to Sydney in 1953 after graduation and I have remained there ever since.'

In recent years Ian has done research into the history of the Battle for Hong Kong and this has given him a greater perspective on his own evacuation in 1940:

I realise now what a big impact the evacuation has had on my life. I have not lived in Hong Kong for sixty-one years but whenever I read a book or newspaper the word 'Hong Kong' springs out of the page at me. I even sometimes watch the Hong Kong news on our multi-national TV channel. Cannot understand any of it because it is conducted in Cantonese but I enjoy the images. Friends here in Sydney are always interested in my story and when asked about Hong Kong I probably go on a bit too much. I have had a very happy life in Australia but I sometimes wonder what it would have been like to have had a career in Hong Kong. Of course I have visited over the years but regret the glitz and sheer overcrowding of the place. [The] pictures [I] collected always seem to centre on the old Hong Kong. I regret its passing.

For thousands of expatriate families living in Malaya, the war in Europe did not touch them for over two years and they believed Churchill's promise that they were safe. Malaya was vitally important for supplying rubber and tin to the Allied war effort and the Governor General of Singapore, Sir Shenton Thomas, put a brave face on the impregnability of the 'naval fortress'. As Geoffrey Brooke, a former naval officer and author of *Singapore's Dunkirk* wrote: 'The sad thing is that this took in our own people, especially regarding evacuation, but not the Japanese, whose intelligence was excellent.'[2] Sir Shenton felt he was responsible for all the races in Malaya, not just the Europeans, and thought there should be no preference shown for the latter. He believed Europeans should stay and Lady Thomas made broadcasts to the effect that the place for women was beside their husbands. It was clear that General Arthur Percival, General Officer Commanding Malaya, felt the same about the service families and although subsequently Churchill twice proposed the evacuation of women and children, this was ignored. After the war Percival wrote: 'It was more than once suggested to me that arrangements should be made for the evacuation in the last resort of important personages and as many others as the available transport could take. This I refused to countenance. Our job was to hold Singapore for as long as we could and not to evacuate it . . .'[3] Life carried on as normal and the children of those families today have fond memories of the lovely lifestyle that suddenly had to be abandoned at the end of 1941 when the world came crashing around them in the dramatic aftermath of the Japanese bombing of Penang.

Shortly after the outbreak of hostilities in Malaya the Colonial Office suggested that evacuation might take place on a limited scale and that there should be no racial discrimination. In the event mostly Europeans, civilians and military families, applied. Destinations were to be Britain, India, South Africa or Australia. The fact that this was not officially sanctioned by the Governor spread confusion and forced decisions about arrangements that were later deemed to have cost many lives. Before the end of 1941, 1,500 women and children left and a further 4,000 left on four ships on 30 January 1942. At this stage evacuation was still voluntary and remained so until three days before the surrender. One of the reasons for this late and messy evacuation is the shame felt when the European population of Penang was evacuated, under military order, following the big bombing raid in December.

When the attack on Malaya came the Allies found themselves hopelessly ill-equipped to fight the Imperial Japanese Army. Advancing at an average rate of 9 miles a day the Japanese landed at Singora and Pattani in Thailand on 9 December 1941 and by 15 February 1942 were in Singapore, taking the surrender from a humiliated Allied army under General Percival. The attack had taken just ten weeks.

Conditions for the evacuees trying to leave Malaya and Singapore during December and January were difficult but not yet desperate. Most people succeeded in getting away safely albeit on overcrowded ships and in cramped conditions.

Their main worries at this stage were what would happen to those who were staying in Singapore and what would become of their homes in up-country Malaya, now occupied by the Japanese. As Percival ordered the general retreat to Singapore on 27 January so the situation began to deteriorate and the civilian population was vulnerable to Japanese air attacks.

Does the evacuation in the Far East count as part of the wartime evacuation story? After all, most children were evacuated with their mothers and therefore the trauma was much diminished in respect of separation and its attendant problems. The answer must be yes, since the effect of this evacuation, though different, is that it left over a quarter of the families involved without husbands and fathers and the majority of the rest without a home after the war. So the effect was felt in a complete change of lifestyle in the post-war era and, for many, a change in fortunes that shaped their lives, without a father to provide for them.

Most people leaving Singapore had so little notice of evacuation they hardly had time to grab the bare essentials before they left their homes. One young woman was told to pack one suitcase, take her bedding and be ready in a quarter of an hour to leave for the harbour: 'Being eighteen I couldn't bear to leave some of my things, so I packed my suitcase full of evening dresses.' Another, Mrs Enid Innes-Ker, was phoned by her husband at breakfast-time and told she had to be at Clifford Pier within the hour. 'I was so choked I could hardly speak, and I can hear now Philip saying calmly, "Take it easy Enid, take it easy." I could wait no longer. We were off, leaving a fully furnished home and many prized possessions. Actually there is only one thing that to this very day I regret having left and that is Tam's rugger honours cap. It would have meant so much to him if only I had thought to pack it.'[4]

As the emergency evacuation accelerated, people made their way down to the docks in cars, on bicycles and on foot, desperate to get away from the battle that was raging in the city. The scenes at the docks were equally Dante-esque.

All the time burning godowns (warehouses) sent up clouds of smoke round those struggling towards their ships, enemy aircraft droned continuously and shells from both sides whined overhead. The plight of terrified children was heartbreaking. All these present a tempting target and the inevitable occurred. A string of bombs landed on the edge of the crowd and a good number were killed or wounded; one man about to embark was seen to take his small child from the arms of his dying wife and go on board in tears, leaving her body on the ground behind him.[5]

A naval officer described the scenes even more vividly: 'The air-raids were following in quick succession and causing heavy casualties among the evacuees. To the noise of the guns was added the screams and cries of the dying and wounded. Smouldering and dismembered bodies lay everywhere among the pathetic remains of scattered, burst-open suitcases.'[6] The Japanese had put out a message in Tokyo that they were not going to permit the British 'another Dunkirk'.

The evacuees fled as best they could. When there were no more ships they took whatever vessels they could commandeer and set sail for Java, 600 miles south of Singapore or some, more adventurous, through the Malacca Straits for India. But their passage was by no means certain, for even if they did succeed in running the gauntlet of the Japanese Air Force and Navy, they still had to negotiate the mangrove swamps of Sumatra's east coast.

As the ships, boats, fishing vessels all made their escape, so the tragedies began to unfold. Oswald Gilmour, a worker in the Public Works Department in Singapore, was shipwrecked when his ship, the *Kuala*, went down. In his book *Singapore to Freedom* he described the horror in the Malay archipelago at the close of Valentine's Day:

Men, women and children in ones and twos, in dozens, in scores and in hundreds were cast upon these tropical islands within an area of say 400 miles square. Men and women of many races, of all professions, engineers, doctors, lawyers, businessmen, sisters, nurses, housewives, sailors, soldiers and airmen, all shipwrecked. Between the islands on the phosphorescent sea floated boats and rafts laden with people, and here and there, the lone swimmer was striving to make land. All around the rafts and swimmers were dismembered limbs, dead fish and wreckage, drifting with the currents; below, in all probability, were sharks; and above, at intervals, the winged machines of death . . . It

278

was a ghastly tragedy, a catastrophe beyond measure.[7]

In total, 8,000 women and children were evacuated from Malaya and Singapore and around 3,000 from Hong Kong. The majority were sent to Australia but others went to New Zealand, South Africa, India, Canada, Ceylon (Sri Lanka) and Britain. Fortunately most had not had to suffer the desperate plight of the evacuees shipwrecked in the Malayan archipelago but almost all of them were abruptly uprooted from their homes to face an unknown future. For the mothers evacuation was initially a much greater worry than for the children. Many of the children of expatriate parents had been used to separation for long periods as the majority would have been sent home to Britain or Australia to boarding school at eight, eleven or thirteen. The shock of separation, therefore, was not as keenly felt amongst this group of children, as their memoirs attest. What was significantly different for these evacuees was the uncertainty of their future after the Japanese invasion and the return from evacuation after the war was over. 'First we lost our homes, our status and our independence and later we lost our way of life. We didn't know that at the time but it became all too clear after the war was over,' said one evacuee from Penang.

On 6 December 1941, Ann Daly was due to sail back to Malaya with her mother, Norah. They had been on six months' leave in Western Australia and were to join Ann's father who was working as a stockbroker in Kuala Lumpur. The sailing was cancelled. A day later the Japanese attacked Pearl

Harbor and any prospect of their returning to their home was shelved. From that moment their lives changed. Ann's father had belonged to the Federated Malay States Volunteer Forces (FMSVF) for many years. Now he was in command of the Ambulance Brigade in Singapore. They received a letter just before he left Kuala Lumpur to say that he had buried all the silver and 'glass'—an Irish term for jewellery—and was on his way with the Ambulance Brigade to Singapore. They were not to worry. But of course they did. Augustine Joseph Daly was already fifty-two years old. By 1943 he was working as a slave of the Japanese on the Thailand–Burma Railway. Nicknamed the Death Railway, it ran from Bangkok in Thailand to Moulmein in Burma, a distance of 258 miles (415 kilometres). During its construction 12,000 prisoners of war and more than 80,000 Asian labourers lost their lives. Ann and her mother received four postcards from him during the war but no more money. The Australian government stepped in and forwarded small amounts to families who were unable to extract funds from Malaya or Singapore and Ann remembered that her education in Australia was funded by her school, Loreto Convent. They moved to ever smaller houses near Perth and eventually they lived on a covered verandah consisting of two rooms, a tiny bathroom and a minute kitchen. Everyone was kind to them, she recalled, but she knew instinctively that she did not belong:

My five years in Western Australia were the most extraordinary mixture of terrible sadness, insecurity, and worry over the future. Would my father survive? What would happen if he did not? How would my mother cope with life if the worst came to the worst? I felt responsible all the time for my mother. For her it was so difficult whereas I, as a child, had friends and was able to have fun but she was always in the back of my mind.[8]

After Japan surrendered in August 1945 friends of Ann began to hear, one by one, that their fathers had survived and would be returning. Every time the news came through there was a surge of optimism that the next bout of news might be good for them. On 24 September Norah Daly received the shattering news that her husband had died on 15 May 1944. The shock was immense. She had been clinging onto the hope that he had survived and yet he had been dead for over sixteen months: 'It must have been awful for my mother, as it was for me. Her married life over, security non-existent and our future a blank. All those plans for their retirement gone in one instant.'[9] Like many war widows from the Far East, Norah had little choice but to head back to Britain. There was no future for her as a non-working widow in Malaya and her daughter needed to be able to complete her education and establish a life for herself.

Ann and Norah left Fremantle in March 1946 and sailed to Britain via Aden. They arrived in Southampton on a grey, dismal day in April. There was no one to meet them. It was Ann's first visit in ten years. The last time she had been six years old and her father had been with them, a whole lifetime of experience away from where she was now at sixteen. She was sent to St Mary's School, Ascot, and remembers her mother telling the headmistress that she would not be able to pay the fees. These were waived. Eventually they were able to get some money out of Malaya and could contribute towards the school fees but Ann never forgot that generosity. Her main worry, however, was her mother: 'People were kind, but Hoddesdon was so unlike Malaya, and our future, Mummy's future, seemed to stretch meaninglessly ahead without any structure.'[10] For a young girl, on the brink of adulthood and with a future full of possibilities, life in Britain had its highpoints and possibilities. For a widow in her fifties, living in a country no longer familiar and without her lifelong companion, it was a depressing existence.

Ann met and married John Bartleet in 1951. 'I could hardly believe it was happening. For so long, since I was ten in fact, most of my hopes for the future had always been dashed. I could not take in that all those sad years were now over. For the first time in years I had something to look forward to that I could really believe would last.'[11] For Norah Daly the relief and joy of knowing that her daughter was happily married was a great consolation. She died in 1955 never having gone back to Malaya. In 1988 Ann and her husband John went to Chungkai War Cemetery in Thailand where Captain Augustine Joseph Daly MC had been buried in 1944. For Ann it closed a chapter but it also reminded her of the terrible sacrifice of the war and the cost, over decades, to widows and their families.

For other children the effect of evacuation was dislocating only in as far as it upset the natural rhythm of their lives and years later they looked back on their experiences and realised how much they had been protected by their mothers, many of whom had coped in difficult circumstances with great bravery and determination.

Robert Arbuthnott only learned of the strength of anti-British feeling as a result of the fall in Singapore at his grammar school in Sydney when he was beaten up by four seventeen-year-old Australian boys who broke his nose and sent him home looking very sorry for himself. Robert, his older brother John, and their mother had arrived in Australia in January 1942 from Singapore and after several unsettled months had rented a cottage in a Sydney suburb where Mrs Arbuthnott got a job teaching elocution while the boys went to Knox Grammar School.

Robert's father, Archie, had been a chartered accountant in Kuala Lumpur since 1926, having been invalided out of the Army after losing an arm and an index figure in the trenches during the First World War. He had joined the Malayan Volunteers before the war broke out, and Robert remembered overhearing him saying to his mother that she had better leave for Singapore by the next day's train as it would probably be the last. With just one suitcase between them they joined thousands of other civilians trying to escape. Eventually the three of them were offered two seats on a flying boat to Sydney via Java, Darwin and Townsville.

Arriving in Sydney, the family was offered a home on a large sheep station in the Blue Mountains by Australian friends from Malaya. But after a few months, finding that she was destined to spend the war as an unpaid cook for the farmhands, and because the children were bullied by their hosts' older children, Mrs Arbuthnott decided to go to Sydney to find work.

In the meantime, following the retreat down the peninsula, Archie Arbuthnott was made a liaison officer on General Percival's staff. Following the surrender he was taken prisoner and sent to work on the Thailand–Burma Railway. His wife was to hear nothing from him, apart from one postcard just before the surrender, until 1944.

After a time with a hostile landlady, Mrs Arbuthnott finally moved to the cottage where her Australian neighbours became lifelong friends. In March 1945 the family accepted the offer of free passage on the *Stirling Castle*. They sailed via New Zealand, to pick up frozen lamb, then across the Pacific and through the Panama Canal to join a convoy to cross the Atlantic. Robert remembers the excitement when the European war ended and German submarines surfaced and surrendered.

Arriving at Liverpool to be met by an uncle in RAF uniform, Robert was struck by how grey and dull everything was. After warm and plentiful Australia, rationing and rain were a real contrast.

But as a child you accept a lot of what you see and experience, so we just got on with it and began to find out what England was like. I had absolutely no knowledge of it at all. Of my father there was still no news. V.J. Day came and went and we heard nothing, and after two months when most of the ex-POWs were on their way home, my mother feared the worst. Then one day, at the house of a friend whose husband had returned, she heard him say, 'I saw Archie in Bangkok the other day', which came as an overwhelming relief to us all.

Robert's father eventually returned by ship and the family was reunited in Britain.

After months of medical treatment, Archie was fit enough to return with his wife to Kuala Lumpur and resume his job there. Robert and his brother were left at boarding school, and saw their father only twice in the next five years, and their mother only once a year. Like most children at the time, they coped with this separation as they had coped with being evacuees. As for Archie Arbuthnott, his appalling experiences had induced a kind of serenity and calm acceptance. 'He was a wonderful father, never angry, always interested,' Robert said.

Robert Arbuthnott's story is typical of many evacuees in the Far East. It was only years later, when events of the past had become a part of history, that they considered how this period had had an impact on their lives. At the time they thought relatively little of it. For children who had lost their parents, as Ann Daly did, the disruption caused by evacuation was as nothing compared with the impact of this loss. For many, understanding what happened to their fathers has been a lifelong search.

Audrey McCormick was ten when she and her mother were evacuated from Singapore to South Africa. Her father was one of those who felt sure that the Japanese were a much greater threat than others liked to believe and he sent his wife and daughter away in the autumn of 1941. During 1944

Audrey kept a diary, which she re-read over half a century later. In the autumn of that year her mother decided they had to leave South Africa and go back to Britain so that Audrey could finish her education. It was, she felt in retrospect, a terrible mistake. South Africa had been a good place for them to live. Scotland was cold, wet and strange. 'The houses, the pebbled paths, the high box hedges and rain. And the enormity of being with my father's parents but without him.' The thing that struck her as she re-lived her childhood was the running theme of her worries about her father, left behind in Singapore. She recorded his birthday in the diary—11 October 1944. 'Wish Dad was here' she had written the day before and then 'the weather is mostly wet'. This perpetual concern with her father's well-being came from her mother's anxiety, sometimes expressed, sometimes suppressed, about his safety. As the war came to an end there was still no mention of him. Looking back, she empathises with her mother: 'My mother's life suddenly faced a reality which was bleak, unless my father turned up alive. But he did not—ever. She never did learn what happened to Dad . . . whereas long, long into the future I did.'

Audrey's father had been killed in a bomb blast on a raid on the docks in Singapore in February 1942 and he was buried in a mass grave. 'But my mother never learned that. Eventually she received access to my father's estate some long time after the end of the war. She went to court to have Bob, her husband, declared legally dead.' Audrey's mother remarried and the two of them lived their lives seeing one another quite regularly but never for long enough, she later realised: 'I do not believe I ever thanked my mother adequately in word or deed for all the love, care, concern and hard work she gave me in lieu of the father I had most certainly doted on. Alas, I gave her too little time in my hectic life.'

For children such as Audrey McCormick who had lived in the Far East the legacy of their evacuation was anxiety and uncertainty about what had happened to their fathers and the eternal question of what might have been. For Nigel Stanley the search has never quite ended and his story is one of the most remarkable to come out of the Far East.

At Christmas 1945 two small boys, intent on climbing Lochnagar, crept downstairs in the dead of a bitterly cold winter night. They had packed biscuits and cake into their satchels, left a note for their parents to say they had set off on an adventure, and unlatched the door. At that moment Nigel's mother appeared on the landing. Her long, dark hair, usually pinned up neatly on top of her head, was flowing down her back. She towered above them at the top of the stairs. Eight-year-old Jim Fisher was awestruck. He had never seen Mrs Stanley with her hair down. 'Who's that?' she hissed. 'We're burglars,' returned seven-year-old Nigel. They were sent back to bed.

Dorothy Stanley was a widow. Her husband had died in December 1943 and she was visiting one of the men who had been imprisoned with him during the war and who was going to tell her how he had died. For Dr Elliott Fisher this task must have been one of the most harrowing experiences of his life. Nigel never heard what Elliott Fisher told his mother. All he knew was that for the rest of that visit to Jim Fisher's parents he was forced to share a room with her. She had no intention of letting her son out of her sight.

The Stanleys and the Fishers were neighbours in Penang in Malaya before the war. Both men had been doctors working at Penang General Hospital, employed by the Colonial Office. When the war broke out in Europe Dr Elliott Fisher and his wife were in Europe on leave. They had been in the Far East since the mid-1930s and were entitled to a home visit. As soon as war was declared, Elliott applied to join the Royal Army Medical Corps (RAMC) but was turned down on the grounds that he was needed in Malaya. Eventually they returned to the Far East in January 1940. Dr Stanley became eligible for his six months' long-leave in November 1941. This was owed to him due to his six previous years' work without a break. Nigel Stanley explained:

My father decided to go with his family to New Zealand. My sister Erika had been brought home from her boarding school in the Cameron Highlands [in Malaya]. As we were about to sail from Singapore my father received telegram from the Colonial Office which stated that the replacement due to take over from my father was ill and would not be able to fulfil his duties. My father immediately agreed to stay on in Malaya and postpone his leave. We all disembarked and headed home. Now, I think that this was one of the terrible ironies of the war. So fateful! Had we all gone to New Zealand our lives would have been completely different.

The 11th of December 1941 was a lovely sunny Thursday, Kitty Fisher remembered. It was her son Jim's fourth birthday—Penang was terror-bombed at eleven o'clock that morning. Both Jim and Nigel remember the bombing of Penang with unusual clarity. In fact for Nigel it was his first memory. He recalls standing on a chair looking out of a window at the great spectacle in the sky. Jim talked of Japanese planes and the extraordinary sight of the fires above the town. Neither boy has any recollection of fear. Just fascination. For their parents the scene was much more sinister. Both mothers went straight to the hospital. There Doctors Stanley and Fisher operated non-stop to save lives while their wives did what they could to help with the 700 casualties lying in close rows on the floor of the admission room 'just like soldiers at Atlanta in *Gone with the Wind*,' Kitty Fisher explained later. Over 120 people had been killed in the bombing and two days later Lieutenant General Heath, with the agreement of Sir Shenton Thomas, the Governor General of Singapore, ordered all European women and children to evacuate Penang and get to Singapore, though their final destination was still undecided.

Although evacuation elsewhere was still voluntary at this stage, it was officially decided that civilian women with children, from Penang, should not be allowed to stay in Singapore. Thus the day after they arrived on the island, Dorothy, Kitty and their three children left aboard the *Nellore*. From Singapore they sailed, in the filthy, hot, overcrowded hold, sleeping on straw palliasses, to Batavia (now Jakarta) where they spent Christmas

289

as guests of Dutch families and British expatriates in the city. From Batavia they sailed on the same ship, now equipped with a few makeshift bunks and lavatories, to Fremantle. The ship docked in Fremantle on Friday 2 January 1942 and a new phase of their lives began. The Stanleys and the Fishers were now evacuees dependent on the hospitality of their Australian hosts. The Salvation Army was the first to provide them with sustenance.

Life for the children and the adults became very different. There was the constant worry about money. The Colonial Office paid half the husbands' salaries to the wives, but it took many months for this money to come through and in the meantime the women had to eke out an existence, coping with hosts who were only partially friendly, and living in much less comfort than they had been used to in Malaya. For the children it was exciting. Nigel explained:

We lived a feral existence. There were no men around to discipline us and act as role models but we had a very strict pecking by age order amongst the children. We boys much admired John Grey, another ex-Malayan evacuee. Joy-riding on passing goods trains was one of his epic tales. He was an utter scamp, but he was five years older and therefore someone to be looked up to and learned from.

Fortunately the local state school gave us an excellent education. We also learned how to swim much earlier than boys brought up in wartime Britain. My mother instilled great patriotism into me; that being English was very special and that one day I would return to this faraway land of superheroes. My pride swelled when I was taken to wave flags as the Duke of Gloucester swept by in an enormous car during his royal visit in 1944. There was also a very brief visit by my mother's brother-in-law resplendent in the uniform of a colonel in the Royal Engineers on his way from England to join the Far East war. Alas, my self-esteem took a knock later when I was spectator at a swimming match between British, Australian and American troops—my heroes were trounced in every event.

In Perth the two families' lives diverged for a time. Kitty Fisher, who had been three months pregnant when she left Singapore, gave birth to a little girl, Anne, in June 1942. By that time she had moved to Busselton to live in a hotel where she had her baby. Jim remembers little about that time except that his mother was fixed on getting back to Britain to show her father his granddaughter. Sadly her father died before they returned so never got to meet Anne.

Dorothy Stanley remained in Perth with Erika and Nigel. Initially she received regular letters from her husband, Bertie. He wrote on 28 January 1942 that he and Elliott Fisher were working in Singapore's Kandang Kerbau Hospital. Less than three weeks later the impregnable fortress had fallen to the Japanese and Doctors Stanley and Fisher were to end up in Changi Gaol with the rest of the civilian prisoners of the Japanese.

Not content to sit back, Bertie Stanley worked

291

hard providing medical services for his fellow civilian internees and working out practical solutions to a host of problems. Although a doctor by profession, he was also a fettler and innovator. Within a short time he had made a grandfather clock from bits and pieces he had salvaged. It kept perfect time. He made cigarette lighters from the magnetos used in the ignition systems of diesel engines, which he scrounged from wrecked lorries, and put them up around the camp for communal use and he even built from scratch a radio to receive news from India and Britain. Although never discovered this last item was to play a part in his undoing.

The first eighteen months or so of captivity passed relatively quietly for Dr Bertie Stanley. He continued to make utensils and gadgets for the hospital and other communal use from bamboo, rubber tyres and various odds and ends. As an eye specialist he discovered that smoking increased the risk of blindness caused by malnutrition. His ensuing anti-smoking campaign was a failure though. Perhaps his communal cigarette lighters were partly to blame, and the smokers continued to smoke. In June 1943 he sent a radio message which was picked up by the wireless operator aboard the HMAS *Ambon*. The message went: 'Father, Fisher, John[s] and myself are very well. Love to Erika and Nigel.'[12] This referred to Dorothy's father, who was imprisoned in Changi Gaol, as well as Elliott Fisher and Brian Johns, who were Bertie's cellmates there. The month prior to this he had sent his third postcard from Changi, which was eventually received by Dorothy on 9 January 1945. In it he wrote: 'Looking

292

forward to seeing you all again. The children will be quite big then. I hope they will not forget me . . . I wish we had gone on leave when we had the opportunity.'[13]

Meanwhile, Major Ivan Lyon of the Gordon Highlanders, who believed his wife and young child had been lost in their attempt to escape from Singapore, was plotting his revenge on the Japanese. He succeeded in persuading the military in Western Australia to allow him to launch a commando attack, codenamed Operation Jaywick, on the Japanese at Singapore. The team, fully equipped and trained, made their way to an island 20 miles from Singapore where they transferred into two-man canoes. 'Paddling under cover of darkness, three separate crews, each covering various areas of Singapore Roads, attached their limpet mines to seven of the largest ships at anchor. They then made their escape. As an example of single-minded determination, the story has few equals.'[14] The attack was successful. Seven ships were destroyed and Lyon and his men got back to Australia undetected. The fall-out was disastrous. The Japanese were convinced that the raid had been carried out by guerrillas operating in Johore helped by intelligence radioed from the civilian internees.

On 10 October 1943, in an event that became known as the Double Tenth, the Japanese secret police, the Kempei Tai, swooped on Changi Gaol and arrested nineteen inmates. Thirty-eight others were taken in the next few months. Bertie Stanley, Elliott Fisher and Brian Johns were amongst the first to be arrested, as was Leonard Wilson, the Bishop of Singapore. Stanley was believed by the Japanese to be a mastermind behind an intelligence ring responsible for the attack. His inventiveness had been well known to them and, for a time, admired, but now they viewed him with suspicion. He was thrown into a cage in the Kempei Tai headquarters at the YMCA building and held there for a month before he was questioned.

Dorothy Stanley knew nothing of her husband's arrest by the Kempei Tai, nor of his subsequent interrogation and horrific torture. The first news that she received was a letter dated 12 May 1944 from the Malayan Government Agency in Sydney informing her, with the deepest regret, that they had received a telegram from the Secretary of State for the Colonies 'stating that official information has been received from Tokyo through the International Red Cross that your husband has died in Malai Camp'. The letter went on to say that the cause of death was not given. The International Red Cross had been informed by the Japanese that he had died of diabetes. Two days after the official letter had been written Bertie Stanley's mother wrote to Dorothy saying that she doubted the cause of death was correct. A fortnight later she wrote again, showing remarkable intuition and prescience as to the true nature of her son's last weeks: 'I think death came to him as a blessed release. Roger [his brother] said don't mourn for Bertie, Mum. I think he longed to die even if it meant the sacrifice of his dear ones and, Dorothy dear, I think and believe it was merciful when death took him from what must have been an unendurable existence.'[15] 'She could not have known how right she was.'[16]

Nigel was five and at school when the news of his father's death arrived. He remembers being brought home from school and there being other people at the house, which was unusual. However, the thing that made the most impact on him was the fact that his mother was crying. 'This was the first time in my life I had seen an adult displaying such distress and this was my mother. It is indelibly etched on my memory,' Nigel explained, over sixty-five years later. She never broke down in front of him again. Kitty Fisher told her son, Jim, that she only ever once recalled Dorothy Stanley weeping and admired her stoicism. Nigel was told by his mother that he was the senior male and as such he had a duty to live up to his father's name. This was no small pressure for a little boy and he remembers feeling a great weight of responsibility descend upon his shoulders. Despite this, his last year in Australia and his journey back to Britain in 1945 included some very happy times. But throughout his childhood he was aware that he must not let his father's memory down.

Of course it is true that my father's death had a huge impact on my life in all sorts of ways but I must stress that I did not feel badly affected materially due to the generosity of relations, family friends and my mother's self-sacrifice. My education was provided for in part by my father's old school, Aldenham in Hertfordshire. Its war memorial fund paid 30 per cent of my fees. A further 30 per cent came from the Rajah of Sarawak's charitable fund. My generous great-aunt helped out with some of the remainder, so that my mother only had to pay what she could.

Nigel did well at school and at eighteen he won a scholarship to Cambridge where he studied medicine, emerging with a First in 1960.

Nigel had four uncles, but his closest male relative was his mother's father, who had been imprisoned in Changi with Nigel's father. Nigel said:

He lived with us from 1946 until he died in 1962. In Changi my grandfather had been starved of news and food. I used to have to go out every Sunday morning to buy him all eight Sunday newspapers. I also remember being fed lots of vitamins so that I would not suffer from pellagra and beriberi as he had done. I now regret that I never questioned him about his wartime experiences. Like many Far East captives he rarely talked about them spontaneously, a habit I even acquired myself.

The Fishers used to have Nigel to stay during their summer holidays in Scotland. He became part of their family and the two boys grew up like brothers. They are still extremely close, despite being, by their own admissions, chalk and cheese. 'Nigel's the quiet, thoughtful one, I'm the noisy gregarious one,' explained Jim Fisher in 2010. 'He was an avowed atheist, I was a religious bore. We could not be more different and I'm not sure if we met one another now we would get on so well together but our paths are so irrevocably intertwined that I cannot imagine growing up without Nigel.'

Jim's return to Britain had been in its own way unsettling and different from what he had grown used to in Australia. Jim, his sister Anne and his mother went straight from London to Scotland to stay with Kitty's widowed mother. 'I went to school in Ballater and had quite a culture shock. We had slates to write on, not books, and there was a lot of corporal punishment at the school.' When Elliott Fisher walked back into Jim's life in the autumn of 1945 Jim did not recognise the man he was supposed to call Daddy. 'Somehow I knew it was Daddy but it was difficult. I didn't know how to behave—whether to hug him or hold back. And my sister, of course, had never seen her father. She came out with her broad Australian accent and it must have been quite a shock to him.'

Elliott Fisher was granted six months' leave by the Colonial Office before he was sent back to Malaya in March 1946. His back pay was eventually sent to him by the Office with the deduction for 'free board and lodging' for the time he had spent in prison in Changi. The irony was not lost on him.

On the first trip to Ballater at Christmas 1945 Elliott Fisher introduced Nigel and Jim to the mountains. Here was something they could really enjoy. 'It was very exciting and made me feel like an explorer,' Nigel elaborated, 'I learned to love the mountains triggered by the sheer beauty of Lochnagar. That winter its snow went pink in the sunset and I was enchanted.' Jim remembers his father walking and climbing a great deal as part of his recuperation from his incarceration by the Japanese. For Jim it was a way to get to know his own father. They had last seen each other in

December 1941 when Jim was four.

From then on and for every summer from 1947 Nigel would join the Fisher family in Scotland for all or part of the school holidays. For the boys it seemed completely natural. 'It was as if he were my brother. Nigel was so much part of the family that he was treated with the same rigorous discipline as my sister and me,' Jim recalled. 'We had to peel potatoes and pump water into this cottage. It had neither electricity nor water. We even had to scrub the floors.'

From Cambridge University Nigel completed his training at St Thomas's Hospital in London and it was there, in his early twenties, that he finally learned exactly how his father had died. It came about in a most unexpected way. Nigel's girlfriend, also a medical student, attended a teaching clinic held by a plastic surgeon called Richard 'Dickie' Dawson who had been a captain in the RAMC and a Far Eastern Prisoner of War. During this clinic he told the students how the doctors in the prison camps used to play tricks on the Korean guards. Nigel's girlfriend then asked him what he knew about Dr Cuthbert Stanley. Dawson replied hesitantly: 'Well, it's not a very nice story but if your boyfriend wants to know he should read a book called *The Double Tenth Trial.*' The book was duly borrowed from Brixton Public Library and Nigel and his girlfriend sat down to read it together. One glance in the index showed Nigel that this was packed with references to his father's name and he read, for the first time, the true and gruesome story of his father's murder by the Kempei Tai.

Nigel learned that the two most damaging

298

pieces of circumstantial evidence against his father had been, on the one hand, his inventiveness with mechanical equipment such as the clock he had built and the cigarette lighters he had improvised and on the other that he had belonged to a radio group in Changi. It was of no interest to the Japanese that the radios they found could only receive, not transmit.

Bertie Stanley had not been questioned for the first month of his imprisonment. Then, on 13 November, he was interrogated for about three hours although not ill treated. Two days later he was 'made to kneel all day upon a duckboard with a billet of firewood tied behind his knees. This forced posturing was continued daily whilst punctuated with savage beatings. The Kempei Tai also broke from their standard procedure of allocating one team for each suspect. All their teams had a go on Bertie, who they dubbed the master spy.'[17] The torture was then supplemented by all the other ghastly methods in the Kempei Tai's repertoire. He would be brought back to his cell with his legs cut and swollen, his face bruised to pulp, wet due to the water torture and with terrible burns inflicted by the electric shock treatment. 'Each night Bertie whispered details of his interrogators' questions to Sam Travis so that he and others could have time to prepare their responses.'[18] Gradually he weakened so that he was unable to walk back to his cell. So the Kempei Tai carried him to and from his interrogations each day in a rattan chair, callously tipping him back into his cage each evening. The days became weeks and Bertie tried to end his life. The Kempei Tai had at last extracted a confession from him, signed

299

under duress described in the Double Tenth war crimes trial by the prosecuting counsel as 'beyond the limits of human endurance'.[19]

The next day he managed to get away from his tormentors and hurled himself from a first-floor window. Tragically for Bertie Stanley he did not succeed in ending his life. He broke his pelvis and from then onwards had no use of his legs. After this attempt to kill himself the Kempei Tai carried on torturing him, but he continued to deny all their accusations. The last time his cellmates saw him he was badly burned and bleeding, with his wounds suppurating, delirious and clad only in his vest. They were told to carry him to a truck outside. 'When I read how my father had died almost twenty years earlier I was almost insane with hatred and rage,' Nigel said. 'For many years I wouldn't buy Japanese goods and I loathed the lot of them. But over time my attitude has changed.' One catalyst actually came from the Fisher family. Jim's brother-in-law married a Japanese woman and Nigel got to know and like her.

In the last twenty years I've met more of them as individuals and have realised they are not personally responsible for their nation's historical baggage. Hopefully their curiosity as intelligent decent people will eventually break through Japan's state-manipulated amnesia about the war years. All these years I've had this duty to emulate my father in my mother's eyes. Just there, in the background. But I've also felt a sense of injustice. My father went through something unspeakably horrible yet he has been erased from our national memory. My father was not on the school memorial. His grave was in Bidadari civilian cemetery at Changi and it was only when I went on my first visit to the Far East forty years after he died that things began to fall into perspective.

Nigel's first visit to Singapore came in 1983. By the time he arrived he had already been to several war memorial sites, so he made straight for the immaculate Commonwealth War Graves Cemetery at Kranji, which has the graves of nearly 4,500 servicemen and which houses the Singapore Memorial that commemorates a further 24,000 who have no known grave, casualties of the battle on land and in the air or from terrible treatment in the prisoner-of-war camps. Next he went to Bidadari Cemetery for civilians where he knew his father had been buried: 'What a contrast! The grave was covered with lalang grass eighteen inches deep which I tried to cut back with a penknife. For me this was one example of various painful moments where I have been confronted with the lack of national commemoration for our civilian war dead.' His indignation was mollified when he learned that one of the three main buildings at the Singapore General Hospital had been named the 'Stanley Block' in his father's memory, albeit about to be destroyed during modernisation of the hospital.

One of the things that jarred most was that Nigel's father had been forbidden from joining the RAMC by the Colonial Office: 'The doctors in the Malayan Medical Service were told that there was a greater need for them to maintain the colonial

301

infrastructure, and the revenue from its exports to finance our war effort.' Also he had stayed in his post and faced the consequences, even though he had several opportunities to get away both before and after the Japanese invasion. Had he died as an Army doctor, Bertie Stanley would have been accorded a grave in a Commonwealth war cemetery in perpetuity rather than in an overgrown patch in a civilian cemetery.

Other information about his father's torture emerged during the investigations before the Double Tenth Trial in 1946 and Nigel began to piece together the terrible tragedy that was the last month of his father's life. He discovered how the Japanese tried to cover up the fact his father had been in extremis when taken from the Kempei Tai headquarters and had been dead on arrival at Kandang Kerbau Hospital. A Eurasian doctor who had worked with Dr Stanley prior to the war had seen the Japanese bringing in the dead body in 1943 and had recognised him despite his battered state. Dr Sheares had been warned by the Japanese matron to keep quiet about what he had seen but he gave testimony at the Double Tenth Trial and this helped to uncover the web of lies spun by the Japanese. Nigel also discovered that an undertaker called Walter Neubronner had seen the body of a tall European covered in bruises and had watched from a distance as the Kempei Tai dumped his coffin unceremoniously into an unmarked grave. His identification of the site allowed Dr Stanley's wife and friends to erect a headstone there in 1946. Later still Nigel met the son of a civilian internee who had driven the truck that had transported his father's body from the

Kempei Tai headquarters to the hospital.

In 2002 Nigel read an announcement in *The Times* that Bidadari Cemetery was to be redeveloped for housing and that all graves would be dug up and human remains cremated and disposed of at sea unless descendants arranged for those remains to be interred elsewhere. So he and members of three generations of his family flew to Singapore to hold a little ceremony before the remains of his father were exhumed. These he had cremated and he brought the ashes back to Britain where he had them buried beside his mother's ashes and those of her parents. Meanwhile in Singapore the headstone was relocated to the Garden of Remembrance in Old Choa Chu Kang Road.

Evacuation from Singapore had that terrible twist for Nigel Stanley that had his father taken the leave entitled to him rather than staying to fill in for a colleague their lives would have been completely different. It left a scar that has taken a lifetime to heal. 'Fate was unkind to my father', Nigel said, 'and his treatment by the Kempei Tai was horrific. For many years I had repeated ghastly flashbacks about his suffering, but at least now their pain has been tempered by admiration for how he conducted himself undergoing such barbaric torture and how much he did for his fellow internees in Changi Gaol.'

Nigel's experience is extreme but not unique. As many as 3,000 children who were evacuated also lost their fathers and had to adjust to a completely new way of life. Mary Harris, who settled with her parents in Britain after the war and never returned to the Far East to live, explained in 2009: 'I have an

303

incredibly strong pull to Singapore, where *my* house still stands and I go through huge emotional upheavals every time I go back. It's a mega-colossal sort of longing for home. It's not a longing to return to an age gone by, but one for the sights, sounds, smells of the climate and vegetation of my childhood. Even though my father came back we three children became colonial orphans.'

9

READING BY A DARK LAMP

For those who experienced the negative effects of evacuation throughout the sensitive years of adolescence, the legacy has been a lifelong effort to cope with the feelings of isolation, loss of love and affection, a numbness, a deep searching for home and belonging.[1]

Margaret Woods

In 1975 a psychologist specialising in adults with severe emotional disorders described his work as similar to 'reading by a dark lamp'. His interest lay in the layers of complexity that his patients would place over the stories of their lives. The fact struck him that a high proportion of such people who were children in the 1930s and 1940s chose to change their history as a result of the Second World War. He found that they spoke about their childhoods with a sense of distance, as if they were describing something they had observed rather than experienced. And many of them, he commented, had great blanks in their memories of events that had occurred at significant moments, such as the day they were evacuated. These mental blocks were subconscious defence mechanisms to shut out the most painful experiences.

To some extent we all write our own narratives to suit the image we wish to project to the outside world. Sometimes these are just tweaked to make us seem more interesting or better educated but in some cases whole new personae are created; this happens for myriad reasons but often the construction placed on childhood experiences shapes the adult form. Childhood narratives are fluid until adulthood when they become increasingly fixed in the memory and as a backdrop to an individual's life. Thus, in the normal run of life, it is possible for two children living in the same family to have completely different childhood experiences, even to the extent that one could claim to have been wonderfully happy while another might feel their own life was bitterly unhappy and ruined by some cataclysmic event that overshadowed everything.

Thus evacuation, as for many just such a cataclysmic event, shaped many children's lives for ever and the experiences they had in those months or years influenced everything that came afterwards. Some were lucky and, though affected, put the past behind them and moved on after the war. For a significant number the changes were too great to assimilate and the long-term effects are still felt today. For an unfortunate few the effects were so devastating that there is no getting away from the past.

The single defining feature about evacuation for young children was that it happened very suddenly, and for most without warning. Few children recall being consulted about whether they would like to be sent away or not. Partially this had to do with the culture of the time when children had little or no say in such matters, though a number of older children sent abroad remember talking through the pros and cons with their parents and deciding for themselves that it would be a good thing. Some younger children remember being told that they were to go on an adventure or a holiday, something exciting to look forward to, which is why the shock of what happened to them was often delayed by hours and even days as children worked out what was really going on. Evacuation was to last for an unspecified amount of time and the children were to go they knew not where to live with, by and large, they knew not whom. Nor did their parents know where their children were going when they left on the official scheme, nor for how long they would be gone. It constituted for many the single most significant event in their lives to date. Some of the children who were the most disturbed were already trying to cope with troubled family relationships, bereavements, unhappiness or concerns about school. They might have been in the middle of a house move, or had just begun to get used to a new brother or sister, or had recently lost grandparents.

Added to this complex backdrop was the element of a lottery in the overall experience. As clinical psychologist Stephen Davies wrote in 2008:

> Generally, luck divided those with a good and a bad billeting experience. Herding unaccompanied, emotionally vulnerable children into a hall in a strange community and asking a local population, unscreened for suitability, to take their pick is a potential disaster for their psychological health. It placed the protection and psychological well-being of these children at risk. In scenes that

would make modern child protection professionals blanch, thousands of children were . . . given to the first set of foster parents who offered to take them.[2]

Six-year-old Lilian Evans remembered being prepared by her mother the night before she left Liverpool. Between them they had torn up one of her father's shirts and pulled her beautiful long hair into ringlets, binding it in strips of cotton. She remembered being so thrilled and proud of her appearance as she left home for her evacuation to Wales. She hoped that someone would take to her pretty looks and give her a nice home. However, this was not to be. She was picked, in her words, by a great, burly Welsh farmer who marched her and another girl back to his cottage. There they were ordered to strip off all their clothes and were put into a bath of green disinfectant:

> He told us to get in it and we got in, smelling awful and she [the farmer's wife] was pouring the jug over our heads and the dog came in from the back and went to sniff our clothes and she screamed and she kicked the clothes out of the back door. These clothes were new, my mother had bought new things for us. They were thrown out the back and she was washing us and then when we got washed she put a big towel round us and sat us on a chair and he got a razor and he was shaving our heads and if he cut you with the razor she put gentian violet on the cut so you had a bald head with purple dots on your head which used to burn when they cut us.[3]

The two girls were shown to their bedroom and told that on no account could they go into any other room in the house. The next day they were sent to school and not allowed to wear hats to cover their heads. The farmer had burnt all their clothes so they were dressed in a motley selection of what could be cobbled together in a hurry. As they arrived at school they were bullied for being nit-ridden townies: 'You bring germs to Wales' they were taunted. They were not the only children from Liverpool in that school to have shaved heads. It appeared to be common practice if the householders suspected the children might have lice.

The combined shock of being away from home for the first time, having her head shaved, being made to bathe in front of adults and then sent to school with clear evidence of stigma was utterly bewildering and terrifying for Lilian. The horrors of her stay in Wales did not end there. She remained with the farmer and his wife for five years and in all that time she was starved of affection and humiliated on a regular basis. On Friday evenings the farmer would sit on a chair with his pipe in his mouth and watch the children having a bath in front of the fire: 'The lady used to say to us—oh God, I'll never forget it—she would say "Here's the flannel, I'll put soap on it, stand up and do between your legs" and we had to do that and he used to be sitting with his pipe, watching.'[4]

Lilian did not return to live with her family until she was eleven years old, at the very end of the war. In all that time she had only received cards for birthday and Christmas, so that she had felt completely cut off by her parents and her four sisters. She learned later that they were told not to visit her for fear of upsetting her but the result for Lilian was that she felt abandoned and uncared for. It seemed that the farmer and his wife had stolen her innocence and deprived her of a normal childhood. Everything that might have made her enjoy life in the countryside was either forbidden or shut out. Apart from being let out to go to school she was given, she said, only half an hour a day to do something for herself. She felt more of a maid than a child and it made her grow up far too quickly because she had responsibilities way beyond her age.

Tragically her homecoming was as lonely as her time in North Wales and her sense of abandonment continued:

The bus was met by our families by the school yard and every child that got off never went near their mother and father because they must have thought that they had been shoved out, they didn't want them. There was no joy in it, no hug or anything. I didn't hug them because I thought they'd left me. Never came to see me and it ruined my life because after that we were all strangers in that house. I was little, that was the best part to be brought up with a family, instead of that I was somewhere else and when I came back I was older in my mind but my family, they were strangers to me.[5]

Lilian concluded: 'I know it ruined my life, it really did because after that I had no family and I

310

still haven't got any family. There is only me and my two boys. That's all. I have got no family.'[6] The great tragedy of Lilian's story is that what began as a terrible shock turned into a long, dark, loveless era of emotional starvation from which she never fully recovered. Other children who had undergone the same shock treatment of head shaving and de-lousing on arrival in North Wales found a way to turn their lives around. Many went back home to Liverpool very quickly in the autumn of 1939 but others became hardened to the way of life and determined to make a virtue of their new existence in the farming communities. They put up with being sent to Chapel rather than going to mass and they soon gave as good as they got at school, to the extent that when a second batch of evacuees arrived in one village in 1940 they were teased by the 1939 children for not being Welsh.

In July 1940 a report on the evacuation of children to Cambridge was completed. It was published the following year and became one of the most important studies into the effect of wartime evacuation. The report was as critical as Tom Harrisson's book, written six months earlier, had been and the main complaint, as for Harrisson, was that no one in officialdom had listened to the warnings given by distinguished psychoanalysts and experts in child care, of the impact on the psychological well-being on evacuated children. The editor of the *Cambridge Evacuation Survey: A Wartime Study in Social Welfare*, Susan Isaacs, wrote in her introduction: 'If we had planned for these problems with a tithe of the labour and intelligence which we put into questions of transport, if human nature had been

311

taken into equal account with geography and railway timetables, there would in all likelihood not have been so serious a drift back to the danger areas.'[7]

The survey established that psychological profiling—though it was not described in exactly those terms—would have helped on both sides. The researchers found that 'on the whole, depressed or anxious children seem to prosper most in quiet, rather conventional homes, where they are by themselves and free to follow their own devices. Whereas more aggressive boys and girls do better in homes with a more lively atmosphere, where there are others of much the same age and the children can be kept actively interested and employed.'[8] The other thing that the study concluded was that the strength of family ties had been seriously underestimated and the trauma that this would cause had not been taken into account. Stephen Davies, writing sixty years on about his work as a clinical psychologist working with older people in the NHS, agreed: 'Long term separations from attachment figures in childhood . . . pose a significant challenge to the development of a secure pattern of attachment.'[9] He observed in the course of his work how adults who had been traumatised by separation as a result of evacuation often found it more difficult to establish meaningful relationships in adulthood.

The Cambridge report was highly critical of the planners in Whitehall who, it was pointed out, had had at least one year's notice after the Munich crisis yet they did not seem to think that planning for social services for children, especially those who were already difficult or disturbed, was necessary: 'In especial, the strength of the family tie, on the one hand, and the need for skilled understanding of the individual child, on the other, seem to have lain too far outside the ken of those responsible for the scheme.'[10]

When the children who took part in the Cambridge survey were asked to make a list of what they missed most about their home lives in London the vast majority put their families at the top of their list, followed by friends, pets and homes. This did not surprise the authors. Individual children wrote comments that were perhaps less expected. One young boy wrote that he missed 'thick fog and fish & chips'; another said: 'I miss getting hidings from my dad when I get into trouble.' A social worker explained that children almost always prefer to stay with their parents, no matter how abusive they are.

Although the survey was limited to children arriving in Cambridge from the London boroughs of Islington and Tottenham in 1939, it is nevertheless possible to apply many of the observations made in the report to the country as a whole. At the time in Britain around 40,000 children a year were taken out of the family environment and 'boarded in private facilities' for a variety of reasons on the recommendation of the Child Guidance Clinics. These had been set up in the late 1920s to deal 'with that group of children and young up to the age of 17 who show behaviour and characteristics deviating so much from the normal as to be disturbing to themselves and to those with whom they associate'.[11] The Cambridge Evacuation Survey authors wrote: 'Their work showed that the emotional difficulties of children expressed as anxiety, temper, upsets in feeding, sleeping and elimination, were generally bound up with the child's relationship with his parents.'[12]

Today the understanding of the importance of a child's emotional development is a great deal more advanced than in the late 1930s. It is difficult to look back on the apparent inability of the evacuation authorities to understand the impact of their plans on individual children without the benefit of hindsight. Nevertheless psychologists such as Susan Isaacs and her colleagues in 1940 had a clear idea there would be a long-term effect on the children:

> there has been a great deal of discussion as to whether the sudden separation of children from their parents will give rise to serious emotional disturbance, and to undesirable behaviour. The question is far too complicated to be answered in any one study, or after only a comparatively short period of time. We do not yet know enough about the changes which the war may produce in children staying at home to speak with any confidence of the effect of separation. It is possible that apparently good adaptation may be at some cost to future stability.[13]

Stephen Davies's research points to the accuracy of Susan Isaacs's conclusion. When writing about what should happen if there were evacuation in the future, he wrote: 'Children are not adults—their psychological needs require separate attention. Families should be followed up psychologically at the end of an evacuation event. They may need both practical and psychological support in the longer term.'[14]

The Cambridge researchers were certain that the problems they encountered could not be treated in isolation but rather the background of the children had to be taken into account when serious behavioural problems arose. Teachers interviewed for the report, who had accompanied the evacuees from Tottenham and Islington, were frustrated that their in-depth knowledge of the children had not been made use of. They complained that much time had had to be spent working through problems that could have been avoided if they been asked at the outset which children needed careful handling.

The Cambridge survey went on to cite case studies that underlined their conclusions, including the following:

Case V Hysterical girl of twelve, placed in good billet: This girl was excitable and irresponsible. She complained that she was left hungry, and that she had been assaulted. Her foster parents were elderly, and very kind, though being childless themselves they were unused to children. This girl had been brought up in a Public Assistance Home. Her parents' marriage took place after the mother's pregnancy, and she deserted the home when the child was five years old. The father was left with three children and was himself very immature.[15]

Thus the seeds of unhappiness were already sown. The authors of the survey were critical of the fact that none of this information had been available prior to the billeting officer placing the girl with the elderly couple. Such situations arose with too great a regularity and were disturbing for the child but also for the foster families who took them on. Another foster mother struggled with a small boy who came from a home where, it was discovered, his father was unstable and the relationship with his mother was poor because she was of below average intelligence. The boy was exceptionally able academically and had been fortunate enough to find a foster home with a highly intelligent woman. The result was that he felt overwhelming affection for his foster mother. At first she enjoyed his intelligence but quite quickly found his affection suffocating and eventually rejected him, which had a consequent distressing impact on the child. Again, the report makes clear, if this had been known in advance, concessions towards the child could have been made and upset avoided.

Other cases that came to the notice of the Child Guidance Clinic in Cambridge and which were reported to the survey were instances of unfortunate misunderstandings. One little boy was referred to them for his 'filthy habits'. He had been spotted by his foster mother masturbating. When the child was examined he was found to have scabies in the pubic region. This was treated and the problem was solved. Another boy had been caught stealing and was in serious trouble with his foster parents. When his case was more closely examined it became clear that his foster family treated him with contempt because they believed he came from a lower social stratum than they did.

The boy was moved, on the suggestion of his teacher, to a family with a background more like the one he had come from in Tottenham and the pilfering stopped immediately. He settled down quickly and within days began to show improvement in his schoolwork.

One of the most troubling aspects of the evacuation is the dark area of child neglect, abuse and sexual molestation. It is hard to conceive of anything more upsetting in the context of this subject than the thought that some children were mistreated while they were in the care of foster families. Having sent their children away from home and into an unknown family, parents had to believe and trust that they would be cared for with kindness, not abused. And by and large they were treated well. As already demonstrated, rural Britain opened its homes to millions of children, mothers, and families and a very large percentage of those who did so were doing so out of generosity and in the spirit of helping one another out in difficult circumstances. Nevertheless, abuse happened and it has to be acknowledged as part of the evacuation story.

While it undeniably occurred, there are no accurate records of the number of children who were abused nor detailed accounts of what form it took. All too often unsubstantiated percentages are bandied about and the figures vary wildly. In the case of physical abuse the water is muddied by the definition of the term abuse. What might have been considered normal, if tough, practice in the 1930s and 1940s, such as corporal punishment, would now be considered abusive conduct towards children. Whether, therefore, it is correct to add to

317

the figures children who were punished by being sent to bed at night without food, caned for disobedience at school or clipped around the ear for scrumping apples is just one question of interpretation.

A form of sharp practice, though not necessarily abuse, that was widely employed and acknowledged later was the use of young boy evacuees by farmers who wanted cheap or free labour to make up for the shortfall in help as a result of farmhands going to the war. In the early part of evacuation this became a problem and it was first spotted by the teachers of evacuated schools that some of their charges were not turning up in the mornings. In the initial weeks of confusion and settlement it was not readily apparent to the teachers who was absconding from school, who had returned home and who was being held back from attending. It has to be said that some of the boys put to work on the farms were not as sad as their teachers might have hoped that their schooling was neglected.

Dennis Thomas was one evacuee who was kept back from school by the family who had taken him and his sister, Pat, into their home. Their evacuation is a story of survival on the one hand and of long-term emotional distress on the other. Dennis was born in 1931 and Pat in 1936. The two had been brought up in Gorton, on the east side of Manchester. Their father, Leslie, owned a butcher's shop, which he and his wife, Bessie, had been given by Leslie's father soon after they were married. Dennis described his parents as having a wild and busy social life with little time for the children. By the time the war broke out Dennis was well practised in playing truant and his slick tongue had got him out of various scrapes: 'I started by playing truant when my father dropped me at school on his way to collect the meat from the market. I began to do it more and more often. My father did not seem to notice, he was far too busy and my mum just did not seem bothered.'

By 1939 Dennis had already been sent away from home once to live with his grandparents in Barrow-in-Furness. He was, by his own admission, quite a handful as a little boy. In 1940, when the invasion of Britain seemed imminent, the subject of evacuation came up within the family. Dennis heard about the CORB scheme and was excited about it. He fancied himself in New Zealand or Canada, he explained, so he got the forms and filled them out himself. This required both his parents' signatures. Leslie was pleased that his son showed enthusiasm for travel so agreed to sign but Bessie was dead set against it so she marched down to the school and tore the form up, putting a stop to Dennis's ambitions for distant lands. However, Manchester was considered to be a likely target for the Luftwaffe so, after a false start in a house in Bollington, Dennis and Pat were sent to Mount Pleasant Farm near Leek in Staffordshire. This is where their extraordinary ordeal began.

Mount Pleasant was a working farm run by two sisters and their mother. One of the women, Elsie, was kind and decent but she was cowed by her slave-driving older sister, Nancy, who Dennis described as 'a psychopath who reminded me of an SS commander'. She ruled the house with an iron fist and dominated her mother and sister. Dennis later heard that Mr Deville had died while his

319

daughters were in their teens and his widow and girls had been left almost destitute. It is possible, he suggested, that the tough life they had had to endure had hardened them all, but in particular Nancy, who seemed the most bitter. This did not excuse their behaviour towards children but it might explain, Dennis felt, why Nancy was such a tyrant.

In all there were fourteen children on Mount Pleasant farm. Pat was one of the youngest, at just four years old, and Dennis one of the older ones at nine. Dennis described the life there as cruel

with the children being used for slave labour, nothing more. We had to work the farm in the absence of any adult farmhands. Aunt Nancy made us pick potatoes by moonlight, we did back-breaking field work and even the little ones like Pat had jobs. She had to do the chickens, you know, feed them, clean them out and collect the eggs and things. We were only allowed to go to school if there was no work on the farm, and that did not happen very often.

A regime of terror was enforced by Nancy by a leather strap. Children would be beaten for any misdemeanour and Dennis remembers as particularly callous the public beatings administered to the little children who wet their beds. He remembered one boy being so badly beaten that his legs bled.

The sisters and Mrs Deville had adopted a boy called Peter, who was used as a farmhand. He had already been at the farm for some time by the outbreak of the war and he appeared to be treated just as badly by Nancy as any of the evacuees who went to live there.

The daily routine was grim. There was no running water or electricity in the house so that one of the boys' jobs was to empty the lavatory pans onto the fields, a filthy task shared out between them. Mrs Deville did the cooking and the food was basic at best and there was never enough. Often the children just had bread and jam if there was nothing else. Children who didn't like what they were given and refused to finish what was on their plates were sent to bed with no food, which was particularly harsh on the little girls who were terrified of Nancy's rages. This did not happen very often as the children soon learned better than to go hungry. Dennis explained how Pat was frequently locked in the girls' bedroom for one reason or another and he would try to be kind to her but there was little he could do in the face of Nancy's harsh temper.

In the winter it was so cold at the house that many of the children developed chilblains. Dennis recalled that his shoes were often frozen in the mornings and his socks were always damp, which exacerbated his chilblains. Sometimes they were in such a state that he was unable to walk to school and had to take a piggyback from one of the bigger boys, Clifford Tucker. There was no medical service in the village and Nancy took no interest in their health provided they could work, except to the extent that she appeared to believe in the various immunisations that were given during childhood. Dennis loathed injections and he was taken to Leek at least once to have his top-ups.

He remembered how Aunt Nancy was disliked in Elstone, the small village of some half-dozen houses on the outskirts of which lay Mount Pleasant Farm. 'Thus we too were tarred with the same brush and the villagers did not like us evacuee children either. As a result we ran riot on Sundays when we were allowed out on our own and this of course just underlined their impression that we were a bad lot.'

Dennis and Pat were at the farm for four years. It was Pat, he felt, who suffered the most. He explained:

I was a bugger from an early age. I knew how to survive and I soon learnt to develop a shell that would protect me from the worst of Aunt Nancy. In fact, in the end, when I was about fourteen, old Mrs Deville wanted me to live on at the farm and I think I might well have stood in line to inherit it from her. It was a very strange experience for me but it taught me a great deal. In fact, I'd go as far as to say the war made me, despite the hardships I had to endure at Mount Pleasant Farm.

Pat had a completely different experience: 'I must have blanked it all out in my mind,' she explained. 'I cannot remember any of the children. In fact I can remember almost nothing about the whole four years except fear. Real, deep down fear. The only person who was ever kind to me was Dennis.' Dennis agreed: 'Pat was a lovely little girl when we went to the farm but she was so young and could not cope with the ill-treatment and lack of affection, which I seemed to cope with better. I was older and tougher. Yes, Pat had a very difficult time indeed.'

Nancy's sister, Elsie, who had failed to exert a moderating influence on her sister, had occasionally been able to spend a little time with the very youngest children before they went to bed. Even this drop of kindness evaporated when Elsie married and went to live in Leek. Peter, the adopted son, went with her and so Nancy and her mother were entirely reliant on the evacuees for help. By the age of nine Dennis could tack up and ride a horse, prepare it to pull the cart and generally handle it with any equipment on the farm.

Some of the children received visits from their parents and Dennis observed how calculatingly delightful Aunt Nancy could be in their presence. But as soon as they had gone her true character would re-emerge. One or two children left but the majority stayed. In all the four years Dennis and Pat received only a couple of visits from their parents, in the early days. Then one day in 1944, apparently out of the blue, Grannie Thomas and Leslie, their father, turned up at the farm without warning. 'Get your clothes, we're going home,' Leslie announced. 'That was a bit of a shock, really,' Dennis explained. 'We had absolutely no idea they were coming to fetch us and although I'd got used to the life at the farm and could handle Aunt Nancy by now, I was just thrilled to see my grandparents again and to be going home with them was the best thing that could have happened to us.'

The surprise was to grow when the children learned that their parents had split up and a decision had been taken that Pat would go to live with Bessie, their mother, and Dennis would go back to Moss Side and live with his grandparents and his father. Pat was mortified. 'I didn't know her. I was just dumped on my mother and left to live there. She left me at home when she went out to work and all I wanted to do was to run "home" to Dennis.'

The result of her miserable experience of living at Mount Pleasant Farm was that Pat found it very difficult to form close relationships with people and to trust them. Her first marriage ended prematurely when her husband died of a heart attack. Although she loved her children, she said, she found herself unable to show her feelings towards them. Her second husband, John, explained: 'Pat had serious attachment problems. She could never show affection to her children even though she felt love for them "inside". She had never had love shown to her so she did not know how to express it to others. It would not be wrong to say that evacuation at the age of four shaped her life and affected her from then onwards.'

Pat once went back to Mount Pleasant Farm to see if she could make any connections there or revive any memories but she was unable to do so. Her only comment was that the house was much smaller than it had been in her memory. Dennis too returned, on a separate occasion, about ten years after the war. By that time Aunt Nancy's mother had died and to his surprise Aunt Nancy had married. Her husband was much older than she was and she waited on him hand and foot. When he died he was buried in the local churchyard, as was Nancy's mother. Dennis visited the churchyard and saw that the old lady's grave had no headstone, just the husband's. He learned later that when Aunt Nancy died a former evacuee, who had gone to live in Canada after the war, came to her grave and danced on it, so bitter were his recollections of what she had done to the children at Mount Pleasant Farm during the war.

Dennis concluded,

In fact, I don't think it really affected me at all except that it really made me appreciate my home life with my grandmother. Without her the family would have disintegrated. I think it also made me determined to succeed. I have always been a very strong character from the word go and it was my grandfather, and not my father, who was the role model in my life. It was he I looked up to. And my grandmother was far more of a mother to me than Bessie ever was. I was her young son and she my 'mother'. When Bessie and my father died I was sad, of course, but when my grandmother died I was devastated. She and my grandfather had shaped my life.

When Dennis left school he wanted to become a butcher but that did not work out. So he got a job in a warehouse until he went into the RAF to do his national service. There he was in the motor transport section and this seemed to him to be a good fit. When he left the RAF he took a course in engineering, joined the motor trade, launched his career and has never looked back.

If physical and emotional abuse occurred for

some children and its legacy has stayed with them ever since, for others it is the spectre of sexual abuse that lurks in their memories and continues to haunt them. A few stories came to light during the war when prosecutions were brought, as they were in Swanage in October 1941 when a man was jailed for twelve months for indecently assaulting three evacuee children in his care. The claim he made that he was using the children as 'human hot water bottles' was not accepted by the jury.[16] However, in the main the stories came out only years, often decades later, when the evacuees who were tormented were finally able to speak about their experiences.

Joan Zilva grew up in an emotionally constrained household where one result of her parent's unsatisfactory marriage was that her father discouraged her from kissing her mother on the grounds of hygiene. She was an only child. 'My father was a research biochemist of Jewish extraction with numerous relatives so that I grew up spending most weekends with a surfeit of aunts surrounded by what seemed to me as a child at the time an atmosphere of uncontrolled emotion and chaos.' Her mother was the daughter of a non-practising Methodist family in Leeds who, on her father's encouragement, had read history at Cambridge before becoming a health visitor in London, which is how she met Joan's father.

For the first few months of the war Joan and a friend were educated by their mothers. The friend's mother had been a teacher before she got married. At least half of the children at the school in Croydon she had attended before the war had been evacuated to the south coast but Joan's parents had not thought it necessary for her to go. Eventually the school was relocated to Purley and Joan spent the rest of the academic year there.

However, as the invasion of Britain became more likely Joan's parents decided that Jews would not fare well under a Nazi regime. Joan, at fourteen, was old enough to know that if there were an invasion the family might end up in a concentration camp. So her parents took advantage of an agreement between the universities of Cambridge and Toronto and she was duly evacuated on the *Duchess of Atholl* in August 1940. On arrival she was sent to live with a wealthy family. From the outset it was a disaster as the couple, who had no children of their own as they had lost twins before the war, had nothing in common with their evacuee, who, at the awkward age of fourteen, was timid, anxious and bitterly unhappy. Mrs H was cold and Joan said that she liked her least of anyone she had met in her life thus far. Mr H seemed a warmer character than his wife but that brought with it its own problems. Mrs H was 'a glamorous housewife who talked and thought of nothing but coats, hats and clothes'. On the third day Joan was taken on a three-hour shopping expedition to buy hats with Mrs H. Nothing could have been further from the way of life she was used to in Croydon and she found that whenever she spoke about it to Mrs H, in particular her enthusiasm for the Girl Guides, she met blank stares. Mrs H wanted to dress Joan up in pretty clothes and treat her like a six-year-old child. It appalled her and it made her want to cry. The clash of cultures was clearly felt on both sides.

She wrote home to say that if she did not see her parents after six months she thought she would almost certainly die, so unhappy did she feel in this enormous, smart house where fridges, two cars, double beds in every room and fresh wallpaper had replaced her familiar home. As news came of the increasingly severe bombing of London so Joan became more and more anxious for her parents. She wrote to them in a letter on Sunday 8 September 1940:

> Almost every night I dream that the war is over, and that I am either coming home or am home. I nearly cry when I wake up and find myself still here, and I go down and read in the paper of nothing but air raids on London. I get a beastly sort of feeling in my throat when I think that it may be years before I see you again, and that you may now be sitting in an air-raid shelter. Whenever I do anything, I think of the times I did it at home, and wonder when I shall do it there again. Time seems to go so slowly. It is under two months since I left you, but it seems like two years, and the thought of two years seems like centuries.[17]

Not long after Joan wrote this letter things with Mr H became complicated. He was the one member of the household who seemed prepared to treat Joan like the teenage child she was. She grew to quite like him: 'He does his very best to make me happy,' she wrote to her parents. 'He plays Chinese Chequers with me the evenings he's home, takes me for drives, and tells me funny stories. He never misses a night to kiss me.'[18] The kissing soon got out of control as Joan explained in her autobiographical writings sixty years later:

'Kiss me' hides a multitude of sins! In fact, he came up after I was in bed every evening, felt me all over and French kissed me at length. I was physically mature but knew nothing about the sexual act. I only knew there was something wrong, but thought it was just me. The fact that I didn't mention it in my letters shows that I was confused and I said I liked him because I had to like someone and he, at least, was kind to me, whatever the motives. I think that Mrs H knew and thought I was leading him on.[19]

Joan wrote to the man in charge of the scheme between Cambridge and Toronto and a few weeks later she was moved to another family in the city but the saga with Mr H continued. Mr H had written to her parents to complain that their daughter was cold and unresponsive. Her parents, who were of course quite unaware of Mr H's attempts to seduce Joan, reproached her for upsetting her Canadian hosts. Joan had already begun to feel guilty that she had asked to be moved and now she was left with the feeling that somehow she was to blame. The fact that she could not talk about it to anyone else at the time underlined her certainty that there was something wrong.

Eventually, after two and a half reasonably happy years with her second foster family, the Bartletts, she managed to convince her family and the authorities to let her come home. She was by now seventeen years old and it was May 1943. Although the war was far from over and the dangers in London were to grow rather than diminish during 1944 they allowed her to return. She remembers calling them from Victoria Station to say she was looking forward to a breakfast of bacon and eggs and to being collected from the station by car, which provoked hollow laughter since rationing of food and petrol made both impossible.

> I had expected to see both my parents, but on the almost deserted platform was my father, but not my mother. She had been ordered to stay at home in case I phoned. My father and I did not kiss, touch or show any outward emotion and as we walked home I can remember my sinking heart as he said that he couldn't understand my accent. Here was I was, after years of waiting, battling and longing, at home and yet a foreigner in my own country. Then the goal was achieved. As we turned into our own drive, so long remembered and longed for, my mother was waiting impatiently on the doorstep and I got the first welcome hug and kiss since I had left Liverpool nearly three years earlier.[20]

Although relations with her father continued to be strained and never improved she always felt that the decision her parents took to evacuate her to Canada was a difficult one for which they could not be blamed. 'I have never regretted returning when I did. I was old enough to have foreseen that life would not be easy and young enough to take each day as normal, even if, by today's standards, life was unimaginably difficult and hazardous. Our parents were the most deserving of sympathy; they had experienced two major wars in their adult lives.'[21]

The main concern for Joan was her final exams at school. She was intelligent and determined to go to university to study medicine. However, just before the examinations the V bombs began to fall on London and Croydon was badly hit. This time the school decided that pupils should be evacuated once again. Joan pointed out that this was not just for their safety but also for fear that they might cheat in their exams when in the shelters. This time she was sent to Llandeilo in Wales, west of the Brecons and out of harm's way. Her parents joined her there after a flying bomb landed in the back garden of their house. On her return to London she learned, to her shock and sadness, that Mrs Bartlett, the second foster mother she had lived with in Canada, who had been extraordinarily kind to her after her experience with the Hs, had died very suddenly after an operation at the age of fifty-six. To her it felt like a family bereavement.

That year Joan went to medical school. She had a long career in medicine and was a consultant and professor in chemical pathology at the Westminster Hospital and Medical School. Looking back over her life she concluded that the experience in Toronto, coupled with her difficult relationship with her father, left her unable to form close relationships:

I never married, though came close to it: I desperately wanted to and to have children,

331

but when it came to commitment I was wary. In my youth most of us did not sleep around and for a long time I was uncomfortable with physical intimacy, especially of the kind I had received from Mr H. I think that this was the greatest influence of those years. I have, also, always felt an outsider and have found it difficult to believe that I could be loved for myself: I desperately want affection, but find it difficult to respond . . . I have always felt on the outside of other people's families, as I did in Canada, however kind they may be. I am lonely when others talk of their families. On the plus side, I learnt self-reliance, which, for an only child, is a valuable asset. My outlook was broadened and I have many good Canadian friends. I adapt to the customs of others more easily that some do. I do, however, feel that I must always be in the wrong unless I am totally sure of my facts, and this may express itself as apparent aggression. All in all, I do feel that the war undermined my self-respect and confidence in the responses of others to me, but that there were also very positive aspects to my experiences.[22]

Rose Clarke had a similar experience to Joan Zilva. Her first foster family was warm and kind to her. There were children of her own age and although she was an anxious child by nature she settled down well in Wales and the greatest concern was whether she could keep up her schoolwork to a sufficient level that it would not suffer when she got back to London. In 1941, without any explanation as to why, she was moved from her first foster family to a second home several miles away. This was an altogether different and deeply unpleasant experience. To begin with she was treated like unpaid help and was expected to look after the younger son and clean the shoes of the older boy. This demeaning workload continued and the children of the house soon became used to treating Rose as if she were a maid. In addition to the two sons there was a thirteen-year-old daughter, M, in the family. As the girls were the same age the parents had put them into a room together where they had to share a bed. Rose would wake up on cold nights to discover that all her bedclothes had been stolen and she was called names and subjected to low-level but insidious bullying on a daily basis. All this could perhaps have been stomached if it had not been for the church youth club:

Each week, M and I went to the church youth club. The club leader kept the room in virtual darkness and then proceeded to sexually abuse us to differing degrees. Looking back I suppose I was fortunate personally, as I was not subject to too much, other than the man fondling me. But some of the others experienced much more. I knew it was wrong but there was no one to tell and I was always afraid of getting other people into trouble. I suspect too, that it was a comfort to think, somewhat misguidedly, that someone liked me when no one else seemed to. I was also sworn to secrecy by the bully, M, who used to pinch me to enforce the point.[23]

The exploitation of children in an environment that might once have been considered to be secure—a church youth group—is not new. An experienced social worker, on reading this story, commented: 'Children who have been sexually abused often feel guilty about the feeling they experienced—but the adults have clearly exploited children who are vulnerable and the guilt means children do not "tell". Paedophiles are very skilled at picking children out who they can use and also very skilled at putting the blame on the child.'

For all the years she lived away from London, Rose never cried. She promised herself that she would not give in to her emotions either in private or public: 'I was too much hurt inside to let my feelings out,' she said. The result was that this bottled up emotion caused all sorts of problems later on when she found herself unable to express her feelings, unable to talk about what had happened to her and unable to trust anyone in a relationship: 'Overall, physically, I did not suffer unduly. I enjoyed the countryside and the new experiences. I loved the sound and the feel of the Welsh language and especially the male voice singing. However, I did not fare well emotionally, as I was already a very nervous and anxious child. I think the fact that I never felt able to talk to anybody about my fears did not help. Also, although very immature in many ways, I felt like a premature adult.'[24] When she went back to living with her mother and siblings she found it almost impossible to re-establish her relationships with them. Quite often she would break down and cry for no reason, something that her mother could not understand and found increasingly irritating.

334

The sense of distance grew between mother and daughter.

Untangling the sad and complicated layers of Jennifer Renter's past has taken a lifetime. A concatenation of circumstance and personal traits led to a deeply troubled adolescence. When Jen left Hastings along with hundreds of other local children on 21 July 1940 she was already an anxious child. Her early childhood had been mostly happy, although her father was a part-time heavy drinker, which had a dire impact on his various attempts at a career. 'Most of the time he was a marvellous father,' she said. 'He repaired our shoes on a shaped iron, could turn basic ingredients into a gourmet meal and would help my mother with the washing but when he had a drinking session it was as though he was bent on self-destruction.' Nevertheless something that he cherished was his children's education and, unusually for the era, he was as keen that Jen should receive a good education as he was that his son Fred should go to the grammar school. So Jen took the eleven-plus and passed in 1939.

That September she had her first premonition of disaster. It was 3 September. Her mother had taken her to the cinema and they watched the Pathé News when Chamberlain announced that Britain was at war with Germany. Jen had a terrible, desperate feeling that this meant something sinister beyond her childish experiences. She could not articulate it but she wanted to go home immediately. Her mother, who had paid to watch the film, wanted to stay. So they did. But all the while Jen was worrying. Later that day she saw the first London evacuees arriving in

Hastings and remembers asking her mother what it was all about: 'Poor little children,' her mother replied. 'They had had to leave their mummies and daddies and come away from London.' Jen's family was poor and lived in a tiny flat so that there was no room to take evacuees since all the available sleeping space was already occupied. The evacuation meant almost nothing to her at that stage. Ten months later the London evacuees left Hastings and two weeks later she and hundreds of other children set out from the coast for safety inland. They had no idea where they were going and since the names of the train stations had been removed to confuse the Germans it was only when they disembarked at their final destination that she learned they had been deposited in Hertfordshire.

Jen was sent to one home and then to a second billet, where she stayed for four and a half years. 'This couple were East Enders from Bow in London. They had been sent down to Hertfordshire on a scheme for rehousing the slums. They had one son who was younger than I was. They spoke in rhyming slang and half the time I did not know what they were talking about.' But the family was kind and they determined to draw her into their world. She soon learned rhyming slang and although the household was poor and the accommodation basic, Auntie fed her properly; in this she was more fortunate than many of the other girls from Hastings who had ended up on the same council estate.

Jen had the sense that she was being subsumed by her foster family and losing her privacy and her own identity. It was not, she felt, unkindly meant, it was just that it suited them to mould her into a familiar type that they could handle. All the while she was desperate to see her mother and in their copious correspondence they wrote incessantly about how she could afford the ticket to see Jen and her brother, Fred, who was living in St Albans, 13 miles away, the place that now housed Hastings Grammar School. There was not sufficient money for Jen to go back to Hastings for the Christmas of 1940 but in the spring of 1941 Jen's mother finally managed to make the journey to see her two children. It was a joyous reunion: 'I can't remember the date but I know I waited for her all day and when I saw her coming up the long road I ran like the wind to meet her and saw her brace herself to withstand the impact as I threw myself at her. After a long cuddle my tongue was loosed and I could not stop talking as I held onto her.' This heavenly visit was over all too soon but Jen's mum promised to return and this time she would come to Jen first and take her over to St Albans to meet up with Fred.

Not long after that first visit the Germans began dropping their loads on the coast as they returned from bombing London. It was in one of these raids that the cinema where Jen's mother worked as a cleaner was hit. She was thrown across the street but was apparently unhurt. A fortnight later her foster mother received a letter from Jen's father. As Jen carried it through to her 'Aunt' she had a terrible premonition that her mother had died. Auntie retired upstairs to read the letter. Jen was eventually called for: 'I remember climbing those stairs but I can't remember who told me my mother was dead. I started to cry and just couldn't stop. It wasn't just an ordinary bout of crying, it was a terrible, wild wailing that seemed to be coming from someone else.' There was no money for Jen to go back to Hastings for the funeral so she had to stay with her foster family and come to terms with her loss. She recalled that her foster father's attitude was 'Cheer yourself up.'

About ten days after this terrible shock her father came to the house with the dreadful news that her brother had been badly injured in a bicycle accident and was not expected to live. She and her father visited Fred in hospital 'to say goodbye'. This time life took a kinder turn and Fred recovered. After weeks in hospital and even longer convalescing he was back on his feet and almost as fit as he had been before the accident. Two more deaths shook Jen's world that summer. The first was that of Fred's foster mother, who Jen had grown to like on her visits to St Alban's while her brother was recovering. The second was her grandmother who died not long afterwards. She suddenly felt terribly alone and when her own foster family continued to keep her close to them she felt all the more cut off from her old life: 'I was totally absorbed into this family, and for some reason they didn't seem to want me to have a family of my own, and in a way they were right because I had very little else in my life from that other world at all, but I still fantasised about going home one day.'

All of this could have been dealt with in the natural course of life, Jen felt, had not the final twist of the knife occurred. She never told anyone about it:

One night when I'd gone to bed, my foster

338

father came into my bedroom and sat on my bed, which he had never done before and started saying things he'd never said before, and then he kissed me. I was absolutely terrified because it wasn't an ordinary kiss, it hurt my lips against my teeth and I couldn't move to escape from it. He left but I didn't move for hours and hours. I was completely and utterly immobile. I was paralysed with fear. The next time he came back I can't remember whether he kissed me first but he started moving his hands across my body and holding my breasts in his hands. He never raped me but he just used to handle and kiss me. I could never tell anyone.

Gradually she developed insomnia. She would lie awake at night in the fear that he might come to her room again. 'He would stand, silhouetted in the doorway, his arms akimbo on the doorposts before making his way to my bed.' Auntie knew Jen was not well but she did not know what was wrong with her. However, when she took Jen to the doctor and the young woman GP asked her what was worrying her, Auntie said, 'There is absolutely nothing worrying her,' and yanked her out of the surgery. Jen came to the conclusion that her foster mother worked out what was going on but for some reason chose not to, or did not know how to, put a stop to it.

At the end of 1944 Jen persuaded her father that she should come home to Hastings. It was to be her first return visit since she had left in 1940, nearly a year before her mother had died. 'Everything in our house was spotlessly clean.

339

There was nothing in it of ours. He had got rid of every toy I possessed including my teddy bear, and there was no vestige of my mother either. I couldn't bear it. I had waited four and a half years to come back and now I could not bear to be there.' Jen moved in with her grandfather, who lived in a small flat around the corner from her father and the two of them set up home in a state of mutual understanding. He had lost his wife and daughter, she her mother and grandmother.

It was not until Jen met her husband that she was able to fulfil her determination to put the experiences of the war years behind her. She explained:

I have recovered from all this because I was determined to. I felt when I met my husband I had got to marry him. I knew he was the one for me. We got engaged on Easter Sunday, married in September and had children right away. We were married for a long time. He was safe and solid and we stuck to each other. When he died I thought I was going to die too because all this stuff about the war and evacuation came back, this huge sense of insecurity which I have never lost. The betrayal was the thing that came to me through it all. This deep sense of betrayal by my foster father, of course, and somehow by many others, including the authorities responsible for our welfare. I was left with this deep sense of betrayal, abandonment and disillusion. It is so confusing because we were all caught up and moved around in this system of evacuation.

The sense that evacuee children were at the mercy of random circumstances comes up in many stories, but no more so than for three young girls evacuated from a poor home in Hull and sent to live in an isolated farming community in South Yorkshire. The girls were nine, seven and five when they arrived in Hatfield, near Doncaster, in 1939. To begin with the girls were submitted to emotional abuse. The couple, who (scandalously for the time) were not married, went out of their way to suggest to the children that they had been abandoned by the parents and were not wanted. They taunted them with comments and jibes about their parents and the children felt isolated, afraid and intimidated. The farmer was a swindler and a bully. He was also a black marketeer and used to supply the local police, amongst others, with petrol and other black market goods. This fact had a very serious impact on the girls later. Initially they were put to work on the farm and worked hard as free labourers, fed bread and dripping and deprived of all comforts and affection. All this was troubling enough but the three girls shared a bedroom and could comfort one another when they were alone. The unpleasantness grew when the farmer turned his attention to the attraction of having young girls on the farm.

One night, when Marie, the middle daughter, was about ten, the farmer came into their bedroom and began to make overtures towards her. Marie was terrified and screamed for her life. The mistress came running and the farmer scarpered. He never attempted to touch Marie again and was consistently unkind to her for the remainder of the

341

time she was at the farm. But at least the unwanted attention disappeared. Unfortunately, however, he turned to the older girl, who was then twelve, and who had begun to go through puberty. Marie was aware that her sister had developed a new smell about her which the farmer used to complain about. It was the smell of sex she told her interviewer fifty years later: 'that was the smell that was on her and he used to say this to her and I always used to feel sorry for that because there was nothing she could do about it.' Unbeknown to Marie, the farmer had begun to take advantage of her older sister and was spotted by the youngest sister having sex with her behind one of the barns. The little girl, then just eight, did not understand what she was witnessing. She told Marie later that she knew instinctively it was wrong so she kept quiet about it.

Several weeks later at the girls' school a teacher noticed Marie's older sister taking a shower and observed that 'my sister was an abnormal shape for a girl of her size. So they put my sister in the car and took her back to the farm and said to the farmer's wife, would you please take her to the doctor's. The doctor lived in Doncaster and away she went to the doctor's and she never came back. We wondered why. Nothing was said to us. There was quite a lot of talk and the police were round but initially we were kept strictly out of the way.'

The police then questioned both girls but could not get to the bottom of the story. Marie had seen nothing, and even though her little sister had, she did not talk. She explained to Marie later in life that she had lived in fear of making their lives at the farm even more unpleasant so she did not tell

342

anyone she'd seen the man having sex with their sister several times in the barns. So in the end, when pressed by the police, she said she had seen an airman kissing and cuddling with her sister. She knew it was a lie but it got her off the hook.

At the time that their older sister was taken away from the farm their father was in prison so there was little he could do for his daughter. When Marie's mother and grandmother came to the farm to see what was going on they were chased away by the farmer and told they would not be allowed to see the two little girls. It would seem, from conversations held much later, that the villagers who lived around the farm and who had children at the same school were well aware that the farmer and his 'wife' were mistreating their evacuees. One woman said later that she had been so concerned for the safety of the little evacuees from Hull that she had thought of reporting the farmer to the authorities but the fact that he was a man with powerful friends in the police meant that no one who complained about him stood much chance of being believed. So a situation that was clearly desperate for the children involved was allowed to go unchecked.

Marie's older sister was sent to a home where she had her baby who was then taken away from her for adoption because she refused to name the father of the child. He turned out, Marie explained, to be a very difficult and disturbed little boy who got into endless trouble and scrapes in his life. This she attributed to his father.

As a result of her evacuation Marie felt guilty and anxious all her life. When she had children of her own she was unable to let them out of her sight. Sending them away to camp was unthinkable and she was always on the lookout for someone who might be intent on doing something evil towards them. Her evacuation has affected her whole life and left her with a great sense of bitterness and distrust of people. She felt sure that people who met her would know about her sad past, about her father's prison background and her sister's illegitimate baby. She felt guilty that she had not known what was going on with her older sister and had not been able to put a stop to it. She also felt deep, intense hatred and revulsion towards the farmer who had destroyed her sister's life and scarred hers and her little sister's for ever. Most of all, she said, she was incredibly angry that her sister was so afraid of him that she would not name him as the father of her child. 'He destroyed four lives and he got away with it. He was never named for his crimes.'

These distressing cases of abuse are the exception in the evacuation story. However, accounts of abuse have been late in coming to the fore. Stephen Davies suggested that it could take decades for submerged memories to rise to the surface. Understandable reluctance, fear of reprisals, guilt and feelings of shame have all played a part in suppressing them, as has the inability to find ways to articulate those memories. One historian of evacuation who lectures regularly has been surprised that in recent years an increasing number of ex-evacuees, a high proportion of whom are men, tell her that they were emotionally, physically or sexually abused as evacuees. She said, 'It was clearly more prevalent than one imagined. So sad that these children have had to live with the horror of those memories for a lifetime.'

10

FORGOTTEN VOICES

Here are your children . . . Mother and I have loved them with all our hearts. We ask you to keep alive their loyalty to us as we have kept alive their loyalty to you—may they never forget that they have two homes.

Hosts of Rex and Anita Cowan to their parents

As the Second World War drew to a close—there was no sudden end as there had been in 1918—children began to make their final journeys home. Their return coincided with a series of interlinked events: the cessation of hostilities first in Europe, then three months later in the Far East; a general election in June 1945 that gave the Labour Party a landslide victory; the return over the next twelve months of 4.5 million servicemen, many of them fathers of children who had been evacuated and, at the same time, the ushering in of a period of austerity as Britain, almost bankrupted by war, tried to adjust to peacetime conditions. There was no time, no energy, no desire to assess the impact of the war on children's lives any more than there was to consider the impact of the war on society as a whole. It was something the Cambridge Evacuation Survey had argued was highly desirable but now the war was over people were focused on looking forward, not backwards. People were encouraged to put up and make do. It is therefore

346

not surprising that for children, families and foster families the whole subject of evacuation was set to one side.

As the children left the countryside and Britain began to re-establish itself there was a great deal of readjusting to be done. First and foremost, family life, still considered the mainstay of society, had to be rebuilt. Over 1 million families were without homes as a result of the bombing; over 500,000 children had never met their fathers, and many of those who had been evacuated at a very young age had little memory of their fathers even if they had known them before the war; rationing got worse, not better, and the overriding message to all was 'get on with it'.

Of the 3 million British evacuees, just 55,000 were officially repatriated by the government in 1945. A year later, on 31 March 1946, when evacuation, to all intents and purposes, came to an end, there were only 5,200 unaccompanied children left in all reception areas of England and Wales, a figure smaller than forecast by the Ministry of Health who three months earlier in Parliament had estimated twice that number. About 3,000 were living with foster parents, 1,000 were in residential nurseries and special schools and the rest were in hostels of various kinds.

So where did the former evacuees fit into this pattern of life in post-war Britain and how did the foster families and communities come to terms with their leaving in 1945? Undoubtedly many were very sad to see the children go home, children who had been part of their lives and communities, had sung in the church choirs, played in school concerts, worked on the local farms and established firm friendships with local children. Those families are almost never mentioned, except in personal memoirs, yet there were hundreds of thousands of them. One woman told Norman Longmate in 1975 that she did not know who cried more when the two little sisters that had been billeted with her mother had to go home. They had arrived late at night in Sherborne, cold, frightened and in rags, terrified they were going to be drowned when they were first put into a bath. A year later when they left they had become contented and treasured members of the family, 'particularly delighting in frequent baths'. Their foster mother was absolutely devastated by their parting, as were the girls. A significant number of foster parents attempted to adopt children who had been in their homes and some, but not all, were successful.

Few children had any understanding of the impact their return home would have on their host families. Clara Smith was eleven when the war ended. She said:

We did not manage to get home until just before VJ Day, 15 August 1945, as there was so many children's homecomings to be organised. When the coach arrived to take us to the station and HOME, I did not even wait to say good-bye, but just ran and jumped onto the coach. I now realise how wicked my actions in doing so were, as we had spent all those years with Mrs Harris and she must have formed some attachment to us, as proved in later years, as she always wanted and did keep in touch.

348

Earlier in the war Peter Shepherd was equally hasty in leaving his foster family. He had been evacuated once in 1939, at the age of seven and for a second time in 1940, this time to Nantyglo in South Wales. He was very happy with his foster family, the Lewises, but he missed his parents, so that when his mother came for a visit in 1941 he was so emotional about her leaving him again that when she offered to bring him home, he accepted. They left in a great hurry and he knew that he had upset Mrs Lewis, who could not understand why he was so anxious to get away. For years he felt an overwhelming need to go back but for one reason or another he did not. Then in 1989 he finally revisited Nantyglo:

Everything looked a lot smaller than I had imagined . . . The people were still friendly however and many would say hello as I passed them even though I was a complete stranger. I had a strong yearning to make some contact with my former foster family. I eventually made contact with Rae, Mrs Lewis's granddaughter, who was 6 years old when I was there and who was now in her mid-50s. I was surprised that she remembered me after 50 years as she was only a very young child at the time. It was very exciting as she was able to bring me up to date with all the events that had happened over all those years. My two foster parents had died over 20 years ago and also one of their sons, Eddie. The other three children, Tom, Winnie (Rae's mother) and Griff were still alive. They all wanted to see

349

me again. I was thrilled with this so we arranged a meeting at the old pub where my enquiries first started. They were all waiting for me. We greeted each other with open arms. It was a highly emotional moment for me. We each brought out our old photographs to show how we used to look. For a brief moment I felt I was being transported back in time. Some of the old emotions I felt as an evacuee came flooding back. It was a most strange experience, difficult to put into words. A sense of nervousness and excitement combined.[1]

Sadly Peter never had the opportunity to talk to his foster mother again and explain why he left in such a hurry.

Michael Bailey, who similarly left his foster family in a rush when he was called back to London by his mother at Christmas 1940, plucked up the courage, twenty-four years later, to return to Wootton Rivers in Wiltshire where he had been so happy with the Carter family for six months. He told his story in 2001:

Late summer and early autumn 1940 were with us. I had been with the Carters for three months already. Very late nights reaping the corn. Physically I was feeling great, I had a nice tan and my scurvy face had long gone. I was healthier now than at any time of my life. I now went everywhere with Mr Carter. I think he partly accepted me as his son, he certainly treated me as such and I looked upon him as a father.

Now Mrs Carter: I don't think I could ever find words good enough to describe her. I fell in love with her from the first moment I set eyes on her at the village school on the first day I arrived. My love and affection grew for her, she would sit down in the evenings with me and I would enjoy talking and playing word games, something I had never been used to before I came to the farm. She had everything a child could wish for, YES, she became my loving mother.

In December 1940 Michael was told by Mrs Carter that he and his sister Dolly, who was billeted in the manor house nearby, would be going home for Christmas.

We got to our home about nine o'clock, back to the old dock area. The first thing we came across was sheets hanging up in the front room and it was dark and smelly. As we opened the door to the kitchen my mum was sitting on the floor with my two young sisters by the fireplace. Mum wasn't looking too clean and my sisters only had their vests on and they looked filthy. It looked as though they hadn't seen soap or water for months.

I felt sickened. What had I come home to? Were the beds just as dirty? Was it still bug-ridden, rat and mice infested? The man that my mum was living with came home from shift work. He was just as filthy, they all seemed to blend together quite well. I could have cried.

Mum was now getting back to her vicious

ways and we were quite frightened of her. A few days had gone by, then I asked my mum, 'When am I going back to Mrs Carter?' The biggest shock of my life came when she said 'You are not going back any more'. . . I was heartbroken.

Michael left school at fourteen and then worked in various jobs until he was called up into the RAF in Compton Bassett in Wiltshire, some 16 miles from Wootton Rivers. He thought about dropping in to see the Carters but could not muster the courage:

The Carter family had still never left my memory. I told the story of my evacuation so many times. It was on one of these occasions—my cousin Violet and husband had a car and said they would take me to Wootton Rivers. It was Easter 1964. I told my family to wait at the canal bridge just in case I got rejected. I walked up the lane to the farm. After knocking twice the door was opened by Mrs Carter. I said, 'Could you spare me a minute? I know you won't remember me.' Before I could say any more she said: 'You are Michael.' She said, 'Come in and I'll call Mr Carter.' I was now so excited. Mrs Carter said we were welcome there any time. I didn't want to lose contact now.

The bond, which had been so warmly formed in 1940, was not broken and Michael felt grateful to the end of the Carters' lives that they had been so kind and welcoming to him. He remained in touch and continued to visit the village twice a year, even after they died, always making a point of going to their graves in the local churchyard to pay his respects and say a few words of thanks.

Other couples who fostered children left stories behind. Stanley and Linda Miller were a childless couple in their late twenties at the outbreak of the war. They lived in Church Street in Chard, a typical Somerset village where the terraced houses were made of stone and the street ran into the village centre in one direction and directly out to the fields in the other. In 1939 they agreed to foster two little girls, Pamela Elwood and her younger sister, Jessica, who arrived a few days after her sister, having recovered from a bout of chicken pox. On her arrival in Church Street, Jessica Elwood announced through her gap-toothed smile: 'I thall thoon be thix.'

For the Millers the little girls became the family they never had: 'When little things went wrong we felt responsible for moulding their characters. So that when they left us they would be as good as when they came to us. We could, of course, never guarantee their safety, but felt they were safer with us than in London. I suppose it could be said that whilst we were trying to teach the little girls the right way to live, we were, ourselves, learning about life.'[2]

As the war drew to a close the girls had to return to London and they all felt bitterly sad. For the Millers it was particularly stark because they were left with what Stanley described as 'a great void in our hearts'. Even though the girls kept in touch and continued to visit the Millers as they grew up and had their own children, nothing could diminish the fact that for four years they were a family and then suddenly Stanley and Linda Miller went back to being a childless couple.

John and Iris Allis fostered a ten-year-old girl, Lilly, from Bow. She came to their family farm in Devon as a nervous stick of a child with wispy, tangled fair hair and bright-blue eyes that had a permanent look of fear in them. The Allises already had three children, two of whom were grown up but one, their son Jim, was just two years older than Lilly. At first there was friction and resentment between the two children and it took Iris a long time to talk Jim into being tolerant of their young 'vaccie'. Gradually Lilly began to feel at home and Iris was delighted to see how she put on weight and lost the hunted look in her eyes. By the spring of 1940 Lilly had developed a natural instinct for life in the countryside and she had settled into the local school. In March, Iris received a letter from Lilly's mother saying she was coming down to collect her.

> I had this uncomfortable sense that things would not go right for Lilly if she left us but there was nothing I could do, so I told her that her mum was coming to collect her. She seemed to accept it and we packed her bags. Off she went the next day, almost without a backward glance. Her mother did not come into the house; she merely stood at the door and waited. I was sad that there was no display of affection, no hug for Lilly. After all they had not seen one another for nearly six months.

Iris Allis thought that was the last she would see

of her little 'vaccie' and she was surprised how much she missed her. She was even more surprised that Jim seemed to miss her too. As news of the Blitz on London filtered through, Iris thought about Lilly and wondered how she was managing. Then, in November, she received a letter asking if Lilly could come back to the country as the bombing was getting more serious. The Allises collected her from the station in the first week of December. Lilly was pale and thin but clearly thrilled to be back in Devon and she soon settled happily into life on the farm and everyone was pleased she had returned. The child would never be drawn on the subject of her life at home, she only said that both her parents worked. Her father was a casual labourer and her mother worked in a factory. There were several older siblings, one of whom was in the Merchant Navy. Letters from home were few, parcels fewer, but Lilly seemed completely content in Devon. Iris said:

In late 1942 we decided we should try to adopt her. John and I didn't quite know how to approach the subject so I spoke to the vicar and he told me to talk to my doctor who passed me onto a social worker who warned me that it would be very difficult. I wish I'd listened more carefully to what he said but I had made up my mind I wanted to give this little girl a happy, healthy life. So eventually I plucked up the courage and wrote to Lilly's mother and father, suggesting that as she was so happy and settled in the country they might consider allowing us to adopt her. For weeks we heard nothing and then suddenly, out of the blue, in early 1943 a man knocked on the door and demanded to see his daughter.

Iris was taken aback by the anger in the man's voice so she summoned John who was working in the yard. Lilly's father was standing with his arms firmly crossed in front of the door, not moving but also not coming in. 'John tried to encourage him to come in and engage in a conversation but he was adamant he had come for his daughter and we people had no business interfering in his daughter's life, trying to turn her head with our country ways. She would be coming home with him that day and she would never be allowed to contact the Allises again.' Lilly came back from school to see her father and John Allis arguing in the garden. She ran to Iris for comfort but her father pulled her away. 'It was a terrible scene and I felt so sorry for the child. She was being torn in two directions at once. It was awful.' Eventually Lilly's father turned to John Allis and announced that he would return in two hours to collect Lilly and all her belongings and take her back to London.

He was as good as his word and Iris never saw Lilly again. Her last memory is of Lilly walking away from the farm, holding her father's hand and waving to her with an expression of deep fear on her face. 'I'll never know what happened to that child, whether she lived or whether she was killed in the bombing. I had a very strong sense of foreboding, however.' After the war Iris made some efforts to track Lilly down but the part of Bow where the family had been living had been badly damaged in the bombing and all contact with her was lost. The school could not help as they had

356

no record of her beyond 1944 when she had left. Jim Allis, Iris's son, knew that it bothered his mother off and on until the end of her life that her little 'vaccie' might have had a very different life if only they had been able to adopt her.

Foster parents were always in a difficult position, a tight-rope act as one described it. The attitude the foster mothers adopted towards the evacuees could have a major impact on the relationship and the future. If they were motherly and they offered a child unconditional love and total security they risked usurping the place of the natural parents and incurring their wrath, as Iris Allis clearly did, and causing pain for all three, mother, foster mother and child. However, if it was a kindly but distant relationship, then the children were starved of affection and they ran the risk of feeling unloved. In an era when overt displays of affection were less common this led some children to feel that they were being held at arm's length. Many talked about how they wished they could have been embraced and kissed and how they missed the warm physical contact of their own parents.

One girl who had been evacuated to Canada said: 'Not having anyone to hug or relax with made me bottle up feelings, which then threatened to be overwhelming. I do feel that I was affected adversely by the separation from my own parents.' Others felt they had no right to 'bother' their foster parents and withheld affection which they might otherwise have shown and later came to regret the fact that their coolness might have been misinterpreted as ungrateful behaviour. 'How can I pay tribute to all this goodness?' one former evacuee wrote to Faith Coghill in 1991, 'such kindness, trust and sheer hard work expended on one rather unresponsive child? It must indeed have been, at times, thankless and saddening work. At the time I was only half aware of the efforts made on my account. I can see now a great unpaid debt.'

When the relationship between evacuee and foster family worked, however, it was often a lasting success and there were several thousand children who never returned to live with their natural parents. Many had reached the age when they would naturally have left school and looked for work, and they found that the countryside offered them more than the cities. Some even seemed to have felt from the moment they arrived in their foster homes that this was for keeps.

Stanley Wilson was evacuated at the age of nine, in May 1941. He was the youngest of four boys from Bootle in Lancashire and was sent to Beguildy near Knighton in Powys and placed with a farming couple, Mr and Mrs Bright and their only son, Harold.

It was a good way of life for a boy. From the day I arrived I was expected to do my duties on the farm and in the house but I also went to school. I learned about the countryside there as well as with the Brights. I used to love Christmas at Beguildy—frosty outside and cosy warm indoors. Yet I didn't forget Bootle and my parents. They wrote to me and I remember the excitement of my monthly parcels from home containing comics and sweets.

In 1945 the Brights moved to a larger farm in Bucknell, 15 miles away from Beguildy and Stanley went with them and from the day he left school he worked for them on the farm. In 1972 he moved into one of the cottages that belonged to the farmhouse and his mother came from Bootle to live with him until her death in 1979. There was no question in Stanley's mind about staying in the countryside since he felt completely at home and in harmony with the way of life: 'I was so lucky. Mr and Mrs Bright and their only son Harold accepted me as part of the family and were very kind to me. How lucky I was to have such a loving home.'

Mrs Bright was a warm and generous woman but she never tried to take the place of Stanley's mother and in many ways that was the secret of the success. When Mrs Wilson used to visit from Bootle, which she did during the war and afterwards, she was always made to feel welcome by the Brights so that Stanley felt no conflicting loyalties. He remembered only one moment of anxiety in the Bright family and that was when he returned to Bootle for his first visit. 'I think Mr Bright was concerned that I would not come back after visiting my parents but he need not have worried. I knew where I wanted to live and I have never wanted to go back to the town.' In 1988 Stanley was presented with a forty-year long-service medal at the West Midlands Agricultural Show. He retired from the farm but still lives in Bucknell: 'As I look back over my lifetime I never did return to the city and to this day I still remain living among the rolling hills of Shropshire and class myself as a true "Shropshire lad".'

Like Stanley Wilson, Gordon Abbott was also evacuated to a farm. An only child, he had been living in a flat in Battersea with his parents when war broke out. At the age of seven he was sent with his primary school to the West Country. After a year with one family he was transferred to live with a childless couple, Mr and Mrs Newton, who lived in Grimscott near Bude in Cornwall. His foster parents soon became 'Uncle' and 'Auntie' and they treated him as one of the family, adopted in all but the legal sense. Gordon grew up on the farm and enjoyed an idyllic childhood milking cows by hand, trapping rabbits, feeding the calves and carrying out chores such as chopping wood or peeling potatoes. 'My foster parents came from a hard-working farming community. They were loyal to their family background and this lifestyle was gradually instilled into me as a young boy and later into adulthood.'

In 1942 the family moved to a larger farm and Gordon went with them. He had received one visit from his parents that year but he did not see them again until after the war. By then he was so completely absorbed by his country existence that the wrench of leaving Cornwall was far greater than it had been to leave London five years earlier. He remembered the pain of leaving his Auntie and Uncle on Bude Railway Station as one of the saddest times in his life. He arrived back in London and felt 'like a fish out of water'. His parents had split up and his mother was living with another man. Fortunately for him his mother realised how desperately unhappy Gordon was in London and she wrote to the Newtons to ask whether they would be able to have him back. It was one of the luckiest things that happened to him and he felt grateful to his mother for being generous enough to recognise his needs and send him 'home'.

'I returned to Shernick Farm and I remained there until after I left school and entered the RAF for my national service.' After five years in the RAF he spent a year at the Kent Farm Institute in Sittingbourne and became a farm manager in Berkshire and later Buckinghamshire. There is no doubt in Gordon's mind that he owed the way his life developed to the foster parents who looked after him as their own son for a decade.

I remained in contact with Uncle and Auntie until their death and they kindly left me a legacy when Uncle died in 1980. I shall always have great respect for them and I loved them dearly, and thank the upbringing they gave me which helped me into my adult life. There have been many stories written by evacuees about their childhood experiences and the effect it had on their lives. Some were happy, some were appalling and some were just unhappy. I was one of the many happy ones and my years as an evacuee from London to the West Country were filled with many wonderful memories.[3]

Other children moved back to the country from the cities as soon as they were old enough to leave home. Kay Dandridge was billeted, with her sister and two cousins, at a big house, the Clock House, at Denchworth near Wantage. Her experiences living with a strict and unlovable woman did not put her off the countryside and she would return regularly to visit the area after the war. On one of these visits she met a young man, who she soon married, and they settled down to live in East Hanney where they stayed until 1997. 'The war made me love the countryside. There is no doubt about that. We grew up in Bow and I was already twelve at the outbreak of the war but I never liked London as a child. I know it's a horrible thing to say, but the war did me a favour in introducing me to the delights of living in the country.'

Patricia Kelly felt the same way. She was evacuated from Manchester to Cressbrook in Derbyshire where she lived with an elderly widow, Mrs Lomas. She lived in Cressbrook for three years until she took her scholarship exam to senior school and was awarded a place at Manchester High School for Girls in June 1942. 'My parents were quite sophisticated townies and so was I in my own way, so that when I first arrived in Cressbrook I didn't find it very easy to settle in.' The house had no electricity and no bath but Mrs Lomas was welcoming and she soon made Pat feel at home. Her parents visited her in Cressbrook and she is amused now by what must have occurred when the families met.

Mrs Lomas was a widow. Her son was a minister and she was very religious. She thought alcohol was sinful. As a child I thought my parents would never go to heaven as they used to drink. My parents were very young by comparison; my mother had been nineteen when they married and was working as a hairdresser in Manchester, running her own salon. It was really as if I inhabited two worlds. The one was Cressbrook—a magical place, so calm and pretty and right in the most beautiful countryside and the other was Manchester, the scene of so much destruction during the war. My bedroom in the cottage in Cressbrook was high in the roof and I could see the red glow in the sky when Manchester and Sheffield were being bombed during the autumn of 1940. Sheffield to the right and Manchester to the left.

That Christmas her father came to bring her home and she witnessed the Blitz at first hand. She was staying with her parents on the nights of 22/23 and 23/24 December when the heaviest raids came. 'It was a terrifying experience; it was a completely different world to Cressbrook, which felt so very far away. We spent the night of the first raid in an underground canal while the world exploded all around us.'

Cressbrook was a haven after the experiences of the Blitz and Pat spent a further eighteen months living happily with Mrs Lomas, receiving visits from her mother and not feeling any sense of conflict between her two complementary worlds of home and safety. When she returned to Manchester to go to the high school she missed Cressbrook but visited Mrs Lomas quite regularly. Once she was old enough she joined a youth group that used to hike in Derbyshire. 'The geography of the place is gorgeous and Cressbrook is almost completely unchanged, even today. I remember so well the smell of the wild garlic and the carpets of bluebells and lily of the valley in the spring.

Although I was glad to be back in the city and surrounded by schoolfriends, I still had a longing for the countryside. As I got older it grew and I slowly began to dislike the idea of settling in the city. I wanted to be in the country.'

After the war her father got a job in Herefordshire as a salesman for Ferguson tractors and she found that there was the perfect mixture of access to towns but glorious countryside, so she and her husband eventually settled in the county where she ran a hairdressing business, as her mother had done before her. 'There is no doubt that my evacuation to Cressbrook changed my life and my understanding of the countryside and it is because of those three years there that I have now settled in the country rather than living in the town. That was the effect of my evacuation. A happy outcome.'

Like Pat, Barbara Southard felt that her evacuation helped to broaden her horizons and it gave her above all a belief that life could be different from what she had been brought up to accept.

When the war broke out Barbara's father was out of work and life at home in Greenwich was tough with little money and domestic unhappiness. There were four children born to the Dawson family within four years and Barbara, at five, was the oldest. Evacuation of a sort happened at the beginning of the war when the family went to live in the Chislehurst Caves in Kent. 'It was a very strange existence because we used to sleep in the caves at night, in a partitioned-off section, so that we were out of the way of the bombers. In the daytime we could be above ground.' That lasted for several months until they were sent to stay with their grandmother in Downham. 'Mum moved about a lot and it was difficult for us to settle anywhere. Eventually Dad got a job as a driver in the RAF and the decision was taken to send us oldest three children away. By this time I was seven years old.' They were taken by bus to King's Cross Station and it was there that a photographer snapped a picture of them huddled together in a forlorn little group, Rosie examining her luggage label and John looking anxious while Barbara sat with her arms around her siblings protecting them.

I have no recollection of that photograph being taken, nor even of getting onto the train that would take us to Northampton, but I do remember being told by my mum to sit between John and Rosie at the very front of the bus and listen out for her when she went upstairs. She said she would stamp her feet on the floor so I would know she was with us. But she never did, of course, and I think I probably knew that she wasn't coming with us but it left me with the feeling that I just desperately wanted to be with her.

The children were split up between two families, John going to an elderly widow while the girls went to a couple who lived in a farm labourer's cottage. She recalls the smell of the house where she and her sister were billeted in 1941.

It smelled of lavender polish and it was a beautifully clean house. That is what struck me when I first walked in through the door and it is a clear memory that has stayed with me ever since. Mr and Mrs Rice were kind people. They were not well off but they were a great deal better off than we were and I remember being amazed by their lovely clean house and clean sheets on my bed. They used to take us for walks on a Sunday afternoon and I learned so much about the countryside. I felt safe with Mrs Rice. She didn't cuddle us but she was kind and she ran a calm home, so very different from what I had been used to. When Mum came to visit us Mrs Rice made her feel welcome.

The children remained in Northamptonshire for eighteen months until their mother came to collect them. Their father had been posted to Ruislip and the family now had a house with a good-sized garden. 'This was the happiest period of my young life, without any doubt. Dad was in the RAF so not around too much and my mum had a job in the local munitions factory so that we had some money for a change. Mum used to take us to the cinema and give us treats, which we had never had before. It was so good to be back with her.' Then things began to fall apart. Her parents had split up as her father had taken on a girlfriend but, after six months of separation, her mother agreed to take her husband back and they returned to live in Greenwich. Life once again became difficult as Barbara's father only had sporadic work. It was a period that stood in sharp contrast to the previous three years. She remained in Greenwich until she married at nineteen, by which time she had been working in an office at Woolworths for four years.

Barbara feels that if evacuation did one thing for her it showed her there was a different way from what she had been used to. 'Mum was lovely. She was a good mother to us but it was very hard for her with so little money.' The very first item Barbara bought for herself when she had a job was a hand-towel so that she could have her own, clean towel when she wanted. When she had children of her own she would always buy them socks in threes so that they could have one clean pair, one to wear and one in the wash.

I look back on my evacuation with fondness. Mrs Rice ran a peaceful home and I liked that. I think it probably helped me to get my values sorted. I realise that for me it is people that count more than material possessions. I like simple things and I love my family. My philosophy has been that if you can think of something that makes others happy then that makes for a better world. Ted and I have always put the family and the children first. I was determined to give them the childhood and life that I would have liked to have had.

The photograph of the three Dawson children, which was chosen for the cover of this book, was unknown to them until 2005 when it appeared in the *Daily Mirror* and was spotted by Barbara's daughter. The Royal Mail used it as a postage stamp in their Britain at War collection and it has appeared in several publications. For Barbara it is an image that reminds her of the conflicting feelings she had as a child when she was evacuated: 'Although I was happy in Northamptonshire and well looked after I never quite lost that nagging sensation of sadness that I would so very much rather have been with my mum, despite all the difficulties of life at home.'

Happy outcomes, sad stories, changed lives—but one thing is quite clear and that is that wartime evacuation has affected the children involved for a lifetime and the fact that so many of them are only now, in their late seventies and eighties, assessing the impact it had on their lives, is perhaps one of the most revealing stories of all. They often attest to it being a period of their lives that remained in sharp focus even as the passing of years blurred other memories.

For Sylvia Mills the years she spent evacuated to Wheatley in Oxfordshire remain fixed in her memory as the happiest time of her life. She can still name all the teachers and children in her class at school. 'It was a really, really lovely experience and I have only got happy memories. The bluebell woods, the fields at harvest time, the walks in the countryside became part of my life. Yet life there was very simple. Mr and Mrs Edwards lived in a house with an outside loo and they grew vegetables in their garden, so they were not a wealthy couple. But they taught me everything I knew and were wonderful.'

Going home was not easy. She had to return to London quite suddenly when Mrs Edwards died and she was disturbed to find that she felt less comfortable with her own parents than she had with the Edwards family: 'I had had a really good, Christian upbringing in Oxfordshire but my parents were different. We seemed not to have the same values any more. My sister was the pet now and I was considered to be the bad 'un in the family. I tried to join the Girl Guides in London, but that was a disappointment. I then joined the Church briefly but that was no better than the Guides, so I gave it all up.' The result was that she continued to be a regular visitor to Wheatley. As soon as her two sons were born she took them to show Mr Edwards and both remember meeting him and having lunch with him on their regular visits. When he died Sylvia was devastated but she is forever grateful to the family that gave her some of the happiest memories of her life.

Josephine Gunn emigrated to America with her new husband in 1952. He had been in the RAF during the war and she had been evacuated as part of the Oxford University scheme to send children to New Haven. Her experience of life in America over the four years was so wholly positive that she knew, when they were offered the opportunity, that it was one they should take.

Had I remained in Oxford during the war, I'm sure I should have had all sorts of different opportunities in my life, but going to America and living with Uncle Paul and Aunt Libby opened my eyes to a quite different world. When we left Britain in 1952 I thought we should probably stay in America for five years but in the end my husband was offered a job in St Louis, Missouri, and we remained, so that our four children could finish their education there. I have never had any doubt that education was of the utmost importance.

It was not merely an academic education that

369

impressed Josephine, it was also the opportunity to benefit from a broad view of the world. By the time they retired to Oregon she had lived in three different states, east, midwest and west coast, and travelled all over the world, as well as keeping up their links with Britain. 'There was no way I could have foreseen any of this happening when I was an evacuee in 1941, but happen it did and I am profoundly grateful for every moment of my life and now of my family's.'

Looking back over the literature and studies on evacuation, there seem to have been three separate strands to the assimilation of evacuation into the story of Britain, and so into the cultural legacy of evacuation. The first is sociopolitical, the second is literary and the third is personal.

In the immediate post-war era the impact of the evacuation programme was on social policy and changes to the Education Act. Richard Titmuss wrote in 1950: 'Evacuation dominated social policy for at least the first nine months of the war. The debate on the condition of the people continued much longer, though on a quieter note . . . it affected in various ways the development of certain welfare services, while the Education Act of 1944 and other legislation bore witness to its deep influence.'[4] The Act introduced a tripartite system of secondary education and made secondary education free for all pupils. Entry to grammar school was selective, based on the old scholarship examination, and renamed the eleven-plus and then there were secondary technical and secondary modern schools to cater for those who were less academically inclined. Until that date only one fifth of all children were studying beyond the then school leaving age of fourteen and one result of the Act was that a greater proportion of children than ever before went on to higher education. The Act also brought with it the additional benefits of free school milk, free medical examinations and transport paid for by the local education authority. Its aim was to take into account the 'whole child'.

The other development, which was partly as a result of evacuation but has also to be seen in the broader context of the war itself, was the change in the government's attitude towards the health and well-being of the population. During the war steps had been taken to increase the numbers of free school meals and free school milk, such had been the shock that the 1939 evacuation had revealed about the state of the cities' mothers and children. It was, however, the Beveridge Report of 1942, with its aim to tackle 'five giant problems—want, disease, ignorance, squalor and idleness'—that laid the foundations for the provision of state welfare, including the National Health Service.

A less noticeable, subtle but fundamental change was felt in the provision of social services. The needs of individuals were considered more carefully and dealt with in a humane way. This contrasted with the treatment of people during the Great Depression and in the period of prolonged unemployment that followed in the early 1930s. Social welfare policy developments after the Second World War laid the bedrock for what we know today.

Reports by psychologists and social welfare officers began to appear both during and immediately after the war but they found it almost impossible to establish common ground, let alone agreement, on the effect of evacuation on the 'child'. It depended on so many different factors that in the end it was not possible to form an overall picture. Some psychiatrists had been at the time and remained post-war vehemently opposed to evacuation. John Bowlby, the British expert on separation anxiety told the *Sunday Times* in 1987: 'Evacuation was a bad mistake and it was the child guidance people who had to pick up the pieces. The result was the writing into the education bill of 1944, the Butler Act, that there be "a child guidance service throughout the country".'[5]

Dame Josephine Barnes, a contemporary of Bowlby's, disagreed and was of the opinion that children had probably even benefited from being evacuated from the cities to the country. She said two years later:

> The idea that the only one who should look after the child is the mother is nonsense. Being sent away from your home could be beneficial. The towns were terribly smoky and dangerous in the 40s and going away to cleaner air definitely improved children's health. In some cases, children were sent to a farm where there were two parents, whereas the children might have only had one in town, especially during the war when the men were away fighting. It taught a child independence. And of course it also taught children how the other half lived—in this case, rural people— which was a good thing. It wasn't always a success but then every real family is not a success, either.[6]

The war had created disorganisation and the separation affecting family life led to difficulties in re-establishing relationships during the post-war years. For some the war had meant excitement, for others stress and anxiety interspersed with long periods of boredom, and, later, many people were conscious of a sense of restlessness, a lack of ability to settle down and resume humdrum ways. All the unusual and varied personal experiences of life in wartime, the different situations and new relationships, and all the new opportunities, obligations and pressures had played a powerful part in shaping the character and personality of children and their parents, all six years older. As such it was almost impossible to isolate a single issue, such as evacuation, and point to how it had affected the children caught up in the war as a whole.

There can be no doubt that the evacuation scheme succeeded in its primary aim, which was to save life. Thousands more civilians would have died had it not been for evacuation. It also served as a safety valve for several million mothers and children, who could leave the cities for the countryside and escape from the bombing for weeks at a time, thus not only putting them out of physical danger but also reducing mental anxiety. This was especially the case during the evacuation in 1944 when Londoners, desperate to protect their children from that most sinister of menaces the V1 Doodlebugs, left in their tens of thousands.

Individual, autobiographical tales did not begin to appear for many years after the war, as the effects of evacuation took years to gain shape within the story of a lifetime. Even then, many chose to write about themselves and others, taking in the broader picture and looking at the overall scheme. The collections of memories are valuable snapshots of the time in which they were published and it is interesting to read, for example, Ruth Inglis's book *The Children's War*, published in 1989, when the people she spoke to were either working or coming up to retirement. Not yet grandparents but looking back on their lives, many were addressing for the first time the whole question of how evacuation had affected them.

Some pointed to behavioural quirks that they only understood with hindsight must stem from their wartime experiences. One woman, who had lost everything in the bombing and had been evacuated twice as a ten- and eleven-year-old, was an inveterate hoarder. She could not bear to throw anything away. Another woman always touched wood many, many times before she travelled on a train. It was only when her daughter-in-law commented on it that she remembered her mother had told her not to worry and to 'touch wood' that they would all be safe at home as she set off for her exciting journey to Wales.

The photographer Penny Tweedie left London in 1944 and was sent to a children's home in Norfolk where she was fed on cabbage and sheep's brains. She was only four at the time and the whole experience made a strong and negative impression on her. Fifty years later, she told Ruth Inglis, the smell of carbolic soap and overcooked cabbage still brings back vivid memories of the horrible experience in Norfolk.

Historian Dr Martin Parsons noticed an

idiosyncrasy in many of the people he interviewed for his research into evacuation and that was an inability to say goodbye. 'I sometimes say to an audience of former evacuees: "How many of you wave until a car or train carrying one of your children disappears out of view?" There is invariably a loud muttering and dozens of hands shoot up. Even seventy years on many of them find parting difficult and do not like to say goodbye.'

It was not, it seems, until the fiftieth anniversary of the end of the Second World War that the former evacuees began to see themselves as a unit or group. In 1995 a small number of them wearing what has become their emblem, the tied-on luggage label, took part in the Great Parade in London and out of that was born the Evacuees Reunion Association. Through its newsletter, conferences and reunions it has encouraged thousands to look back at their evacuation experience, to get in touch with foster families, to contact former fellow evacuees and to meet up. Fifteen years on the interest is greater than ever and when in September 2009 a memorial service was held to mark the beginning of the September 1939 evacuation in St Paul's Cathedral some 2,000 former evacuee children attended.

More attention than ever is given to the 'Children's War' and more wartime children are prepared to speak about their experiences publicly and with enthusiasm. They are welcomed in schools as living examples of the evacuation scheme, there are programmes on television and radio, the BBC People's War website entitled 'Childhood and Evacuation' has more than 550 pages, each with twenty stories, some 10,000 in total and counting. Part of this is due to the extraordinary appetite in Britain for stories about the Second World War but there is also the sense that these children are now assessing the impact of their evacuation not only on themselves but also on their mothers, their families and their own children. Many admit to wondering—when their own children reached the age they had been in 1939 or 1940—what they would have done in similar circumstances. Now they have grandchildren who are learning about their past as a part of history. The subject that was once an element of a personal life is now part of a much larger story.

There are also sub-groups of evacuees which have formed as a result of reunions. The family of the *City of Benares* is a very obvious example. Now numbering less than twenty, they are nevertheless a tight-knit group linked by the worst civilian maritime disaster of the Second World War. The children of the Warren Committee are still linked by the common thread of the generous and energetic spirit of Aunt Sylvia Warren in Massachusetts and the boys who were housed in the camp school at Sayers Croft in Kent held a seventieth anniversary reunion in May 2010 when a dozen out of the boys still living spent three days together talking, listening and reminiscing about their time in the school.

Nearly three-quarters of a century after some three and a half million British children were evacuated from their homes it is clear that the experiences of those weeks, months and years are still alive in the minds of those who went through it. The disruption, the unhappiness and the trauma; the joys, the friendships and the life-changing events are a huge part of what people became post-war. There will always be the question for individual families as to whether parents made the right decision on behalf of their children. And there will always be critics of the government scheme that removed nearly a million schoolchildren from their homes and sent them, unaccompanied, to live with strangers. Also there will always be former evacuee children who felt enormous gratitude to those people who looked after them and helped to enrich their lives. Although there are sad tales and unhappy experiences, a large proportion of the children interviewed for this book, now in their seventies and eighties, wanted to speak about the positive side of their experiences and to emphasise how much they had gained from their foster families. Don Murdoch summed it up when he said:

I am eternally grateful to those kindly couples who took me into their home, shared my joys and sorrows and made me a temporary member of their families at a time my own family was under tremendous pressure. My subsequent life and career was, I believe, profoundly influenced for the better by my experiences as an evacuee. Perhaps one day the nation will acknowledge the thanks it owes to the many thousands of good-hearted ordinary country folk who, for scant reward, upset their domestic arrangements to accommodate children from the cities.[7]

POSTSCRIPT

I am very sad to record that two survivors of the sinking of the *City of Benares*, whose stories are told in chapter 7, Lord Quinton and Bess Cummings, died in June and August 2010 respectively.

ACKNOWLEDGEMENTS

Writing this book has been a journey for me and, I believe, for some of the former evacuees whose stories appear in these pages. Many of the stories told here are revealed for the first time. I am indebted to those who have entrusted their experiences to me and would like to thank them all warmly for adding personal colour to the narrative. They are: Gordon Abbott, Norman Andrews, Robert Arbuthnott, Donald Bayley, Derek Bech, Wally Boater, Barbara Booth, Ron Brandwick, John Brasier, Nigel Bromage, Larry Buxton, Derek Capel, Dorothy Carlile, Beryl Carter, Iris Charos, Doris Cox, Kay Dandridge, Ruth Elliott, Jim Fisher, Patrick Fitzgerald, Faith Garson, Marion Green, Eddie Harrison, John Hay, Ray Hewitt, Patricia Kelly, Eric Knight, Audrey McCormick, Ian McNay, Penny Mare, May Marston, Sylvia Mills, Jessie Nagel, Elizabeth Patterson, Frank Pendlebury, Joan Risley, Bill Rolstone, Sheila Rowe, Juliet Sanger, Sheila Shear, Peter Shepherd, Julie Smith, Barbara Southard, Ann Spokes Symonds, Nigel Stanley, Tim Sturgis, Peter Summers, Audrey Symons, Jean Tabron, Arthur Taylor, Dennis Thomas, Pat Thomas, Shelagh Watkins, Stanley Wilson, Doreen Wright.

*　　　*　　　*

In addition I am very grateful to people who have given me permission to quote from their published and unpublished works and who have given me encouragement and answered my questions. Thank you to Betty Barnes, Felicity Bartleet, Elva Carey, Michael Henderson, Pam Hobbs, Louise Milbourn, James Roffey, Margaret Simmons, David Tett, Mattie Turnbull, Penny Tweedie, Sue Wheatcroft, Shirley Williams and Joan Zilva.

* * *

Several people have been very generous with their time and I wish to thank Chloe Campbell, Martin Parsons, Jonathan Moffatt, Elaine Rockcliffe, and Michele Topham for their feedback and assistance. Warm thanks also to Angela Herlihy, Martin Bryant and Katherine Stanton at Simon & Schuster.

* * *

I have also received help from individuals with expertise and knowledge of different fields including Fran Baker at the John Rylands Library in Manchester, Tina Cunningham at Wycombe Abbey School, Jennifer Glanville at University Museums and Special Collections Services at the University of Reading, Roderick Suddaby, Keeper of Documents at the Imperial War Museum, Keith Andrews, David Fuller, Lucy Garson, Gill Grigg, Charles Hampton, Sean Hollands, Steve Humphries, Angela Kelly, Michael Kinnear, Janet Menzies, Jonathan Moffatt, Clifford Morris and Meg Parkes.

* * *

I extend warm thanks to my agent, Catherine Clarke and my editor Mike Jones. Special thanks also to Stephen Rockcliffe who helped enormously with pictures and research. No book is possible without the support of my family and friends. To Lil, Ali, Jude, Caroline, Zena and Christy I say a big thank you for putting up with me on and off the water. My husband Chris has been a source of enormous strength and sanity and I could not have completed this book without his support.

NOTES

INTRODUCTION

1 These figures are based on Titmuss, Richard, *Problems of Social Policy*, p. 562, and Parsons, Martin, *I'll Take That One*, p. 36: 827,000 unaccompanied primary school children, 524,000 young children and mothers *plus* Titmuss's estimate in the region of 2 million children who were evacuated privately over the course of the war.
2 Henderson, Michael, 'To Escape the Bombing', published in *The Christian Science Monitor*, August 2010, p. 51.

CHAPTER 1

1 Titmuss, Richard, *Problems of Social Policy*, p. 4.
2 Titmuss, p. 5.
3 Hansard, vol. 270, col. 632, House of Commons Debate, 10 November 1932.
4 *The Times*, 28 April 1937.
5 Hansard, vol. 295, col. 859, House of Commons Debate, 28 November 1934.
6 Titmuss, p. 17.
7 Harrisson, Tom, and Charles Madge (eds.), Mass Observation, *War Begins at Home*, p. 23.
8 Harrisson and Madge, pp. 299–300.

9 Harrisson and Madge, p. 303.
10 Harrisson and Madge, p. 298.
11 Harrisson and Madge, p. 23.
12 Crosby, Travis L., *The Impact of Civilian Evacuation in the Second World War*, p. 34; *Spectator*, 8 September 1939.
13 Harrisson and Madge, p. 316.
14 Harrisson and Madge, p. 313.
15 Harrisson and Madge, p. 319.
16 Titmuss, Richard, quoted in Parsons, Martin, *I'll Take That One*, p. 265.
17 Schweitzer, Pam, Andy Andrews and Pat Fawcett (eds.), *Goodnight Children Everywhere*, p. 49.
18 Williams, Shirley, *Climbing the Bookshelves*, p. 26.
19 *The Times*, 30 January 1940.
20 *The Times*, 6 May 1940.
21 Fethney, Michael, *The Absurd and the Brave*, p. 30.
22 Inglis, Ruth, *The Children's War: Evacuation 1939–1945*, p. 137.

CHAPTER 2

1 *The Times*, 4 April 1945.
2 Longmate, Norman, *How We Lived Then*, p. 75.
3 Lin, P. Y., 'Perils Awaiting Those Deemed to Rise above their Alloted Status: The Social Impact of the Overseas Evacuation of British Children in the Second World War', IWM 91/33/1, no. 82.
4 Spokes Symonds, Ann, *Havens Across the Sea*, p. 99.

5 Mann, Jessica, *Out of Harm's Way*, p. 266.
6 UMASCS (University Museums and Special Collections Services, University of Reading) WA101/1–2.
7 UMASCS WA101/1–2.
8 UMASCS WA77/TS/TP/34/1–5.
9 Mann, p. 297.
10 UMASCS WA027.
11 UMASCS WA65/1–3.
12 Hobbs, Pam, *Don't Forget to Write,* p. 193.
13 Hobbs, p. 203.
14 UMASCS WA4/1–4.
15 UMASCS WA4/1–4.
16 Schweitzer *et al.*, p. 12.
17 Schweitzer *et al.*, p. 14.
18 Schweitzer *et al.*, p. 49.
19 Schweitzer *et al.*, p. 49.
20 Henderson, Michael, *See You after the Duration*, pp. 225–6.

CHAPTER 3

1 Simmons, Margaret, 'Paying the Piper: Female British WWII Evacuees Tell Their Mother's Stories' in Parsons, Martin (ed.), *Children: The Invisible Victims of War*, p. 170.
2 UMASCS WA4/1–4.
3 *Woman's Own*, 1941.
4 Mann, Jessica, *Out of Harm's Way*, p. 301.
5 Inglis, Ruth, *The Children's War: Evacuation 1939–1945*, p. 128.
6 Inglis, p. 129.
7 Schweitzer, Pam, Andy Andrews and Pat Fawcett (eds.), *Goodnight Children Everywhere*,

p. 87.
8 Inglis, p. 160.
9 Schweitzer *et al.*, p. 216.
10 Schweitzer *et al.*, p. 35.
11 Schweitzer *et al*, p. 36.
12 Harrisson, Tom, and Charles Madge (eds.), Mass Observation, *War Begins at Home*, p. 333.
13 Spokes Symonds, Ann, *Havens across the Sea*, pp. 96–7.
14 Henderson, Michael, 'North American Evacuation: A Good Idea or a Bad Mistake?' in Parsons, Martin (ed.), *Children: The Invisible Victims of War*, p. 97.
15 Schweitzer *et al.*, p. 107.
16 Schweitzer, *et al.* p. 100.
17 Bayley, Donald, unpublished memoir.
18 Andrews, Norman, *The Dream, the Glass and the Firelight*, p. vii.

CHAPTER 4

1 Tony Challis, www.bygonederbyshire.co.uk.
2 Crosby, Travis L., *The Impact of Civilian Evacuation in the Second World War*, p. 72.
3 Contributor from Solihull, 2005, www.bbc.co.uk/ww2peopleswar/.
4 Wheatcroft, Sue, 'Children's Experiences of War: Handicapped Children in England during the Second World War', p. 18.
5 Humphries, Steve, *Out of Sight: Experience of Disability, 1900–1950*, p. 74.
6 Humphries, p. 88.
7 Wheatcroft, p. 10.
8 Wheatcroft, p. 6.

9 Wheatcroft, p. 11.
10 Crosby, p. 73.
11 Wheatcroft, p. 20.
12 Reiss, Esther, *Balendoch Evacuation Hostel Diary, 1940–45.*
13 Reiss.

CHAPTER 5

1 Spokes Symonds, Ann, *Havens across the Sea*, p. 83.
2 Spokes Symonds, p. 50.
3 Williams, Shirley, *Climbing the Bookshelves*, pp. 36–7.
4 UMASCS WA42/TS.
5 Williams, p. 48.
6 Williams, p. 44.
7 Williams, p. 62.
8 Williams, p. 75.
9 Brittain, Vera, quoted in Henderson, Michael, *See You after the Duration*, p. 228.
10 UMASCS WA42/TS.
11 Spokes Symonds, p. 99.
12 Spokes Symonds, p. 98.
13 Spokes Symonds, p. 97.
14 Spokes Symonds, p. 97.
15 Henderson, p. 224.
16 Quoted in Henderson, p. 222.
17 Henderson, p. 223.
18 Henderson, p. 102.
19 Carey, Elva, *et al.*, 'A Very Hard Decision', p. 1.
20 Carey *et al.*, p. 90.
21 Carey *et al.*, p. 94.
22 Lin, P. Y., 'Perils Awaiting Those Deemed to

Rise above their Allotted Status: The Social Impact of the Overseas Evacuation of British Children in the Second World War', IWM 91/33/1, no. 67.

23 Milbourn, Louise, *A Very Different War*, p. 238.
24 Milbourn, p. 2.
25 Milbourn, p. 1.
26 Milbourn, p. 4.
27 Milbourn, p. 12.
28 Milbourn, p. 21.
29 Milbourn, p. 119.
30 Milbourn, p. 131.
31 Milbourn, p. 158.
32 Milbourn, p. 174.
33 Milbourn, p. 174.
34 Milbourn, p. 176.
35 Milbourn, p. 180.
36 Milbourn, p. 180.
37 Milbourn, p. 181.
38 Milbourn, p. 181.
39 Milbourn, p. 184.
40 Milbourn, p. 198.
41 Milbourn, p. 209.
42 Milbourn, p. 226.
43 Milbourn, p. 232.

CHAPTER 6

1 Fethney, Michael, *The Absurd and the Brave*, p. 30.
2 Fethney, p. 38.
3 Quoted in Cloud, Yvonne, *The Basque Children in England*, p. 165.
4 Huxley, Elspeth, *Atlantic Ordeal*, p. 2.

5 Fethney, p. 77.
6 Fethney, p. 76.
7 Fethney, p. 7.
8 Fethney, p. 160.
9 Fethney, p. 163.
10 Fethney, p. 207.
11 Fethney, p. 211.
12 Fethney, p. 234.
13 Fethney, p. 239.
14 Fethney, p. 239.
15 Fethney, p. 259.
16 Fethney, p. 264.
17 Fethney, p. 264
18 Lin, P. Y., 'Perils Awaiting Those Deemed to Rise above their Allotted Status: The Social Impact of the Overseas Evacuation of British Children in the Second World War', IWM 91/33/1, no. 67.
19 Lin, IWM 91/33/1, no. 67.
20 Lin, IWM 91/33/1, no. 68.
21 Lin, IWM 91/33/1, no. 74.

CHAPTER 7

1 Huxley, Elspeth, *Atlantic Ordeal*, p. 23.
2 Fethney, Michael, *The Absurd and the Brave*, p. 137.
3 Fethney, p. 138.
4 Fethney, p. 139.
5 Geoffrey Shakespeare, statement to the press, 28 September 1940.
6 Menzies, Janet, *Children of the Doomed Voyage*, p. 110.
7 Menzies, p. 113.

8 Menzies, p. 150.
9 Huxley, p. 24.
10 Huxley, p. 25.
11 Huxley, p. 43.
12 Huxley, p. 53.
13 Huxley, p. 55.
14 Huxley, p. 62.
15 *Daily Express*, 24 September 1940.
16 Menzies, p. 206.
17 O'Sullivan, Rory, unpublished memoir, Oblates of St Francis de Salles, p. 4.
18 O'Sullivan, pp. 4–5.
19 Menzies, p. 207.

CHAPTER 8

1 Brooke, Geoffrey, *Singapore's Dunkirk: The Aftermath of the Fall*, p. 7.
2 Brooke, p. 8.
3 Brooke, pp. 9–10.
4 Brooke, pp. 18–19.
5 Brooke, p. 19.
6 Brooke, p. 19.
7 Gilmour, Oswald, quoted in Brooke, p. 23.
8 Bartleet, Felicity, *Ann*, p. 21.
9 Bartleet, p. 23.
10 Bartleet, p. 29.
11 Bartleet, p. 30.
12 Tett, David, *A Postal History of the Prisoners of War and Civilian Internees in East Asia during the Second World War*, p. 286.
13 Tett, p. 287.
14 Tett, p. 288.
15 Tett, p. 291.

16 Tett, p. 291.
17 Tett, p. 288.
18 Tett, p. 288.
19 Tett, p. 288.

CHAPTER 9

1 Mann, Jessica, *Out of Harm's Way*, p. 320.
2 Davies, Stephen, 'Needing Love: What Psychological Damage Did Britain's Wartime Evacuation Inflict and What Do We Learn from It?', in Parsons, Martin (ed.), *Children: The Invisible Victims of War*, p. 277.
3 UMASCS WA89/TS/1–2.
4 UMASCS WA89/TS/1–2.
5 UMASCS WA89/TS/1–2.
6 UMASCS WA89/TS/1–2.
7 Isaacs, Susan (ed.), *Cambridge Evacuation Survey: A Wartime Study in Social Welfare*, p. 4.
8 Isaacs, p. 6.
9 Davies, in Parsons, p. 278.
10 Isaacs, p. 9.
11 Isaacs, p. 109.
12 Isaacs, p. 14.
13 Isaacs, p. 146.
14 Davies, in Parsons, p. 282.
15 Isaacs, p. 115.
16 *Dorset County Chronicle* and *Swanage Times*, 23 October 1941, quoted in Parsons, Martin, *I'll Take That One*, p. 88.
17 Zilva, Joan, *At an Awkward Age: A Teenager's Transatlantic Wartime Saga*, p. 93.
18 Zilva, p. 95.
19 Zilva, p. 95.

20 Zilva, p. 587.
21 Zilva, p. 594.
22 Zilva, p. 623.
23 Schweitzer, Pam, Andy Andrews and Pat Fawcett (eds.), *Goodnight Children Everywhere*, p. 14.
24 Schweitzer *et al.*, p. 14.

CHAPTER 10

1 UMASCS WA136/TP/TP18/1–3.
2 Schweitzer, Pam, Andy Andrews and Pat Fawcett (eds.), *Goodnight Children Everywhere*, p. 141.
3 Abbott, Gordon, unpublished memoir.
4 Titmuss, Richard, *History of the Second World War: Problems of Social Policy*, p. 441.
5 Inglis, Ruth, *The Children's War: Evacuation 1939–1945*, p. 154.
6 Inglis, p. 156.
7 UMASCS WA122/1–2.

BIBLIOGRAPHY

PUBLISHED SOURCES

Andrews, Norman, *The Dream, the Glass and the Firelight* (Peterborough: Upfront Publishing, 2006)

Andrews, Norman, *IPECAC and Old Snapshots* (Peterborough: Upfront Publishing, 2006)

Atkins, Ursula, *Fräulein Tom Tom* (Brighton: The Book Guild Ltd, 1997)

Barnes, Betty, *Belonging* (London: Athena Press, 2007)

Bartleet, Felicity, *Ann* (Durham: The Memoir Club, 2006)

Bawden, Nina, *Carrie's War* (London: Victor Gollancz, 1974)

Bentinck, Michael, *Waving Goodbye* (Cambridge: Fieldfare Publications, 1999)

Brittain, Vera, *Testament of Experience: An Autobiographical Story of the Years 1925–1950* (London: Victor Gollancz, 1957)

Brooke, Geoffrey, *Singapore's Dunkirk: The Aftermath of the Fall* (London: Leo Cooper, 1989)

Brown, Mike, *Evacuees in Wartime Britain, 1939–45* (Stroud: Sutton Publishing, 2000)

Calder, Angus, *The People's War: Britain, 1939–1945* (London: Jonathan Cape, 1969)

Cartland, Barbara, *The Years of Opportunity, 1939–45* (London: Hutchinson, 1948)

Cloud, Yvonne, *The Basque Children in England:*

393

An Account of their Life at North Stoneham (London: Victor Gollancz, 1937)

Colinon, Maurice, '*Sept Petits Naufragés*', *Lecture Pour Tous*, *Numéro Spécial*, No. 84, December 1960

Crosby, Travis L., *The Impact of Civilian Evacuation in the Second World War* (London: Croom Helm, 1986)

Ensor, R. C. K., *The Spectator*, 8 September 1939

Fethney, Michael, *The Absurd and the Brave* (Brighton: The Book Guild Ltd, 1990)

Gardiner, Juliet, *Wartime Britain, 1939–45* (London: Headline, 2004)

Gardiner, Juliet, *The Thirties: An Intimate History* (London: HarperPress, 2010)

Golding, William, *Lord of the Flies* (London: Faber and Faber, 2002)

Harrisson, Tom, and Charles Madge (eds.), Mass Observation, *War Begins at Home* (London: Chatto & Windus, 1940)

Henderson, Michael, *See You after the Duration* (London: PublishAmerica, 2004)

Hobbs, Pam, *Don't Forget to Write* (London: Ebury Press, 2009)

Horseman, Grace, *Growing Up in the Forties* (Newton Abbot: Forest Publishing, 2000)

Horseman, Grace, *Growing Up in the Thirties* (Newton Abbot: Cottage Publishing, 1994)

Humphries, Steve, *Out of Sight: Experience of Disability, 1900–1950* (Tavistock: Northcote House Publishers Ltd, 1992)

Huxley, Elspeth, *Atlantic Ordeal: the Story of Mary Cornish* (London: Chatto & Windus, 1941)

Inglis, Ruth, *The Children's War: Evacuation 1939–1945* (Glasgow: William Collins & Sons,

1989)

Isaacs, Susan (ed.), *Cambridge Evacuation Survey: A Wartime Study in Social Welfare* (London: Methuen & Co Ltd, 1941)

Johnson, B. S., *The Evacuees* (London: Victor Gollancz, 1968)

Kynaston, David, *Family Britain, 1951–57* (London: Bloomsbury, 2009)

Lewis, C. S., The Chronicles of Narnia (London: HarperCollins, 2002)

Longmate, Norman, *How We Lived Then: A History of Everyday Life during the Second World War*, (London: Pimlico, 1971)

Magorian, Michelle, *Goodnight Mister Tom* (London: Puffin Books, 1983)

Magorian, Michelle, *Back Home* (London: Puffin Books, 1987)

Mann, Jessica, *Out of Harm's Way: The Wartime Evacuation of Children from Britain* (London: Headline Book Publishing, 2005)

Menzies, Janet, *Children of the Doomed Voyage* (Chichester: John Wiley & Sons, 2005)

Milbourn, Louise, *A Very Different War* (Oxford: Isis Publishing, 2003)

Nicholson, Norman, *Collected Poems* (London: Faber and Faber, 1994)

Parsons, Martin, *I'll Take That One* (Peterborough: Beckett Karlson Ltd, 1998)

Parsons, Martin (ed.), *Children: The Invisible Victims of War: An Interdisciplinary Study* (Peterborough: DSM, 2008)

Rich Harris, Judith, *The Nurture Assumption* (London: Bloomsbury, 1998)

Roberts, Elizabeth, *Women and Families, An Oral History 1940–1970* (Oxford: Blackwell, 1995)

Rosenthal, Jack, *Three Award-winning Television Plays* (Harmondsworth: Penguin, 1978)

Rowe, Sheila, *Evaporated Children* (Colchester: The Plynlimmon Press, 2005)

Schweitzer, Pam, Andy Andrews and Pat Fawcett (eds.), *Goodnight Children Everywhere: Memories of Evacuation in World War II* (London: Art Exchange Theatre Trust, 1990)

Smith, Lyn, and Imperial War Museum, *Young Voices: British Children Remember the Second World War* (London: Viking, 2007)

Spokes Symonds, Ann, *Havens across the Sea: A Wartime Journey from Oxford* (Calais: Mulberry Books, 1990)

Tett, David, *A Postal History of the Prisoners of War and Civilian Internees in East Asia during the Second World War*, vol. 1, *Singapore and Malaya 1942–1945: The Changi Connection* (Gloucester: David Tett, 2002)

Thorpe, Jeremy, *In My Own Time* (London: Politico's Publishing, 1999)

The Times, 28 April 1937, p. 1; 30 January 1940, p. 7; 6 May 1940, p. 3; 4 April 1945, p. 2

Titmuss, Richard, *Problems of Social Policy: History of the Second World War* (London: HM Stationery Office and Longmans, Greene and Co., 1950)

Weightman, Christine, *Remembering Wartime, Ascot, Sunningdale and Sunninghill 1939–45* (Ascot: Cheapside Publications, 2006)

Wheatcroft, Sue, 'Children's Experiences of War: Handicapped Children in England during the Second World War' in *Twentieth Century British History*, vol. 19, no. 4, pp. 480–501

Williams, Shirley, *Climbing the Bookshelves*

(London: Virago Press, 2009)

UNPUBLISHED SOURCES

Abbott, Gordon, unpublished memoir

Bayley, Donald, unpublished memoir

Bird, Captain G. V. and Mrs D., IWM Documents and Sound Section 65/16/1

Carey, Elva, *et al.*, IWM, 'A Very Hard Decision': A document about girls evacuated to Canada in World War II who attended Branksome Hall School

Hansard, vol. 270, col. 632, House of Commons Debate, 10 November 1932

Lin, P. Y., 'Perils Awaiting Those Deemed to Rise above their Allotted Status: The Social Impact of the Overseas Evacuation of British Children in the Second World War' (BA thesis, Princeton, 1991), IWM, 91/33/1

Masters Sanger, Juliet, 'Mother and Daughter Separated by War', IWM, 03/42/1

O'Sullivan, Rory, unpublished memoir, Oblates of St Francis de Salles

Reiss, Esther, Balendoch Evacuation Hostel Diary, 1940–45, IWM, Misc 261, Item 3551

UMASCS (University Museums and Special Collections Services, University of Reading) WA027

UMASCS WA65/1–3

UMASCS WA4/1–4

UMASCS WA42/TS

UMASCS WA89/TS/1–2

UMASCS WA136/TP/TP18/1–3

UMASCS WA101/1–2

UMASCS 122/1–2
UMASCS WA77/TS/TP/34/1–5
Zilva, Joan, *At an Awkward Age: A Teenager's Transatlantic Wartime Saga*, IWM 02/1/1

WEBSITES

www.basquechildren.org/
www.bbc.co.uk/ww2peopleswar/
www.bygonederbyshire.co.uk/
www.cwgc.org/
www.iwm.org/
www.oldderbeians.org/
www.shipnostalgia.com/city_of_Benares/
www.uboat.net/allies/merchants/532.html
www.warsailors.com/
www.wartimememories.co.uk.ships/
www.youandyesterday.com/

PICTURE CREDITS

The first deliberate targeting of civilians: Bettman/Corbis

31 August 1939: Bettman/Corbis

Doris Cox: courtesy of Doris Cox

Nigel Bromage: courtesy of Nigel Bromage

'Uncle' Harry Mayo and Sheila Ripps: courtesy of Sheila Shear

Joan Risley: courtesy of Joan Risley

Robert and Florence Lenton: courtesy of Norman Andrews

John Brasier: courtesy of John Brasier

A village foster mother: Imperial War Museum HU 0326234

The large dome of St Paul's Cathedral: Corbis

Amber Valley Camp: courtesy of Elisabeth Bowden

Bathing pool in the River Amber: courtesy of the Old Derbeian Society

British evacuee children leaving for Canada: Hulton-Deutsch Collection/Corbis

Faith Coghill: *The Christian Science Monitor*, 23 August 1940

Louise Milbourn: courtesy of Louise Milbourn

Ann Spokes Symonds: courtesy of Ann Spokes Symonds

Mary Cornish: Elliott & Fry, London

Padre O'Sullivan: taken from *Lecture Pour Tous, Numéro Spécial*, No. 84, December 1960, photographer unknown

Dr Cuthbert Stanley, Nigel Stanley beside the River Dee and Nigel and Elizabeth Stanley with

Dorothy and James Fisher: courtesy of Nigel Stanley
Joan Zilva: courtesy of Joan Zilva
Ann Daly: courtesy of Felicity Bartleet
Evacuees return home: Hulton-Deutsch Collection/Corbis